THE
EARLY HISTORY
AND
GROWTH OF CALCUTTA

THE EARLY HISTORY AND GROWTH OF CALCUTTA

RAJA BINAYA KRISHNA DEB

GYAN

Published by

GYAN

Gyan Publishing House
5, Ansari Road
Daryaganj, New Delhi-110002
Phone: 011-47034999, 9811692060
E-mail: books@gyanbooks.com

Distribution Network
gyanbooks.com
India, USA, Canada, UK, Australia

ISBN: 978-93-7169-127-7 (HB)

First Published, 1925

2nd Impression 2025

Printed at: Gyan Press, Delhi.

THE EARLY HISTORY AND GROWTH OF CALCUTTA
Author: RAJA BINAYA KRISHNA DEB

THE EARLY HISTORY AND GROWTH OF CALCUTTA.

BY

RAJA BINAYA KRISHNA DEB.

Calcutta:

ROMESH CHANDRA GHOSE, B.A., 106/1, GREY STREET.

1905.

In Token

OF THE ESTEEM

AND IN

Grateful Acknowledgment of Important Services

THIS BOOK IS RESPECTFULLY DEDICATED TO

The Right Hon'ble Professor JAMES BRYCE,

M.P., P.C., D.C.L., L.L.D., &c.

BY

THE AUTHOR.

PREFACE.

It was during the search for and collection of the materials for the Memoirs of Maharaja Nubkissen Deb Bahadur by Mr. N. N. Ghose, F.R.S.L., Bar-at-law, Editor, Indian Nation, that an opportunity was afforded me to have a peep into the old records of the early transactions of the British in this country. That was in 1894 and 1895. I am glad to be able to say that the facilities thus offered have been usefully employed. Needless to say that I constantly kept the subject before me, never casting it aside, as it has a great fascination for me. It would be too tedious to my readers, were I to describe how fondly and with what dogged perseverance and tenacity I have pursued my favourite study. In the meantime certain articles anent the early reminiscences of Calcutta, etc., which appeared in the *Hitabadi* newspaper, attracted my attention, and my friend the talented editor of the paper allowed me to point out some of the inaccuracies in the articles referred to, and I began to write. The editor was so pleased with my contribution that he pressed me to continue the subject, which he said was appreciated by the public. It was a source of satisfaction to me that other newspapers made extracts from my articles. Thus emboldened, I seriously contemplated to write in Bengali a History of Calcutta. But it was at the suggestion and request of my wife and dear cousin Romesh Chandra Ghose, B.A., that I commenced writing the present volume in English. I am too well aware of the serious venture in which I have embarked, and no one feels the grave responsibility of the situation so keenly as the writer. At the same time, I must say I do not regret the choice I have made. It is no use concealing the fact that I derive great self-satisfaction by studying some of the problems connected with one of the most interesting and epoch-making periods of Indian History. Therein lies my consolation.

PREFACE.

I owe it to myself to acknowledge gratefully the encouragement I received from my esteemed friend Mr. N. N. Ghose, and I shall be wanting in my gratitude were I to omit to record my grateful acknowledgment to Mr. A. E. Mitchell, M.A., Dr. J. N. Cook and Mr. Geo. Coppard, Babus Bidhu Bhusan Banerji, Romesh Chandra Ghose, B.A., Baidyanath Mukherjee, B.A., my nephew Kunja Behari Basu, B.A., and many other friends.

Lastly, it is necessary that I should state here that for all opinions expressed in the work and for the arrangement of the book I alone am responsible. Should my "History of Calcutta" be favorably received, I contemplate to add in the next edition a few more Chapters, such as on "Ancient families," "Sports and Amusements," "Social and Political Revolutions in Bengal."

I conclude with the fervent hope that my readers will pardon me for several mistakes and omissions, for the Mss. were sent to the press when I was afflicted with a serious illness.

The Maps have been taken from Mr. A. K. Ray's History of Calcutta.

SABHABAZAR RAJBATI,
106/1, Grey Street,
Calcutta, the 2nd February 1905.

BINAYA KRISHNA.

CONTENTS:

CHAPTER I.

INTRODUCTION.

CALCUTTA, as it is to-day, may truly be called a great and magnificent city. Its metamorphosis from a small collection of villages in the midst of a swampy land has been characterised as unprecedented. Hardly any comparison can be instituted between its present state and its early condition. A scene quite novel and events quite unique in their character will be presented to our view. History furnishes but few parallels to a change so rapid, so varied, so extensive. The growth and development of Calcutta has been even more striking than that of St. Petersburg since the days of Peter the Great. With the exception of London, no city in the great British Empire can be compared to Calcutta in point of size, beauty, and commercial and political importance. It is not only the recognised capital of British India, and hence the seat of the Supreme Government, as well as the head-quarters of the Provincial Governor of Bengal, but it may be regarded as the second capital of the Empire. In its early days it was dependent on, and subordinate to, the older Indian presidencies, namely, those of Bombay and Madras. In the year 1707 it was declared a presidency town,* and it attained almost the same status as the two other presidencies. We

* Hunter's Imperial Gazetteer of India, Vol III., Edition 2nd.

read that in the year 1773, by an Act of Parliament called the Indian Regulating Act, the Chief of the Bengal Presidency came to be known and recognised as the Governor-General of India, and a new Court, consisting of a Chief Justice and three Puisne Judges, came into existence under the title of the Supreme Court of Judicature. The power of appointing the Judges remained with the Crown, and a superiority was given to the Presidency of Bengal over the other presidencies* in India—thus the Bengal Council began to exercise control over the other presidencies. Calcutta is ahead of all cities in India, not only as its capital, but on other grounds as well. It is now a centre of Commerce and a resort of the highborn and wealthy. The various institutions of public utility, the structural improvements and improved sanitation, the rapid increase of population, and the growing progress of arts and commerce, have transformed this once unhealthy cluster of villages into a town of conspicuous prosperity and grandeur. One is almost staggered and awed at the unprecedented increase of luxury and magnificence that have attended the change when he looks at the innumerable, broad and well-paved roads running symmetrically, and the many houses that have sprung up, whose splendour and beauty have deservedly won for Calcutta the appellation of "The City of Palaces," and conceives its early stage as a land more fit for saurians than for men. The city of Harun-al-Rushid seems to pale in comparison. Calcutta is now acknowledged to be the healthiest place in Bengal. The malaria-afflicted people of the mofussil take up an abode in Calcutta if they can at all afford the luxury. The wealthy zemindar, the prosperous lawyer, doctor or public servant, thinks it one of his

* Annual Register for 1773. Hunter's Imperial Gazetteer, Vol. III...

duties in life to erect a residence in Calcutta, and where he does not altogether abandon the home of his fathers in the country, keeps it only as a summer retreat. The autumn makes it intolerably unwholesome, but generally speaking there is no malaria in the cold weather, and then the attrac tions of the town are overpowering. Commerce has made Calcutta the home of many nations, and, in fact, a mart of the world. Armenian and Jew, Parsi and Marwari, Frenchman, German, Greek and Chinese, are all here for commercial purposes, and several of them come to be permanently settled. Calcutta is to-day as much a European and a Marwari as a Bengalee town.

To students of history, the foundation of a great city, its subsequent growth and development, are matters of deep interest. The growth of a City is connected with the social life of its people, its morals and religion, its arts, industries, commerce and education. By a faithful examination of its history, we find how deep and far-reaching is the influence exerted by circumstances long forgotten or uncared for over present-day life, and how from apparently trivial and insignificant causes events of the highest importance seem to have sprung.

The healthy example of British energy, British far-sightedness, pluck and perseverance, is indelibly written upon the history of Calcutta. It is unquestionable that by British statesmanship, courage and firmness, England has been able to secure for herself her great Indian Empire. Here, in Calcutta, events of momentous consequence have been enacted, which form an important chapter in the history of the world.

The day when Job Charnock, sitting under the shade of a big peepul tree at a place now known as Baitackkhana Bazar, smoked meditatively his favourite *hookah* and selected Calcutta as a most convenient site for the trading purposes of the English merchants, whose agent he then was, little did he calculate that he was practically laying the foundation of a great Empire for his countrymen. Their sole object then was to shake the golden pagoda tree, which, according to a Western superstition, was supposed to grow and flourish in Indian soil. Little did Job Charnock anticipate the consequences of his decision. It is a hazardous task to calculate the destinies of nations. Behind the veil of futurity many forces are at work, which even a deep and penetrative mind is unable to fathom. In proper season they become manifest, when, so to speak, they attain their full maturity and development. When Job Charnock made his choice, it was remote even from the dreams of the most farsighted man that Calcutta would become the capital of the British Indian Empire.

In the year 1599 an association was formed in England, and funds were raised in order to send a few vessels to the East Indies, where the Portuguese then had almost the monopoly of trade.* The jealousies against the Dutch trade in India led the English merchants at home to convene a meeting of their own in September 1599, with the Lord Mayor in the Chair, and they agreed therein to form an association for the purpose of trading directly with India. Sir John Mildenhall was sent over by the Constantinople route to the Great Moghul by the pleasure of Queen Elizabeth to apply for privileges for an English Company. The

* Mill's History of India. Edited by Cowell and Wilson. Vol. I.

reputation of this country for untold wealth moved and stirred into action many an eager soul. In Europe, more especially in England, the spirit of adventure was abroad. To carry on trade in several parts of the world by sea, and to acquire riches in foreign lands, was the chief ambition of the energetic Britons. In the seventeenth century, and at the end of the reign of Queen Elizabeth, the East India Company, after obtaining a formal charter, commenced its trading business. It is said that their capital then amounted to £30,133 5*s.* 8*d.*, and consisted of 101 shares.* During the reign of Charles I the charter was renewed in 1635. For a while, during the days of Cromwell, the East India Company was dissolved; but it was ultimately restored by him with all the privileges it had enjoyed before. His sympathy was drawn to such an extent to the Company's affairs, owing to the repeated losses caused by the Dutch, that in 1652 he espoused its cause and declared war against them. Its capital then rose to £740,000. In 1661 King Charles II granted them greater privileges, and their trade then not only extended to China, but through the good offices of Sir Thomas Roe in the Moghul Court, they began to establish their factories in the Indian Peninsula. Sir Thomas Roe came out to India as a representative and ambassador of King James I of England. The Emperor Jehanghir was then the Sovereign of Hindustan.† Readers of Indian history need hardly be reminded that the Moghul Emperor looked with a most favourable eye on the English. Englishmen were his favourites. Large concessions and privileges were showered upon them.

* Mill's History of India. Edited by Cowell and Wilson. Vol. I.

† The British Empire in the East by Count Bjornstjerna. J. Talboy's History of India.

Originally a committee of fifteen, and subsequently of twenty-four, with a President, was chosen among its share-holders. It was called the Court of Directors. The Court of Directors disposed of all questions touching the affairs of the East India Company. It was divided into three sections:—The first looked after all matters relating to finance, the second attended to matters political and military, and the third to matters administrative and judicial. Each of these committees was composed of eight members. There was also a secret committee, whose functions were to consider such questions as the declaration of war, the conclusion of peace, and the management of other political questions. It need hardly be said that with the rise and growth of the political power and consequence of the East India Company, its laws rules and regulations of conduct were much enlarged, and varied according to circumstances. But its political career in India may be said to have begun in 1756.*

In 1784 Parliament established a Board of Control. Its business was the superintendence and control of the resolutions passed by the Court of Directors of the East India Company. The Government of the Anglo-Indian Empire was thus embodied:—

1. In the Parliament, by this is understood, according to the English acceptation of the word, the King and the two Houses of Parliament, whose joint assent is required to make a law.

2. In the Court of Directors chosen by the proprietors holding a certain amount of stock in the capital of £6,000,000 of the East India Company.

* The British Empire in the East. By Count Bjornstjerna.

3. In the Board of Control, a ministerial authority forming a part of the English Government.

4. In the Governor-General in India, who resided in Calcutta, and was besides local Governor of the Presidency of Bengal.

5. In three other Governors, one for each of the three remaining presidencies—Madras, Bombay and Agra.*

In 1833, Parliament interfered in the following ways, namely, by laying down—

1. That the Company should retain its political rights, namely, of directing the affairs of the East Indian Empire, under the superintendence of a Board of Control.

2. That it should cease to be a commercial Company, and in consequence thereof give up its monopoly of the Trade of India as well as of that with China.

3. That the trade with those countries should be free for every British subject.

4. That British subjects should, on certain conditions, be allowed to settle in British India, which was before strictly forbidden.

The East India Company existed till 1858. In that year, after the suppression of the Mutiny, India became a part of the direct dominion of the sovereign of England.†

* The presidency of Agra was separated from the presidency of Bengal in or about 1840.

† The above facts have been largely taken from Mill's History of India, edited by Cowell and Wilson, and from the British Empire in the East, by Count Bjernstjerna.

CHAPTER II.

EARLY HISTORY OF CALCUTTA.

IT is only two hundred and twenty years or so that Calcutta has come within the range of history. Its career of progress dates from that time. In 1752 Mr. Holwell, on assuming the office of zemindar, was much exasperated in not finding any documents, papers, etc., prior to 1737 A. D. It is said that the great cyclone and inundation of 1738 destroyed important and valuable documents, and that the white-ants also ate up and damaged papers of value. It is also complained that, owing to negligence and carelessness of the subordinate officers, papers of value and importance were lost. There can undoubtedly be no palliation of the circumstances which caused the loss of papers that would have been of immense value; but at the same time it should be acknowledged that the latitude given and carelessness exhibited by the superior officers contributed much to the loss. According to Mr. Holwell, from 1732 he began to look seriously to the preservation of the papers. I quote his own words:—

"I have since, during the arrangement of the few scattered old records that remained, endeavoured, as much as the very limited time at my disposal would permit, to search out such documents as might throw a light on its past history; but the state of chaos in which the records of the office have lain for many years, the gradual decay effected by damp, white-ants and neglect.*" The materials for a history of Calcutta are to be looked for mainly in the India Office Library. One writer observes: "the Government records in the India House in London, amounting to 100,000 volumes, open out rich store-house for the future historian of Calcutta."† The same writer states that in 1717 Calcutta was known as a village appertaining to the district of Nuddea. The husbandmen and fishermen were then its only inhabitants. These simple and inoffensive people used to live together in clusters of 10 or 12 thatched huts. This condition of things, we find, still lingers on in the remote villages of Bengal. Calcutta was then full of jungle, and might not inaptly be termed a part of the Sunderbunds. It was a swamp. It is not to be wondered at that in those times the accumulated refuse and stagnant water added much to the unhealthiness of the place. It was hardly to be expected from those rude people that they should adopt any sanitary measures worthy of the name. Pestiferous ponds were scattered over the place. The jungle, the dampness of the soil, the impure air blowing from the Sunderbunds and the Salt-water Lake standing in its vicinity were all insanitary factors, and Calcutta, in consequence, was the picture of unhealthiness. It is said that the Salt-water Lake extended up to the localities known at the present as Scaldah and Bowbazar. Living creatures were no less a source of danger than the forces of nature. Wild boars, crocodiles, alligators, reptiles and leopards infested the place; and man was as

* R. C. Sterndale's Historical Account of the Calcutta Collectorate.

† Long's Peeps into the Social Life in Calcutta.

much a source of danger as the beast, for thieves and robbers abounded. It seems wonderful to-day that, in spite of these disadvantages, Job Charnock selected the site as the trading centre. It would scarcely be reasonable to credit him with a calculating prescience of the glory of the town, and one can only regard him as the unconscious instrument of a Divine purpose. Whatever the reasons of his choice, it has been justified by the event, and to-day it is possible to describe him as "the illustrious Job Charnock the first conspicuous Englishman on this side of the world."

From a cluster of three mud villages (Delhi Calcutta, Govindpur and Sutanati) modern Calcutta has grown. The areas of the three villages, as mentioned by Mr. Holwell in 1752 A. D., were:—

	Bighas	Cottas.
Delhi Calcutta	1,704	3
Sutanati	1,861	5¼
Govindpur	1,044	13½

"The bounds of Calcutta in 1757 were, to the south, the creek which ran from the site of the Bank of Bengal and Chandpaul Ghat across Chowringhee Road to the Salt-water Lake; to the east, the Lal Bazar and Chitpore Road; the Bara Bazar to the north, and the river to the west; all beyond was called the continent, probably because with Creek Row, the river, and Maharatta Ditch, Calcutta formed an island." "When purchased as a zemindary in 1698, it was only 1½ miles square. Calcutta was then known as a settlement"*

The site of Sutanati is now occupied by that portion of the town which is traversed by the Chitpore Road. The ghat now called Hatkhola was known for close upon a century by

* Long's Peeps into the Social Life.

the name of Sutanati ghat, in immediate proximity to which was a large market known as Sutanati bazar. Under Act XXIII of 1850, the whole of Calcutta was surveyed and the boundaries of Sutanati were thus determined:—The Bagh Bazar khal (Mahratta Ditch) on the north, Upper Circular Road on the east, the river Hughli on the west, and Ratan Sarcar's Garden Street on the south. Govindpur was a straggling nondescript sort of village with clusters of huts here and there, and patches of jungle intervening. It occupied the site of Fort William and the adjacent plain*. The first establishment of the Company was at Hughli. In or about the year 1746 they built a fortress there. A writer in a magazine † observes: "During the earlier years of Queen Elizabeth's reign, a solitary Englishman, a student of New College, Oxford, named Stevens, was wending his way to the capital of the Great Moghul, to realise for himself the gorgeous pageantry of an Eastern Court, of which historians had written and poets sung. The accounts which the young Oxonian sent home gave a fresh stimulus to travellers to the far East, and he was followed, in 1583, by Newbery and Fitch, who travelled overland by way of Syria to India, bearing a letter from Queen Elizabeth to the Emperor Akbar. Fitch's writings are still extant, and form a valuable addition to our knowledge of the country and its inhabitants in the 16th century."

An unfortunate quarrel with the Nabob's troops rising out of an ordinary bazar squabble was the immediate cause that led the Company to retire from Hughli. The circumstances are these. Hughli was then governed by a

* "Indian Empire," December 1859, and Life of Maharaja Nubokissen Bahadur in Bengali by Babu Bepinbehari Mitter.

† "Indian Empire," November 1888.

Mahommedan officer called the Fouzdar, and having been possessed of arbitrary powers and a large retinue, he treated foreigners with insolence and took from them anything he could to satiate his greed. The Fouzdar took advantage of the helplessness of a small body of Englishmen, and his tyranny and exactions roused the wrath of the Court of Directors. They directed their agent to ask the Nabob to grant them some lands in order that they might establish warehouses and strengthen their fortifications, and to represent the matter to the Great Moghal. When affairs were in this condition, the extortionate demand of the Moghal officer brought about a crisis and the aforesaid quarrel ensued. An unsuccessful appeal to the Nabob was made, and afterwards to the Moghal Emperor at Delhi. In the meantime their trade was stopped and their ships were sent away half empty. King James II, hearing of the distresses of the English Merchants in India espoused the cause of the Company and sanctioned their going to war with the Emperor Aurangzeb. An armament, consisting of ten ships of the line, carrying from 12 to 70 guns, was despatched under Captain Nicholson, who was to command the fleet till his arrival in port, when he was to be relieved by the Chief of the Settlement, who was to act as Admiral Commander-in-Chief, and six companies of infantry that were on board were to be officered by the Members of the Council. Nicholson's instructions were to demand a compensation of sixty-six lakhs of rupees, and, if necessary, to enforce payment at the mouth of the guns. A portion of the fleet came up to Hughli, and while the Chief was anxiously waiting for the arrival of the rest of the squadron, a drunken brawl, originating with three of the sailors, brought on a free fight. Nicholson having a fine excuse at hand, bombarded the town and set fire to 500 houses. This of course, precluded the idea of an amicable solution of the difficulty. The frightened Fouzdar begged for a truce, promising to submit Nicholson's demands for the consideration of the Emperor.* Leaving Hughli, the English Company came first to Sutanati, a village to the east(?)† of the Dutch settlement at Baranagor. In the meantime the Nabob's forces appeared on the scene, and Charnock construed this into a breach of truce and commenced a pillaging warfare against the small islands lying between Tanna and Ingellie (Hijlee), which latter he took and fortified.‡ Mr. Sterndale described it as the worst situation possible, being a low, swampy island covered with long grass, subject to salt tidal inundation, and destitute of a drop of fresh water, where, in three months, the English lost half their force and were subject to constant attacks from the Nabob's army: but the Court of Directors were greatly incensed with Nicholson for not sacking Hughli and for making truce with the Fouzdar. They sent Heath in command of the *Defiance* frigate, with a hundred and sixty men on board, either to assist in the war or to bring away their entire establishment if an amicable settlement had been made with the enemy. Heath arrived in 1688, and, landing at Balasore, stormed the batteries and plundered the place. He sailed for Chittagong with the whole body of the Company's servants, and, after entering into negotiations with an Arakanese Raja, he abruptly set sail for Madras, where he landed the Company's establishment. Strange vicissitudes of fortune dogged their steps for some years, the attempts of the Company to establish a footing in Bengal by force of arms proved abortive,

* The "Indian Empire," December 1889.

† It should be worth.

‡ The "Indian Empire."

involving their commerce and settlements in one common ruin.* The English were obliged at length to conclude a peace with the Naboh, and by his permission they moved towards Ulubaria. Ibrahim Khan was then the Governor of Bengal. But the new situation being found to be an inconvenient one, Mr. Charnock for some inscrutable reason, selected Sutanati, and there finally established his factory, paying to the Moghal Government a *pishcash* in lieu of customs of Rs. 3,000 annually.†.

Mr. A. Stephen‡ writes that Ibrahim Khan, the Governor of Bengal, sent pressing invitations to Charnock to return to his old place of trade. The offer was accepted. and Charnock landed at Sutanati with an accumulated stock of goods. On the 27th April he received a *firman* in which the Emperor declared that it had been the good fortune of the English to repent of their past irregular proceedings, and that permission was given to them to carry on trade.

According to another writer, the Emperor Aurangzeb offered a compensation of Rs. 60,000 to the English for the goods which had been plundered, and it was on the 24th of August 1690 that Charnock hoisted the standard of England on the banks of the Hughli, and laid the foundation of the City of Calcutta.§

On the death of Job Charnock in January 1692, Sir John Gouldsborough was appointed the principal Agent at Calcutta. Affairs were in such a desperate condition that

* "Indian Empire," December 1889.

† Sterndale's Historical Accounts of the Calcutta Collectorate.

‡ *Vide* "Indian Empire."

§ "Indian Empire," December 1889.

no one could be trusted; and in 1694-95 Sutanati was declared as a seat of their chief trade in Bengal, and the Court of Directors issued instructions to their chief agents by taking farm of other villages in its vicinity. During the rebellious days of Sobha Singh, Zemindar of Burdwan, in 1696-97, opportunity was not lost sight of to apply to the Moghal authority to permit them to fortify their settlements against the attack of the enemy; and the old Fort William in Calcutta was thus erected, and after its completion in 1699 it was named by royal permission in honour of King William III. About this period the Dutch had built their Fort Gustavas at Chinsurah, and the French had built theirs at Chundranagur. Nabob also sent a *Nishan* to the English for a settlement of their rights at Sutanati, on the basis of which they rented the adjoining villages of Calcutta and Govindpur.*

There is a different version of the transaction which resulted in the selection of Calcutta as the settlement, in Gladwin's "Bengal." It runs thus: "The English factory at Hughli having sunk with a noise into the river in the middle of the day while the English were at dinner, a few lives were lost and the rest escaped with difficulty, but their merchandise and property of every description entirely perished; hence Governor Charnock looked out for another place; he chose another one near it, erected a factory and fortified it, but the native merchants complained that their women were overlooked from the English houses, some of which were two stories high. The natives repaired to Murshidabad to complain, and orders came to prohibit finishing the factory; the workmen hearing this refused to work; on this Charnock

† "Indian Empire."

setting fire to all the houses on this side the river embarked in a ship; the Fouzdar sent orders to the Thanadar at Mukuah Thana (near Calcutta) to seize the ship; he ran an iron chain accross the river, provided some time before, to impede the incursions of the pirates of Arrakan and the Mugs who used to infest the river, but the chain was broken by the English. The ships having provided Alumgir's Camp with corn in a time of scarcity, the Moghal became favourable to Charnock, and permitted him to erect the Calcutta Factory."

In 1698 A.D., the East India Company purchased at Rs. 16,000 only the villages of Sutanati, Govindpur, and Calcutta with their districts extending about 3 miles along the eastern bank of the Hughli and about one mile inland. It is difficult to say when the three aforesaid villages came to be known and recognised under one head "Calcutta;" sometimes it is mentioned as "Puraganack Calcutta," and in documents bearing date 1778, the following passage occurs: "That the villages of Sutanati, &c., situate, lying and being in Calcutta."‡ Now-a-days, no longer one hears of Govindpur and Sutanati. In a neat little booklet called "The History of the Armenians," it is recorded that the well-known khoja surhead Israel rendered yeoman's service in obtaining the permission of the Prince Azim-osshan, grandson of the Emperor Aurangzeb and Subadar of Bengal to purchase the three villages from their owners. The annual rent was fixed at Sicca Rs. 1,195. Khoja surhead Israel was then chosen to represent the interest of the English merchants in the Court of the Subadar. Previously this Armenian as political agent made unsuccessful attempts to secure the lands for the English at the Court of the brave Commander Zaberdust-Khan,

‡ *Vide* Sterndale's Historical Account of the Calcutta Collectorate.

who was appointed by the Emperor Aurangzeb to curb the recalcitrant Pathan Rahim Khan. Malleson says * that Mr. Stanley was deputed to the Subadar's Court not only to secure the aforesaid three villages, but also to get other lands contiguous to and lying on both sides of the river Hughli. It is doubtful whether Mr. Stanley's representation had the desired effect. To Dr. Gabriel Hamilton, a Scotch Surgeon, Englishmen are vastly indebted, not only for his valuable help in securing the three villages, but also for obtaining thirty-seven or thirty-eight villages † on both sides of the river Hughli. Indeed, it is pleasant to observe that the humane art practised by medical gentlemen had been the successful means of obtaining a foothold in India for Englishmen. The successful treatment of Emperor Shah Jehan's daughter by Boughton,‡ and the operation on Emperor Farrukh Seyor by Hamilton, point to a moral which should not be lost sight of. Nabob Jaffer Khan, Governor of Bengal, was very inimical to the interests of the English, and without openly violating the privileges granted to them by Emperor Aurangzeb, employed artifices to distress them. The Company soon found their position in the country very uncomfortable. At last they determined, in the year 1713, to send an embassy to the Court of the Moghul at Delhi with a complaint. Mr. Hodges was then the Governor of Calcutta. Messrs. J. Surman, E. Stephenson and Khoja Surhead were chosen to

* Life of Warren Hastings.

† See Appendix.

‡ In 1645 the services of Mr. Gabriel Boughton, surgeon of Hope Hall, were requisitioned by the Emperor Shah Jehan, who granted many privileges to the Company; and in 1646 the Governor of Bengal was also medically attended by Boughton. In consequence of these services the factories at Baleswar and Hughli were placed on a much more secure basis. Be it stated here that the Hughli factory was established in 1640, and that of Baleswar in 1642. *vide* Hunter's Imperial Gazetteer, Vol. II.

represent their grievances at Delhi. They took with them presents consisting of curious glassware, clockwork, toys, brocades, and the finest manufacture of woollen cloths and silk. While the embassy were on their way to Delhi, the Emperor Farrukh Seyor was afflicted with a disease which required the aid of a surgeon, and by the kind offices of Khan Duran, a confidential minister of the Emperor, who was friendly to the English, Dr. Hamilton's services were asked for. He made a successful operation on the royal patient. The Emperor, to mark his sense of pleasure and gratefulness, expressed his desire to reward the English surgeon. Dr. Hamilton begged the Emperor to grant the representations of the coming embassy, which afterwards reached Delhi in 1715. The Emperor was so impressed with the disinterestedness of the Doctor that he readily expressed his pleasure to consider favourably the representations of the embassy. In the meantime the Emperor's marriage with a Rajput princess, Bai Inder Kumari, daughter of Ajit Sing of Marwar, delayed the audience. At last, in 1716, the representations were delivered to the Emperor. The Emperor granted permission to the English to purchase the thirty-seven or thirty-eight villages in 1717, and also conferred many valuable commercial privileges.*

In its onward march of progress, Calcutta has met with many vicissitudes. We have already seen after what hard struggles, and at times against what almost insurmountable difficulties, the English merchants were allowed to build their settlement and carry on their trade in this country. The jealousies manifested by the Moghul authorities, owing to the growing prosperity of the settlement and the obstacles

* Orme's Hindustan. Vol. II.

thrown in the way, are indeed well known to every student of History. Among the disasters that visited Calcutta may be cited the great cyclone of 1737, accompanied with a violent earthquake; several houses along the river side, said to be about 200 in number, collapsed, and the high and magnificent steeple of the English Church fell to the ground, and 2,000 ships, barques, canoes, &c., belonging to different nationalities were severed from their moorings and sunk or damaged. The water rose 40 feet higher than usual on the Ganges, and it is said 300,000 persons perished;* by a strange irony of fate the year was ushered in as a year of great hopefulness. An old annalist refers to it as "a period when we had opulent merchants, in days when gold was plenty, labour cheap, and not an indigent European in all Calcutta."†

In or about the year 1742, great alarm and consternation was caused amongst all sections of the people by a report that the Maharatta marauders would soon overrun Calcutta. It was determined to dig a Ditch, since known as the Maharatta Ditch, for the safety of the English Settlement. It was resolved to have it dug from the Northern part of Sutanuti up to the Southern part of Govindpur. It ran along the lines now occupied by the Circular Road. After 3 miles had been finished in 6 months, the work was abandoned. Had it been completed, it would have stretched as a semi-circle of 7 miles. It is said that 600 peons and 300 Europeans were engaged in this work, the earth excavated being used to form a road on the inward or town side. The next incident connected with the history of Calcutta is the sack of the town by the profligate Nabob Siraz-ud-doula in 1756. Nowhere

* Gentleman's Magazine, 1788-89.

† Indian Empire, December 1889.

has the adage "coming events cast their shadows before" been so strikingly illustrated as in the thrilling incident enacted on the occasion, which subsequently transferred the government from the hands of the Moghul to those of the English. The Nabob Siraz-ud-doula's early debauchery and profligate habits had created in the minds of the wealthy inhabitants of Bengal a great alarm and a sense of insecurity, and Kissendass, the son of Raja Raj Bullava, Governor of Dacca, fled to Calcutta on a pretext of going on pilgrimage to the shrine of Jagannath in Orissa with gold and other valuables. It was previously arranged with the English that they would offer help and safety if he came to Calcutta. Nabob Siraz-ud-doula hearing that Kissendass could not be fleeced as he had fled from Dacca, demanded peremptorily from the English his person and all his effects. The English refused to comply with the demand. Nabob Siraz-ud-doula had from his early years imbibed a violent hatred towards them, and on the present occasion he was greatly incensed, and he determined not only to give them a severe chastisement, but to drive them out of Bengal. The English were greatly alarmed at the attitude of the Nabob, but Raja Raj Bullava, the Governor of Dacca, assured them that all the sardars and ministers of the Nabob would help the English against him. In the meantime secret and confidential correspondence was opened with the ministers and sardars, and Nubkissen Deb was employed to carry on this negotiation. The Nabob Siraz-ud-doula attacked Calcutta with a large army, and the Governor Mr. Drake and many Englishmen fled on board a ship to Fulta. Nubkissen supplied the English refugees in distress there with provisions, in spite of the prohibition of the Nabob, and brought them valuable information relative to the Nabob's movements. The remainder opposed the attacks of the Nabob and were ultimately made prisoners and consigned to a cell now known as the "Black Hole." At the same time he changed the name of Calcutta to Alinagor, and appointed Raja Manic Chandra the Governor of the place. In January 1758 the name Alinagor was again changed to Calcutta by a Sanad of Mirjaffer. It is not necessary here to describe the horrors of the Black Hole. It will be sufficient to quote here only a few lines from Macaulay's essay on Lord Clive:—"Then was committed that great crime—memorable for its singular atrocity—memorable for the tremendous retribution by which it was followed! The English captives were left to the mercy of the guards, and the guards determined to secure them for the night in the prison of the garrison—a chamber known by the fearful name of the Black Hole. Even for a single European malefactor that dungeon would, in such a climate, have been too close and narrow. The space was only twenty feet square. The air-holes were small and obstructed. It was the summer solstice, the season when the fierce heat of Bengal can scarcely be rendered tolerable to natives of England by lofty holes and the constant waving of fans. The number of the prisoners was one hundred and fifty-six. When they were ordered to enter the cell they imagined that the soldiers were joking; and being in high spirits on account of the promise of the Nabob to spare their lives, they laughed and jested at the absurdity of the notion. They soon discovered their mistake; they expostulated—they entreated—but in vain!! The guards threatened to cut down all who hesitated. The captives were driven into the cell at the point of the sword, and the door was instantly shut and locked upon them!!!" Subsequently, in 1757, Nabob Siraz attacked Calcutta again and encamped in Amirchand's (Omichand's) garden, now called Halsebagan, whereupon Colonel Clive deputed Munshi Nubkissen with an engineer officer (possibly Mr. Amyath*) under the pretence of making proposals of peace and sending presents to the Nabob and his attendants. These two officers of the English brought with them in writing a particular account of their encampment, and Colonel Clive marched his force up to the Nabob's camp at the end of the night and blew up the Nabob's tent and those of his Sardars by the first fire from cannon. The Nabob, however, saved his life by having prudently removed to another tent during the night, and so escaped with the loss of the greatest part of his troops, and Colonel Clive followed him to Plassey, where he fought a dreadful battle with the Nabob's Commander-in-Chief, and slew him, and totally defeated and dispersed the Nabob's troops.

Another account says that the above successful attack on the camp of Nabob Siraz-ud-doula induced him, in February 1759, to conclude a treaty to the greatest advantage of the English; but scarcely had this contest terminated when news was received of a war having been declared between England and France, and the reduction of the French power became an object of importance to the English. Nabob Siraz-ud-doula informed the Council of Calcutta that if hostilities were carried into his country by the English he would assist the French with all his power. However, after a vigorous assault, Chandernagor was taken by the English, and the Nabob having shown

* Broom's History of the rise and progress of the Bengal Army.

marks of displeasure at this event, it was resolved to depose him by supporting Mirjaffer Aly Khan (who had married the sister of Alibardikhan, Siraz-ud-doula's predecessor). This was followed by a decisive action on the Plains of Plassey, in which the Nabob's troops were routed in every direction, and he was obliged to flee from his capital in the disguise of a faquir and was brought to Murshidabad and beheaded by Mirjaffer's eldest son. Jafer Ali Khan, from letters having passed between him and Munshi Nubkissen, did not give battle, but formed an alliance with Colonel Clive, who took possession of Murshidabad and declared Jafer Ali Khan to be the lawful Nabob of Bengal. With the sanction of Colonel Clive, Munshi Nubkissen* settled the terms of the soobadary agreement with Nabob Jafer Ali Khan.†

It is interesting to observe that in recent times there has arisen a class of writers who deny altogether the occurrence of the Black Hole Tragedy, and do not hesitate to insinuate that it was the fabrication of Mr. Holwell, who declared himself before the world as one of the survivors of the tragedy. The arguments adduced to support the contention are indeed quite frivolous. It is said that a room 20 feet square could not possibly contain 146 persons, so one cannot believe the occurrence. There is no attempt to

* The official accounts say that Mirjaffer employed Jogat Sett as his agent, but Nubkissen in his petition to the Council of Revenue, Bengal, dated 14th Nov. 1777, made the following statement:—

His services under the Right Hon'ble Lord Clive (then Colonel Clive) in the resolution which happened in consequence of the capture of Calcutta and subsequent defeat of Siraz-ud-doula, on which occasion your petitioner acted as Personal Secretary and Translator, and was employed in all the most confidential transactions.

This fact was also mentioned in his petition to the Hon'ble Harry Verlest, dated the 16th March 1767, *Vide* Memoirs of Nubkissen.

† Journal of the Asiatic Society of Bengal. Part 1. History. Literature. &c. Account of Moharaj Nubkissen Bahadur by S C Hill, Esq., Officer in charge of the Govt. records.

discuss the motives which could have actuated Mr. Holwell to propagate a false story which, on the face of it, was most horrible. · It is even said that Nabob Siraz-ud-doula was only a simple, inoffensive and inexperienced prince, and after all not a bad type of a ruler. A historical question, however, is not to be disposed of by sentiment, or by a consideration of probabilities, but should be decided only upon evidence. All the available evidence is in favour of the reality of the Black Hole.

Another portentous and terrible incident in the annals of Calcutta was a severe famine. The year 1770 was memorable for the dire famine and the pestilence which afflicted not only Calcutta, but the whole of Bengal. Between the 15th July and the 10th September, according to Mr. Hickey, seventy-six thousand persons died in the very streets of Calcutta. "There was not a corner in the city, or any lurking place in the vicinity of Calcutta, where the living, the dying, and the dead were not mingled or heaped together in melancholy confusion. It was impossible to stir abroad on business or recreation where these offensive or mortifying associations were not in the way. The daily employment of hundreds was to remove the dead, in proportion as they became a nuisance to the living. These in cart-loads, and without any funeral or religious obsequies, were promiscuously plunged into the river. By this increasing and prodigious mortality, notwithstanding the most constant attentions to decency and cleanliness, the town and suburbs were so much infected that, from the raging heat of the weather, the foul *congregation* of vapours which incessantly ascended from the unburied dead, and the torrid or intemperate state of the atmosphere, a pestilential influenza was generally and seriously apprehended." The late Sir W. Hunter states:—"Two years after the dearth, Warren Hastings wrote an elaborate report on the state of Bengal. He had made a progress through a large portion of the country, instituting the most searching inquiries by the way, and he deliberately states the loss 'as at least one-third of the inhabitants.'"*

* The Annals of Rural Bengal, by the late Sir William Hunter.

CHAPTER III.

CAPITALS.

OPINIONS differ as to the etymology of the name "Calcutta." Different writers have suggested different accounts of its derivation. The one most acceptable seems to be that which traces it to the word "Kali Kota,"* *i. e.*, the shrine or abode of the Goddess Kali at Kalighat, close to the old course of the Ganges now known as Adiganga (Tolley's Nullah). From very remote times this place has been reckoned as one of the leading shrines of India. A Dutch traveller connects Calcutta with Golgotha. A legend relates how one-fourth of the European inhabitants were cut off by some disease appearing in the rainy season, and the mariners out of superstition regarded Calcutta as Golgotha, *i.e.* the land of skulls.† According to the late Raja Sir Radhakant Deb Bahadur, K.C.S.I.,‡ the name Calcutta was originally "Kilkila." Grose§ states that "the first

* Calcutta is a place known from remote antiquity. The ancient Hindus called it by the name of "Kali Kshetra."...........According to the Purans a portion of the mangled corpse of Sati or Kali fell somewhere within that boundary, whence the place was called "Kali Kshetra." Calcutta is a corruption of "Kali Kshetra." Indian Empire, Nov. 1889.

† Hunter's Imperial Gazetteer and Calcutta Review, Vol. XVIII.

‡ *Vide* the Introduction and Preface to the Sabdakalpadruma.

§ A Voyage to the East Indies, Vol. II.

town on the river Hughli is Calcutta, a good market for coarse cloth, as also for corn, oil and other produce of the country." Mr. A. K. Roy, in his "Short History of Calcutta," says "that the province of Kilkila is described as being twenty-one jojans (160 square miles) in extent, with the Saraswati on the west and the Jamuna on the east, and containing the towns and villages of Hughli, Bansberia, Khardah, Sealdaha, Govindapur, &c., &c." During the days of Akbar, the name of Mahal Calcutta occurs in the rent-roll of Raja Todar Mall as published in Abul Fazel's *Ain-i-Akbari.** Another story is as follows: The first Englishman on landing here happened to meet a grass-cutter carrying his load and he asked him—"What place is this?" The grass-cutter thinking that the question related to the bundle of grass on his head, replied, *kal kata,* "I cut it yesterday." The Englishman, thinking it was the name of the place, noted it down as Calcutta, hence the name.† There is also a supposition that the name Calcutta is derived from *khal-kata* (excavated canal) or the Marhatta Ditch, which served as a boundary to the land. It is not improbable that when the Marhatta Ditch was excavated the three villages, *viz.*, Govindapur, Calcutta and Sutanooty, came to be known by the single name of Calcutta.

I have given here, as far as I have been able to ascertain, the various notions that are current in connection with the origin of the name Calcutta. To the curious they may prove interesting. In the absence of any certain knowledge, it is not safe to come to any definite conclusion. It is said sometimes with hope, sometimes with fear, that in time Calcutta will

* Mr. R. C. Sterndale's Historical Account of the Calcutta Collectorate.

† H. J. Rainey's Sketch of Calcutta.

not exist as the capital of the British Indian Empire. The shifting of the course of the Ganges and its silting up will in time reduce much of her importance. Pestilence and epidemic diseases will decimate her people like those of Gour. But it is impossible to wipe away the history of about a century and a half. Apart from long-standing traditions and associations, the material development of the town will be an almost insuperable obstacle to any great severance with the past. The capital that has been sunk in it by merchants, the Fort of long standing, the docks and jetties, the offices and the public buildings that have been erected by Government, the residences and places of business of immense value that have been set up by private individuals or companies, the structural alterations made by the Corporation, the University with its Senate House and a host of affiliated colleges, the Railway Companies with their elaborate termini stations and central offices, and the entire system of official arrangements in regard to tours, distribution of work, and such other matters, are not things to be swept away by anything less than an upheaval of nature, or to be transplanted to another soil at the caprice of a ruler. Calcutta will be the Capital of the British Empire if only because it has been such for a long time. Sir William Hunter was happy in his quotation of Virgil, when he said with regard to Calcutta as the Capital: *Sedet æternumque sedebit.*

Calcutta has been called the sixth Capital in Bengal. Gour is mentioned as the first ancient Capital situated on a deserted channel of the Ganges in the district of Maldah, the latitude being 24° 52′ North and longitude 88° 10′ East. The city with its suburbs covered an area variably estimated at 20 to 30 square miles. The origin of the city is lost in obscurity and can only be conjectured; but all agree that it flourished 700 or 800 years before the birth of Christ. The Rev. Mr. Long declares that the city flourished for 2000 years.* Mr. Thomas Twinning remarks: "All India bears infallible traces of a remote antiquity, but nowhere, perhaps, is this evidence more striking than in the instance of Gour." It contained a population of more than a million, and surpassed modern Calcutta in size, building and grandeur. To give an instance of its singular traditions, it is stated "that 30,000 betel shops were daily opened for the supply of its inhabitants with the delicate aromatic plant."† Another name by which it was known was Lakshanabati. Extracts from Abul Fazel's description are here appended :—

"Jenatabad is a very ancient city and was once the Capital of Bengal. Formerly it was called Lakshanabati and sometimes Gour. The present name Jenatabad was given it by the late Emperor Humayun...Goura, or, as it is commonly called Bengali, is the language spoken in the provinces of which the ancient city of Gour was the Capital. It still prevails in all the provinces of Bengal, except in some frontier districts ...When Muhammad Bukhtyar Khiliji conquered Bengal in 1203-4 A. D., he established the then ancient city of Gour as the capital of his dominion.........In 1535 the Emperor Humayun, when in pursuit of Sher Khan, the Pathan, (who afterwards expelled him from Hindusthan) took Gour, then the capital of Bengal. In 1575 the name of Gour hardly recurs." To convey a general idea of its past greatness, I quote a passage from "Sketches of India" by an Officer for Fireside Travellers at Home:

* Calcutta Review, Vol. XVIII.

† Travels in India a Hundred Years ago.

"You are treading on the ruins of Gour. This soil is formed of bricks now mouldered or crumbling beneath your tread, but fashioned by the hand of man, ages, long ages ago. Here, in the dust, lie the temples, the palaces, the dwellings of the city whose memorial you seek. Can you discover at Jerusalem one brick of the famed temple of Solomon? Is one stone left upon another of the second temple of Jerusalem which was rased to the ground 800 years after the day of my strength and pride? What seekest thou? Babylon and Tyre and Sidon were my sisters; Egypt and its idols knew me; empires on empires have arisen and fallen since my day; Carthage, Rome and Byzantium lie low. As in the days of Hezekiah, Isaiah the prophet of the Lord, foretold of other cities of renown, so has it been with me, and with my conquerors since me. My sons were mighty in valor, my towers high, my walls fenced, my treasure full, my daughters fair; music and dancing were in my feasts; I was proud and lifted up, and I am brought low even to the dust."*

Dr. Buchanan Hamilton says that in 1639 Sha Suja, one of the sons of the Emperor Sha Jehan, abandoned Gour and fixed Rajmahal as the Capital of Bengal; and from that time, according to him, dates the desolation of Gour. He thinks that "the city then went to instant ruin, not from any great or uncommon calamity, but merely from the removal of the seat of Government."

Raj Mahal is another instance. Mr. Twinning makes the following statement:—"Raj Mahal is like Hughli and Nuddea, an instance either of the singular instability which

* Sketches of India for Fireside Travellers.

has attended the imperial cities of India, or of the great number of years which must have elapsed during the successive elevation of so many cities or towns to the rank of Capitals of the empire, and their subsequent decline to their former inferiority or insignificance, their celebrated gardens and orange trees entirely disappearing, and the romantic magnificence of their palaces discoverable in the extent alone of their ruins............" Elsewhere he observes: "It is certain that Raj Mahal was once a vast city, the capital of Bengal, but the duration of its pre-eminence is involved in the obscurity which covers the transactions of this distant period. Truth can hardly be expected where the history of a nation is traced with the sword of a conqueror, or by a hand enfettered with the chains of subjection." The same writer goes on: "It stands on the West bank of the Ganges in 25° 2' 25" North latitude and 87° 52' 51" East longitude, is now a mere collection of mud huts with a very few respectable houses belonging to well-to-do Mussalmans. The ruins of the old Mahommedan city, now covered with rank jungle, extend for about 4 miles to the west of the present town." Further on, "Raj Mahal appears to have been chosen on account of its central position with reference to Bengal and Behar, and as commanding both the river Ganges and the pass of Teliagarhi through which the railway now runs. The place is also called by the Mahommedans *Akbarnagar*, and the following story is told to account for the name. The Rajput General returning after his Orissa victories, began to build not only a palace for himself, but also a Hindu temple at Raj Mahal. Fate Jung Khan, the Mussalman Governor of Behar, who had lived at Raj Mahal before the Rajputs arrived, wrote to the Emperor that Man

Singha was profaning the town by building a temple for idolatrous worship, and evidently meditated insurrection. Man Singha, however, on hearing of this letter, changed the name of the town from Raj Mahal to Akbarnagar, and turned the temple into the Jumma Musjid."

The Rev. Mr. Long says: "Raj Mahal, 'the city of one hundred kings,' favourably located at the apex of the Gangetic Delta................" Dhaka or Dacca has also been mentioned. "Its fame dated from Roman times."* Walter Hamilton states in his Gazetteer: "In 1608 A. D. † (?) the seat of Government was removed from Raze Mal (Raj Mahal) to the city of Dacca by the then Governor General of Bengal, Islam Khan, who, in compliment to the reigning Emperor, changed its name to Jehangirnagar........... It is related that during the second government of the Viceroy, Shaista Khan, rice was so cheap at Dacca that 640 pounds might be had in the market for one rupee. To commemorate this event, as he was leaving Dacca in 1689, he ordered the western gate to be built up and an inscription placed thereon forbidding any future Governor to open it until he had reduced the price to as cheap a rate. In consequence of this injunction it remained shut until the Government of Serferaz Khan in 1739."

Now-a-days it is looked upon as the capital of East Bengal, and is considered the fifth largest city in Bengal.

Nuddea has been the "Oxford of Bengal" for nearly five centuries. Mr. T. Twinning in his "Travels in India, a hundred years ago," writes:

* Calcutta Review Vol. XVIII.

† Mr Twinning says that it was in 1639 that Sha Suja removed the capital from Gour to Raj Mahal.

"...Nuddea, a town of great antiquity and celebrity, being said to have been the capital of Bengal more than 4,000 years* before the reign of Akbar in the sixteenth century...... Nuddea was one of the places at which the tobacco plant was first introduced into India by Europeans during the reign of the Emperor Akbar."

Here the great Apostle of the Vaisnava religion, Chaitanya, lived and preached. To Vaisnavas the place is especially holy.

Muksadabad or Mursidabad was the abode of Mursid Kuli Khan. He transferred his seat of Government here, and the city was named after him in 1704 A. D. It continued to be the capital under his successors till 1772, when Warren Hastings, the first Governor-General of India, removed the seat of administration to Calcutta. Many of its finest mosques, palaces and public monuments were built with the bricks and stones quarried out of the ruins of Gour. Indeed, many of the public structures of Pandua, Rajmahal and Tanada were the plundered materials of the ruined city of Gour. It is said that the commercial Residency at the English Bazar of Mursidabad was constructed with the bricks of Gour. And modern Calcutta came to be recognised in 1772-73 as the first city of Bengal and the capital of the British Indian Empire.

---

* It is incredible.
The above is written from the *CALCUTTA REVIEW*, Vol. XVIII.
Travels in India a Hundred Years ago, by T. Twinning.
East India Gazetteer by W. Hamilton.
Sketches of India by an Officer for Fireside, and Imperial Gazetteer by Hunter.

CHAPTER IV.

TOPOGRAPHY AND POPULATION OF CALCUTTA.

"IT has been observed," so writes Dr. James Ranald Martin, "that of all the European nations who have planted distant settlements, the English have invariably shown least regard to the proper selection of localities for the sites of their colonial cities."* Captain Alexander Hamilton, whose visit to the various parts of India embraces the period from 1688 to 1733, says about Calcutta that "a more unhealthful place could not be chosen on all the river."† Indeed, Dr. Martin's opinion, even on the ground of commercial expediency, is pronounced. He says:—"But here, we have not even the consolation of a commercial expediency in favour of the choice of a site for our metropolis; for, I believe, there are many places between us and the sea, better suited for shipping, while there exist none so ineligible as to their immediate and surrounding localities." Rev. J. Long considered the site of Calcutta as the most suitable one from a commercial point of view. He says :—"The question has been often asked, why was Calcutta not placed on the right bank of the Hughli, which the French, the Danes and the Dutch found to be more

* Notes on the Medical Topography of Calcutta printed by order of Government.

† Notes on the Medical Topography &c

healthy? The main reasons we believe, to have been this:— The left bank had deeper water, the weavers who supplied the Company with piece-goods lived chiefly there, and it was not so exposed to the raids of Maharattas as the Howrah side."* Walter Hamilton viewed the aspect in the same way as Rev. Long did so far back as 1815. He observes:— "Calcutta possesses the advantage of an excellent inland navigation, foreign imports being transported with great facility on the Ganges and its subsidiary streams to the northern nations of Hindusthan, while the valuable productions of the interior are received by the same channels." †

Calcutta is situated on the east or left bank of the river Hughli, its longitude being 88° 23′ 59″ East and latitude 22° 34′ 2″ North. It lies about 80 miles from the sea, and it contained in 1901 a population of 542,686 souls, exclusive of the Port and the Fort and the suburban portion amalgamated with the town under a recent Municipal Act.‡ Mr. H. James Rainey describes Calcutta as a "low, flat, alluvial plane, only slightly elevated above the level of high water mark, lying within the lower portion of the Gangetic delta...." "In the Abstract Report of the proceedings of the Committee appointed to conduct the boring operations in Fort William, 1835-40, we find it recorded: 'At 392 feet a few pieces of fine coal, such as are found in the beds of mountain streams, with some fragments of decayed wood were picked out of the sand and at 400 feet a piece of limestone was brought up. From 400 to 481 feet fine sand, like that of the sea-shore, intermixed largely

* Long's "Peeps into Social Life of Calcutta &c."

† The East India Gazetteer.

‡ Mr. A. K. Ray's census of India Vol VII. and Imperial Gazetteer of India Vol. III.

with shingle, composed of fragments of primary rocks, quartz, felspar, mica, slate and limestone prevailed, and in this stratum the bore had been terminated.' This coarse conglomerate, the depth of which has not been ascertained, but is supposed to extend some 80 feet below, clearly indicates the existence of high mountains adjacent to it, which appear to have gradually sunk; and this supposition is borne out by the disposition and nature of the strata discovered at various depths below the surface. Thus, at a depth of 80ft. from the surface was discovered a stratum of peat, which was found to contain seeds of the Madras cucumber......... etc., leaves of the sugar grass,..........etc, and these, according to Dr. Hooker, (*Vide* Himalayan Jour., Vol. II., p. 341) 'indicate a very different state of the surface at Calcutta at the time of its deposition than that which exists now, and also shows that the estuary was then much fresher.' Stiff clay with yellow veins occurred at 159 feet, and at 196 feet, clay impregnated with iron; at 340 feet and again at 350 feet a fossil bone was extracted, and supposed to be the humerus of a dog, and other bones were also found at a depth of 372 feet."

"Again, at a comparatively recent period, the physical features of the country must have been very different from what we now find, as the river Hughli did not then exist, and the main stream of the Ganges, several centuries ago, did not flow down the Padma, but found its way to the sea by Nadiya, Tribeni, etc., and the natives reckon the site of Tolly's Nala as the true bed of the ancient river, and designate it Burhi Ganga, or old Ganges. It is not possible to state exactly when this great change in the course of the Ganges took place; but it was probably, as stated by

Dr. Buchanan Hamilton, caused by the 'junction of the Kusi with the Ganges.' The well-known story related by Valmiki in the Ramayana regarding the descent of the Ganges from heaven, at the intercession of Bhagiratha, the great-grandson of king Sagara, whose 60,000 sons were destroyed by the malediction of the holy hermit Kapila, when about to perform for their father the Asvamedha, or "Horse sacrifice," has caused this river to be held in great veneration by the Hindus, and the lower portion of it to be called the Bhagirathi, which name is still applied to it by the natives, and not Hughli, an absolutely modern designation, derived from the town of Hughli, and that only since that place rose to importance on the decay of Satgoan, known to the ancients as Ganges Regia, which was the Royal Emporium of Bengal from the days of Pliny. Hughli was called by the Portuguese Ports Piquens and it became a royal port in 1632,* from which date, probably, the River Hugli acquired its name."† The humidity of Calcutta is usually considered to be very high.

Mr. Blanford‡ has ascertained that "the mean vapour in thousandths of an inch" in Calcutta during the whole year is as high as ·762, whilst that of London is less than half that, being only ·376; but, on the other hand, the mean relative humidity, Saturation ·100, for the same term is barely ·76, whilst in London it is a good deal more than that, being ·89. Mr. Blanford adds that, "next to the temperature, this is perhaps the most important *climatal* difference in the two places in all that affects health."

*A misprint for 1532.

† A Historical and Topographical Sketch of Calcutta, published at the *Englishman* Press, 1876.

‡ Proceedings of the Asiatic Society, Bengal, November 1873.

The average annual rainfall in Calcutta is, according to Mr. Blanford's elaborate "Table of Average Monthly and Annual Rainfall in Northern India," inches 66·04, whilst less than 100 miles below it, at Sagar Island, it is as high as inches 82·29.

The average atmospheric pressure in Calcutta, 18 feet above sea level, as indicated by the barometer, is 29·793 inches. The people of Calcutta have had a bitter experience of terrible rotary storms, most appropriately denominated "Cyclones" by Piddington, which have at various times committed great havoc in Calcutta. These cyclones are usually confined to two periods of the year— the commencement of the S· W. Monsoon, and the end of it. Those which occur at the latter period are usually generated in the higher parts of the Bay, and the barometer hardly affords any indication of their approach.*

Calcutta, as has already been observed, is called the "City of Palaces." How long she has enjoyed the title it is difficult to say. Enamoured of the rural beauty of the scene, Job Charnock is said to have selected the spot. Fort William and the Esplanade and their surroundings were covered with forests. From Chandpal Ghat to Kidderpur it was all jungle. In 1717 there was a small village with a number of straggling houses surrounded by a pool of water, where now stand the fashionable houses at Chowringhi. Chowringhi was then looked upon as outside of the town, and at night-fall servants returned in parties from these localities for fear of the dacoits who then infested the places. Shooting excursions were made in the midst of Calcutta. Riding beyond Calcutta was then a risky thing. Not only

* Rainey's Historical and Topographical Sketch of Calcutta.

the French, but also the Portuguese, the Mugs and the Mahrattas were sources of great danger. It is said that in 1717, 1700 people were carried off by the Mugs from the Sundarbands and sold as slaves at Arakan at the rate of Rs. 20 to Rs. 70 per head. It is calculated that three-fourths of the Arrakanees were of Sundarbands origin. The alarm continued down to 1770, when a chain was run across the river at Mukwa Thanna fort (near the Botanical Garden) to protect the port of Calcutta against these parties of kidnappers. The Mahrattas were hovering round; they took possession of Thanna fort on the site of which Dr. Anderson's house in the Botanical Garden now stands. There are old people at Uttarparah who have heard from their ancestors how the women had to hide themselves in tanks, with *kulsis* over their heads, to escape the Mahratta horse. *Borgi-hangam* (the depredations of the Mahrattas) is a well known Bengali phrase, recalling the terror of those days.* The slave-trade lingered on in Calcutta and its neighbourhood even to the middle of the nineteenth century. It was a long-standing practice. The Dutch, the French, the English, the Portuguese, the Hindus and the Moslems favoured the custom. It has now ceased to exist. The slaves of Bengal were treated much better than those of the West Indies and America.

During the Moslem rule, not only Calcutta but the whole of Bengal was considered as a most unhealthy place. Gladuria in his account of Bengal sets forth the views of the Mussalmans :—

"In former reigns the climate of Bengal on account of the badness of the air and of the water was deemed

* Peeps into social life. A pamphlet by Rev. Long. Page 13.

inimical to the constitution of Moghuls and other foreigners, and only those officers who laboured under the royal displeasure were stationed there; so that this fertile soil, which enjoys a perpetual spring, was considered as a gloomy prison, the land of spectres, the seat of disease, and the mansion of death." Perhaps Atkinson's poem well describes the condition of the City.

> "Calcutta! what was thy condition then?
> An anxious, forced existence, and thy site
> Embowering jungle, and noxious fen,
> Fatal to many a bold aspiring wight:
> On every side tall trees shut out the sight;
> And like the Upas, noisome vapours shed;
> Day blazed with heat intense, and *murky* night
> Brought damps excessive, and a feverish bed;
> The travellers at eve were in the morning dead."

In 1690 A.D., Captain Hamilton describes a hospital into which many patients went, but from which few came out alive to give an account of their treatment. On an average about one-third of the crew of a ship perished from disease arising from exposure and arrack. One good indicator of the mortality was the immense sums of money that undertakers made; the rainy season was their harvest time; when, in some years, only one-fourth of the European population survived, and when a large dinner party used to be given on the 15th of October for the survivors to congratulate each other on their being alive. Hamilton mentions that in 1700 there were 1,200 English in Calcutta, but in the following January 460 were buried.* Malaria and Dysentery were then rife, and a fever named *pucca fever* carried off its victims in a few

* Rev. Long's Peeps into Social life.

hours. Mrs. Kinderly alludes to it as "the illness of which most persons die in Calcutta; frequently carries persons off in a few hours—the doctors esteem it the highest degree of putridity."*

A writer in the *Calcutta Review* writes :—"No wonder fever was prevalent in Calcutta. People slept on the ground floor; few houses had upper stories, though the first floor was raised and was approached by a flight of steps. There was a disease common to the lower classes of Europeans called the Barbers, a species of Palsy, owing to the exposure to the land winds after a fit of intoxication. Abscesses of the liver were very fatal; one of the charges advanced against Compte Lally was 'of causing himself to be treated as if he had an abscess of the liver before an abscess was formed, which, had it ever happened, would have caused his death.' Though this is absurd, it shows the view entertained by them of abscess."

Dr. Lind writes of the fevers of the middle of the last century, *i.e.*, the 18th century.

"The distempers are fevers of the remitting or intermitting kind; sometimes they may begin under a continued form, and remain several days without any perceptible remission, but they have in general a great tendency to remission. They are commonly accompanied with violent fits of rigors or shiverings, and *with discharges of bile upwards and downwards.* If the season be very sickly, some are seized with a malignant fever of which they soon die; the body is covered with blotches of a livid colour, and a corpse in a few hours turns quite black and corrupted. At

* Long's "Peeps into Social Life of Calcutta," &c.

this time fluxes prevail, which may be called bilious or putrid, the better to distinguish them from others which are accompanied with an inflammation of the bowels. In all those diseases at Bengal, the *lancet* is cautiously to be used. It is a common observation, both at Bengal and at Benocolen, that the moon or tides have a remarkable influence there on intermitting fevers. I have been informed by a gentleman of undoubted veracity, and of great knowledge in medicine, that in fevers at Bengal he could foretell the precise time when the patient would expire, it being generally about the hour of low water. Thus much is certain, that in the year 1762, after a great sickness of which it was computed 30,000 blacks and 800 Europeans died in the province of Bengal, upon an eclipse of the moon, the English merchants and others, who had left off taking the bark, suffered a relapse. The return of this fever was so general on the day of the eclipse that there was not the least reason to doubt of the effect."* As to the time when cholera appeared in Calcutta, Dr. Lind says "that in the great sickness of 1762, in which 30,000 blacks and 800 Europeans died in the province of Bengal, it was marked that a "constant vomiting of a white tough, pellucid phlegm, accompanied with a continued diarrhoea, was deemed the most mortal symptom." Cholera was called mort de chien, "very frequent and fatal," and the treatment was emetics, opiate, hartshorn, and water; it took the patient off in a few hours. Monsieur Dellon in 1698 writes of a disease called the Indian Mordechi, which kills people in a few hours' time, accompanied with vomiting and looseness; the remedies reckoned effectual| are applying a red-hot iron to the feet across the

* Calcutta Review, Vol. XXXV.

ankles, and taking kanji water with pepper. When cholera as an epidemic first broke out in the Marquis of Hastings's grand army, natives were first attacked; in the case of Europeans it was accompanied by spasms, caused intense thirst, but the Doctors did not allow a drop of water, though some men that got water by stealth rapidly recovered. Besides brandy and laudanum, one of the remedies was placing the patient in a hot bath, and bleeding him while there in the arms—provided blood flowed. The Doctors considered the disease was in the air, and it was at first thought to be contagious; the camp followers were cut off so rapidly that the Marquis of Hastings was obliged to pitch a standing camp near Gwalior.*"

How dysentery was then treated can be learnt from a paper "On the progress of European medicine in the East," by the late Dr. Goodeve. He says:—"As the strength must be supported in the dysentery, wine and solid animal food were the most appropriate diet." Patients were ordered in these cases, "pillaos, curries, grilled fowls and peppered chicken broth *ad libitum*, with a glass or two of medicines or a little brandy and water, and dessert of ripe fruits." Native Doctors had their hot and cold remedies for hot and cold diseases—their mantras and philtres, while Dr. Lind states that Portuguese doctors prescribed as the grand cure "the changing all the European blood in their patients' bodies into native's. This they endeavoured to accomplish by repeated venesections till they conceived that the whole mass of this circulatory fluid had been abstracted. And then by a diet consisting exclusively of the productions of the country, they hoped to substitute a liquid entirely Indian, which

* Vide Calcutta Review, Vol. XXXV.

would render their patients proof against the maladies under which they had previously laboured.* In cases of fever, Dr. Bogue remarks, bleeding was commonly used. In 1793 Dr. Leskard opened baths at 37, Chinabazar, price one rupee a bath; they did not pay.† There is no doubt that much of the disease could have been avoided had the English adapted themselves to the mode of living, dress, diet, etc., conformable to the tropical climate. Perhaps hardly a race is to be found among whom the tyranny of custom exerts such dominating influence. The English people are slaves to their own institutions. A writer in a magazine‡ has made a just estimate of the extent to which custom rules English society. He writes:—"The Anglo-Saxon in every part of the world has wished to carry his home system on with him; he is the topiwala in Calcutta as in London; he is like the Dutch at Batavia, who in the swamps made canals or fetid ditches run through their capital because Amsterdam had them—the results were pestilential fever, hence the canals have slain more Dutch in Java than the swords of the natives. We find Calcutta people warned in 1780; from the many sudden deaths which have happened lately, gentlemen should be cautious not to eat too freely during the continuance of the heat (June). The Surgeon of an Indiaman expired in the street after eating a hearty dinner of beef; the thermometer was at 98." Nor were good doctors then available. The manner in which dysentery was treated has already been referred to. The Rev. Long states that Calcutta had two doctors on salaries of £25 a year each, but then they, like others, had a percentage

* Vide Calcutta Review, Vol. XVIII.

† "Peeps into Social Life of Calcutta." By Rev. Long.

‡ Calcutta Review, Vol. XXXV. Page 170.

on various articles, not excepting Madeira.* Hamilton says :—"In these days (1709) doctors were not well qualified or well paid. *Ex uno omnes disce* :—an anecdote is mentioned of one of the Governors of Bombay who, wishing to gain the favour of his Honorable Master in England, by retrenchment, found the surgeon's pay to be forty-two rupees monthly; at which he said there must be some mistake, that the figures were transposed, and so saying, with one stroke of his pen he wrote twenty-four instead of forty-two!†

A squib in a Calcutta paper in 1780 has the following :—

"Such Doctors who never saw Leyden or Flanders,
Run counter to reason, and bleed in the jaundice.
If your wife has a headache let Sangrado but touch her
And he'll jobb in his Launcet like any hog butcher
Tho' in putrid complaints dissolution is rapid,
He will bleed you to render the serum more vapid.
But consider the cause sure, 'twill give one the grip, man,
To see dubbed a Doctor a special good Midshipman,
Who handles your pulse as he'd handle a rope,
And conceives your complaint just as clear as the Pope.
Some Doctors in India would make Plato smile,
If you fracture your skull, they pronounce it the bile,
And with terrific Phiz, and a stare most sagacious,
Give a horse ball of jalap and pills saponaceous."‡

But in 1780 we find Physic as well as Law was a gold mine to its professors. The medical gentlemen then made their visits in palanquins and received one gold mohur from each patient for every common attendance; extras were enormous.§ Medicines were also rated very high; an apothecary's

* "Peeps into Social Life of Calcutta." By Rev. Long.

† Calcutta Review, XVIII page 286 foot-note.

‡ Long's "Peeps into Social Life of Calcutta" and Calcutta Review, Vol. XXXV.

§ Calcutta Review, Vol. XVIII.

shop was opened at the old Fort by the East India Company. The following were the prices set down for some of the drugs:—An ounce of Bark Rs. 3, a Blister Rs. 2, a Bolus Re. 1, &c, &c. At the present day one may ruin one's fortune and pawn his very utensils to preserve one's precious life. Even the modern Kavirajes like their brethren practising in European methods charge their patients for every visit; their charges for medicines are so exorbitant, that it is quite perplexing to determine the method in which the prices are fixed. In former times—say only half a century ago—our Indian Kavirajes used to charge moderately and not in an unfeeling way. Their kindness and sympathy for the genteel as well as for the poorer sections of our community deservedly made them respected. Their attainments were highly spoken of, and to this day they have not been excelled or even equalled. But the old order of things is fast disappearing, and the new presses upon the people in every direction.

It need hardly be said that the defective sanitary arrangements and the impurities of the soil added considerably to the mortality in Calcutta. The "Pucca fever" to which allusion has been made was attributed to the mass of jungle and fetid ponds and jheels which extended through Calcutta in every direction. Not only the dead bodies of beasts, but those of human beings were to be seen for days together lying in the streets in a putrid state and under the blazing sun. Jackals and such other animals ate of these carcases for days together. The dead bodies were then thrown into the river or sometimes into the pond.

According to Mr. Blacquiere, a well-known inhabitant in Calcutta (who shot wild fowl in the Tank Square, now known as Dalhousie Square), there was a small-pox epidemic in 1796 which carried off many men and cattle. It occurred during the months of January and February. In 1802 inoculation was introduced into the Settlement of Calcutta by Dr. James Anderson, the Physician-General of Madras, who inoculated two European boys with cow-pox matter and sent them by ship to Fort William. Mr. William Russel was the first person who commenced the practice of Vaccination in Calcutta, and was appointed by Government "to superintend the further promotion of the benefits of Dr. Jenner's discovery within the Bengal Presidency."* Another salutary measure was enacted about this period (1802) prohibiting the cruel practice of casting the children into the sea off Sagor island, which was indulged in by some misguided Hindus. The inhuman custom has never been sanctioned by the Shastras. A detachment of troops was sent to enforce the order, but no opposition was encountered.

The Lottery Committee rendered very useful services for the improvement of the sanitation of Calcutta. There were in those days the Lottery Commissioners, and in 1794 they advertised for benevolent and charitable purposes a lottery of 10,000 tickets, at Rs. 32 each, and some of the best streets and churches were constructed out of these funds. Rev. Long mentions: "Lotteries were the order of the day; large houses fetching Rs. 1,000 monthly rent were sold by lottery tickets of Rs. 600 each, also garden houses, *a Howrah house is put up to lottery*, situate on the bank of the river where the bore has no effect. The Harmonic house, a celebrated Tavern, was put up to auction by lottery in 1780,

*H. J. Rainey's Historical and Topographical Sketch of Calcutta.

and won by the Hon'ble Mr. Justice Hyde. A garden house in Entally was raffled in 1781 for Rs. 6,000, prize tickets Rs. 75 each. Some of the best roads in Calcutta were subsequently made by the sale of lottery tickets."*

Dum-Dum, Baraset, Chundranagar, Kassimbazar, Chittagong, Suk Sagor, Bircul near Hughli, were then favourite places and considered as sanitariums. Previous to 1749 Calcutta had a municipality. However, "as early as 1749 the Government ordered the drains to be resurveyed to make the settlement sweet and wholesome.† In 1707 the chief

*" Peeps into Social Life in Calcutta."

† Ditto.

¶ In 1793 the practice of raising money for public improvements by means of lotteries first came into fashion. The Commissioners for the Bengal lottery for that year offered a large sum, raised by them by means of lotteries, to the Committee of the Native Hospital, but the latter declined to receive the money, which was thereupon given for the relief of insolvent debtors. The first issue of tickets was 10,000 at Rs. 32 each. The whole of this sum was, after a deduction of two per cent. for expenses and ten per cent. to be defrayed for benevolent and charitable purposes, given away in prizes. In 1805, 5,000 tickets were issued at Rs. 1,000 each. Ten per cent. of the entire sum then raised was taken for the Town Hall and two per cent. for expenses In 1806 the lottery was for 7½ lakhs, and so on. The proceeds of the lotteries were made over to Lord Wellesley's Town Improvement Committee so long as that Committee existed. Between 1805 and 1817 many important works were executed from funds obtained by means of these lotteries, which were under the immediate patronage of the Governor-General himself. Large tanks were dug, the Town Hall was built, the Balliaghata Canal constructed, and several roads including Elliot Road were made. No less than 7½ lakhs appear to have been available for town improvements from lottery profits. In 1817 the Vice-President in Council appointed the famous "Lottery Committee," which took over the balance of the previous 17 lotteries amounting to 4¼ lakhs of rupees. This Committee looked after the affairs of the town (except as to matters relating to conservancy, which remained in charge of the Magistrates as before) for a period of 20 years, *i. e.* down to the year 1836, when lotteries ceased to draw. The effective measures adopted by the Committee to make the settlement "sweet and wholesome" were greatly appreciated. It would appear that it was under the auspices of this Committee that street watering was first introduced. The *Calcutta Gazette* of February 19th, 1818, says:—

"We observe with much satisfaction the great improvement to the convenience and comfort of the residents in Chowringhee, by the road being watered from the corner of Dharamtallah up to the Chowringhee Theatre."

It would be tedious to describe in minute detail all the works of improvement that were done by the Committee; we have space for reference to only the more important of them. It may be truly said that it was under the direction of the Lottery Committee that the work of reconstructing chaotic Calcutta into the regular form of a modern town was not only inaugurated, but pushed on with vigour. That handsome roadway which traverses Calcutta from north to south and includes Cornwallis Street, College Street, Wellington Street, Wellesley Street and Wood Street, was driven through the town and the fine squares—Cornwallis Square, College Square, Wellington Square and Wellesley Square—with large tanks in their centre, agents of the English company of merchants issued an order forbidding all persons to erect irregular buildings within their zemindaries. This was necessary, because many inhabitants made houses and tanks and walls without taking any permission from them. The endeavours of the English rulers to make the sanitation of Calcutta as perfect as possible under the circumstances are beyond all praise. There is no question that modern ideas of sanitation are of Western origin, and the means and appliances of sanitation are therefore also of Western invention. The trouble which the English have taken and the money they have spent on the improvement of Calcutta have changed its character and aspect. Among the early Governors whose labours in this direction are of a more systematic character may be mentioned the Marquis of Wellesley. He appointed a committee of experts, both Indians and Europeans; and their reports embodying schemes of reform exhibit the anxious care which the noble Marquis bestowed on its improvement. He opened the Government purse, and his attentions were early paid to the defects of the drainage system. It is worth while quoting here his own observations: "The defects of the climate of Calcutta during the latter part of the rainy seasons may, indeed, be ascribed in a great measure to the state of the drains and the watercourses, and to the stagnant water remaining in the town and its vicinity." It

---

were constructed at intervals along its course under the auspices of the Committee. Other streets, such as Free School Street, Kyd Street, Hastings Street, Creek Row, Mangoe Lane, and Bentinck Street were also opened, straightened and widened by them. The Maidan was improved by the construction of roads and paths, by the excavation of tanks and erection of balustrades; the Strand Road was made; Coloctollah Street, Amherst Street and Mirzapore Street were laid out, and the Mirzapore Tank, Surtibagan Tank, and several tanks in Short's Bazar, were dug by the same Committee. Several roads were metalled, and arrangements for watering various Streets were also made by them, an engine being fixed for that purpose at Chandpal Ghat.

A. K. Roy's "A Short History of Calcutta." Part I.

was the desire of the noble Lord that "India should be governed from a palace, not from a counting house, with the ideas of a prince, not with those of a retail dealer in muslin and indigo." Governor Vansittart, Lord Clive, Governor Verlest, Governor Cartier and Governor General Hastings have also rendered important services towards cleansing the town and making it wholesome and convenient. Sir William Hunter states: "When Mr. Hastings came to the Government he added some new regulations, and gave a degree more power to the officers of the Police, divided the Black and White Town into thirty-five wards and purchased the consent of the natives to go a little further off."*

Municipal work in early days was managed by the Mayor and nine older men, who were appointed by the Government every December, but they had nothing to do with the drains. Then the Committee and the Government, with the Medical Officer appointed by the Government, used to look after the health of the town. The Justices in the meantime stepped in. They were appointed for life by the Government. The late Sir George Campbell made an infructuous attempt by introducing a Bill whose object had been "the enlargement of the powers of Municipal Commissioners, to lay less municipal work and responsibility on the shoulders of Magistrates, to make Municipal Commissioners elective and in other ways to make more scope for municipal self-government"† His aim was, as he himself said, "not an increase of taxation, but the introduction of a system of self-Government." In another place he stated: "Municipal self-government is not foreign to this country,

* Imperial Gazetteer Vol. III.

† Municipal Work in India, by R. C. Sterndale.

but inherent to it, being the ancient rule and habit of the Hindu race."* His successor, the late Sir Richard Temple, has been able with the concurrence of the India Government to grant the privilege to the ratepayers of Calcutta to elect a certain number of Commissioners with the powers and privileges clearly defined.† Among the many improvements effected by the introduction of self-government in Calcutta may be prominently mentioned the complete drainage works, lighting of the streets with gas and electricity, improvement of the bustee lands and the scavengering arrangements, and the present water works. The municipal administration of the city has a history full of interest. Unfortunately, space will permit us to place before the reader only a very brief account. It appears that from the very commencement of the settlement of the company of English merchants in Calcutta in the time of Job Charnock, they bestirred themselves on the blessed work of sanitation. Strenuous efforts were made to convert this unhealthy locality into quite a habitable one. Lands were surveyed and resurveyed, plans and maps prepared, roads constructed, jungles removed, steps taken to level the land, and other sanitary and structural improvements sketched out and taken in hand. Individual efforts then counted much to make the settlement "sweet and wholesome." In truth, commerce and benevolence led the way to sanitary and structural improvements, and for a long time even after the Government assumed the responsibility and direct control, individual efforts played a very useful part in this direction. Modern Calcutta dates from 1757. After the battle of Plassey, Meer Zafer was elevated to the

* Municipal Work in India, by R. C. Sterndale.

† *Vide* an interesting account of this in a pamphlet by Mr. N. N. Ghose.

musnud of Bengal, and according to the treaty agreed upon he paid money, known as the Restitution money, to the Calcutta merchants and other inhabitants for the loss they sustained when Siraj-ud-Doula sacked Calcutta in 1756 and 1757. The English received £500,000, the Hindus and Mahommedans £200,000, and the Armenians £70,000. From this period the history of Calcutta presents an interesting study. Its prosperity has been smooth and uninterrupted. The once swampy great jungle pervaded by wild beasts was converted into the present Maidan intersected with roads. The old Fort was abandoned and its site was utilised for the Customs House and other public buildings. The present Fort William was planned by Clive, and the English inhabitants gradually migrated from the centre of the town extending from Dalhousie Square to the mint, to Chowringhee and its vicinity, while the Indian population shifted from Govindpur and the adjoining villages (the site of the present Fort) to the northern portion of the town.*

From the foregoing observations it is evident that the successive heads of Government used to take not only a personal interest in looking after the municipal affairs of the town, but they had great direct control over it. But it is impossible for an enlightened Government like the British to shut the people from associating themselves with their legitimate duty of looking after the government of the town in which they are virtually interested, and we find that from the Mayor and Aldermen the Municipal administration gradually passed into the hands of the Justices of the Peace, whose functions among others were "principally repairing

* Imperial Gazetteer, Vol. III, 2nd Edition. Rainey's Historical and Topographical Sketch; and *Calcutta Review*, Vols. XXXV and XVIII.

and clearing the streets." It is easy to observe that, with the rapid growth of Calcutta, the Municipal work of the town increased, and the restricted duties and powers of the Justices greatly hampered the work. Ultimately the Government provided an opportunity to the people to associate themselves more closely with the Municipal administration, and, as has already been stated, the boon of partial local self-goverment was conferred during the administration of Sir Richard Temple, and Government began to keep only a watchful supervision over its affairs. The law creating self-government was amended from time to time, and while the Police duties were taken away, other duties and powers were given to the Municipality. During the Lieutenant-Governorship of Sir Alexander Mackenzie an amending Bill was introduced, which was passed into law during his successor Sir John Woodburn's rule. The Indian population felt keenly the passing of the measure, which they regarded as the death-knell of local self-government. Their protests and representations were of no avail.

It was Job Charnock who in 1690 issued a proclamation inviting various nationalities to come and settle in the Company's Zemindaries—the three villages, Sutanooti, Calcutta and Govindpur. He gave them special immunities and offered advantages to induce them to establish themselves in new settlements. The Portuguese, the Armenians, the Greeks the Jews, the Hindus, the Moslems and other nationalities began to come in. In his history of the Armenians in India, Mesrovb J. Seth writes that, prior to the days of Job Charnock and his founding of Calcutta in 1690, the Armenians had formed a small commercial settlement in the village of Sutanooti. It is not mentioned by Mr. Seth when the

Armenians first came to Calcutta, but he has lately brought to light an interesting inscription in the Armenian language over the tomb-stone of an Armenian lady in the Armenian churchyard at Calcutta, bearing date 11th July 1630 A. D. In the fourth Chapter of his interesting book, he makes the suggestion that long before Charnock set his foot on the soil, the Armenians traded here, and Sutanooti was noted as a commercial mart. This writer also remarks that in compliance with the invitation of Job Charnock, the Portuguese and the Armenians came from Chinsurah. The Armenians settled here enjoying the privileges granted to them in a charter by the East India Company in 1688. Mr. Stark states :—" Many responded to his overtures and congregated at the northern extremity of the settlement. This circumstance is still chronicled in the names 'Armenian Ghat' and 'Armenian Street.' Here they made themselves extremely useful to the British, and afforded an excellent medium through which the English reached the native markets. They enjoyed ths privileges of British citizens, and several of them rose to positions of wealth and influence." This enterprising community came to India at the end of the sixteenth century ; the splendours of the Moghul Court attracted them to share in its prosperity, and there came numerous adventurers from Armenia. When the East India Company set foot on Indian soil in 1601, the Armenian trade was in a flourishing condition. The Armenians became invaluable agents and helpers to the English, when they obtained a firman from the Emperor Jehangir in January 1612. Rev. Long gives the following account of the Armenians:—"The Armenians came to India, some by the Persian Gulf others by Khorasan, Candahar, and Kabul to Delhi. They were among the earliest settlers, coming gradually from Guzerat and Surat to Benares and Behar. They settled in Chinsurah soon after the Dutch settlement of 1625. On the foundation of Calcutta in 1690, the Armenians, in common with the Portuguese, accepted the invitation of Governor Charnock to settle there, and flourished, so that in 1757 they received as compensation for their losses seven lakhs of rupees; they were pioneers in the Central Asian trade, which has yet a great future before it."*

The Greeks came to Calcutta in or about 1750.

I pass on now to take a view of the Portuguese in India. At one time, according to Mr. Hamilton, their language rose to such consequence that most of the Europeans used to learn it to qualify themselves for general converse with one another. It was the *lingua franca* in India. The Europeans who first made an attempt and came to India were the Portuguese. Christopher Columbus's original design was to come to India, but he went to America instead. Five years later, in 1498, Vasco da Gama came to Calicut by the Cape of Good Hope. But the first Portuguese who came to Calicut was Covilham. He came by the overland route about the year 1487. The Arabs showed great hostility to the new-comer. The Delhi Emperor was then an Afghan of the Lodhi Dynasty, and the ruler of Bengal was also an Afghan. The southern presidencies of India were then divided into several satrapies. The most powerful monarch, who was the paramount Lord in the south, was the Hindu King of Bijoynagor, whose influence was then even greater than that of the Emperor of Delhi. Vasco da Gama, after staying for a few months on the Malabar Coast, returned

* Rev. Long's "Peeps into the Social Life in Calcutta."

home with a letter from Zemorin, Raja of Calicut. Like Columbus, he also met with an enthusiastic ovation after his return. The spirit of the people then rose to a pitch of enthusiasm, and the early Portuguese were not petty merchants or adventurers, but they were charged with the sacred and holy mission of converting the pagans and promoting the spread of Christianity. In 1500 A. D., under the command of Cabral, another expedition was sent, whose mission was to begin with preaching, and if that failed, to use the sword. In the meantime the King of Portugal, in 1502, obtained from the Pope a bull constituting him "Lord of the Navigation, Conquest, and Trade of Ethiopia, Arabia, Persia, and India." In the intervening period Cabral, after various reverses, established factories at Calicut and at Cochin. In 1502, Vasco da Gama again sailed to the East and made war with several States and people who were, at first, friendly and hospitable towards him, and at length in 1505 a large fleet with a considerable force was despatched under Francisco De Almeida, who was known as the first Portuguese Governor and Viceroy in India. In 1509 the great Albuiquerque succeeded him as Governor, and it was in consequence of his conciliatory spirit and temperate attitude that the Portuguese were able to gain the good-will and confidence of the natives, so much so that they liked more to be governed by the Portuguese than by the Mussalmans. The Rev. Mr. Long mentions that the Portuguese appeared in Bengal in 1530 as mercenaries in the service of the king of Gour, and acted as a kind of Pretorian Guard to the Native Rajas. The Spanish influence proved to be the precursor of the downfall of the Portuguese in India. The Portuguese Crown was united with Philip II. of Spain in 1530, and from that period the interest of Portugal was subordinated to that of Spain. In the meanwhile the

Dutch and the English appeared in the Eastern lands, and although Portugal in 1640 separated itself from Spain, its destiny had already been played out. Sir William Hunter states that for exactly a century from 1500-1600 the Portuguese had enjoyed the monopoly of Oriental trade. From Japan and the Spice Islands to the Red Sea and the Cape of Good Hope, they were the sole masters and dispensers of the treasures of the East, while their possessions along the Atlantic Coast of Africa and in Brazil completed their maritime empire. Sir William Hunter thus describes the cause of their downfall:—

"But the Portuguese had neither the political strength nor the personal character necessary to maintain such an Empire. Their national temper had been formed in their contest with the Moors at home. They were not traders, but knights-errant and crusaders who looked on every pagan as an enemy of Portugal and of Christ. Only those who had read the contemporary narratives of their conquests can realise the superstition and the cruelty with which their history in the Indies is stained....................The Portuguese at no time attempted to found a Company but kept their eastern trade as a royal enterprise and monopoly."* The only Portuguese possessions now in India are Goa, Daman and Diu, all situated on the west coast. And the Portuguese half-castes—known as the Feringees—live in the quarter now known as Moorgihata or Canning Street and China-bazar. It is very sad to reflect on their downfall. They did the part of a kerani when the English settled in Calcutta, and they performed their task in so slovenly a fashion as to call down the censure of the Court of Directors. They were employed as table

* Imperial Gazetteer of India.

servants, slaves and topazzas. Many of them betook themselves to the profession of bandits and pirates. They in their degenerate days led the life of vagrants and carried off peace-loving people to other lands for sale. Their women are serving the fashionable English ladies in the capacity of ayahs. It is said that such words as Janala, Caste, Compound &c., are derived from the Portuguese language.*

According to Babu Ramkamal Sen, the English first visited Bengal about the year 1620. On their arrival at the first settlement in Govindpur and Sutanooti, the natives did not dare approach them, not being able to understand what they said. Business was accordingly transacted by the gestures and signs of the body. The Basacks or Setts were then a great family and known as piece-goods dealers. The English requested them to send a *dubas* or dhobhasia, which means one who knows two languages. This class of men had proved themselves very useful at Madras. Without comprehending what they meant, the Basacks sent some washermen (Dhobies) in their employ; and the washermen by frequent intercourse with the English learnt somewhat imperfectly their language, and they are said to have been the first who knew anything of the language. One Ratan Sarkar, a Dhobie by caste, was the first Indian who was employed as an Interpreter by the English.†

Although Job Charnock laboured to see his new settlement peopled with various nationalities, he did not unfortunately live long to see it flourish, for, in January 1692 he died and was buried in a vault under the mausoleum which still stands in the old Cathedral (St. John's) churchyard, just

* *Calcutta Review.* Vol. XVIII.
† Preface to Ramkamal Sen's Dictionary published at Serampore in 1830.

opposite the late Collectorate, formerly the old Mint, and which, to the discredit of Calcutta, is the only memorial of its founder extant in this age. Mr. Sterndale observes that the names of many men of less note remain to this day on our streets and lanes; but neither street, square, nor monument exists bearing the name of Job Charnock, the pioneer of British power in Bengal and the founder of Calcutta.* Mr. J. Rainey states:

"According to Bruce, Charnock died much respected, and Orme says of him that he 'was a man of courage, without military experience, but impatient to take revenge on a Government from which he had personally received the most ignominious treatment, having been imprisoned and scourged by the Nawab.' And Sir John Goldsborough, who came out as Commissary-General in 1794, characterised his disposition as irresolute and indolent." But, on the whole, Charnock appears to have been, as stated by Bruce, much respected.

There is an episode in Charnock's life that I must refer to at some length, and which has been termed by a writer to an Indian periodical, "Romance in the earlier history of Calcutta." Some time in the year 1678, Charnock, who was walking about the banks of the river at Hughli, observed a young Hindu widow of beautiful aspect, gorgeously arrayed, proceeding towards the funeral pyre of her aged husband. The too susceptible Charnock became smitten with her charms, and as she appeared to be reluctant to sacrifice herself, he, with some assistance, rescued her, took her to his home, and she became his wife and bore to him several

* Since the publication of Mr. Sterndale's book a street has been named after Job Charnock.

children. She died and her remains were interred in the family vault in St. John's Churchyard, where, says Captain Hamilton, her husband used to sacrifice a fowl on the anniversary of her death."* Between 1742 and 1753 the development of the town consisted chiefly in the rapid increase of native Indian houses, both kutcha and pucka—mostly kutcha—in the outlying parts of the European town within the Mahratta Ditch.

The map of 1756 shows a much greater development of the town. A lot of jungle has been cleared, and very nearly the whole town, from Perrin's Point to the Lall Bazar Road, is dotted with masonry buildings, and the area marked out in the map of 1742, as being under jungle, is shown as being under occupation. We can see that holdings are marked out, though not prominently, for the sites of gardens and orchards, and that jungles have greatly disappeared. And whereas in the map of 1742 there are only sixteen streets to be seen, in that of 1756 no less than 27 big streets and 52 smaller streets are clearly laid down. But the greatest improvement is in pucka buildings. By a rough calculation we find that in the place of only 21 masonry structures (and only 5 of them of any size) outside the fenced city of 1742, we have in 1756 no less than 268 pucka buildings shown in the map. The huts are also shown, but not certainly with care or precision, and a great many are omitted.†

Maharaja Nubkissen Deb Bahadur made also great efforts to induce learned Brahmins and men of other castes to settle in Calcutta. He gave them lands, erected houses

* This custom still lingers on among the low caste Hindus at Behar.

† Mr. A. K. Roy's Short History of Calcutta.

for them, and helped them in various other ways. The Brahmins hailing from the province of Orissa were introduced by him as cooks into Calcutta Society. In these days it was too risky a thing to eat food cooked by the Ooriya Brahmins. Even now many Hindu families do not take rice prepared at their hands. Like the Maharaja his descendants still patronise the Ooriyas by allowing them to live in their houses in large numbers, as free tenants. A writer speaking of the Ooriya bearer says that they are an old class in Calcutta, as in former days *palkis* were chiefly used. We find from a computation made in 1776 that they carried 3 lakhs of rupees yearly to their own country, made by their business. At the present day members of this important labouring class are employed as servants in the houses of the European and Indian inhabitants; as day-labourers they are engaged in different kinds of work. Babu Nagendra Krishna Vasu in his Bengali Lexicon* mentions that during Maharaja Nubkissen's time† about 3,000 families comprising Brahmin, Kayestha, weaver, oilman &c., inhabited Calcutta.

I shall now say something of the origin and nomenclature of the several localities. In 1799 the Circular Road was made. A writer says that "in the Circular Road the young and sprightly, in the fragrance of morning, *in the chariot of health*, enjoy the gales of recreation." "Alipur" takes its derivation from a Mussalman name. Nearly opposite Alipur Bridge stood "Two Trees" called the trees of destruction. Here Hastings and Francis exchanged shots. Park Street owes its name to Sir Elijah Impey's

* Biswa Kosha, Part III.

† Maharaja Nubkissen flourished in the time of Lord Clive and Warren Hastings.

Park.* In Upjohn's map of Calcutta in 1794, it was known as the Burial Ground Road. Chowringhee Road was spoken of by Holwell in 1752 as the "road leading to Collegot (Kalighat) and Dee Calcutta"—a market was held in it at that time. Upjohn in 1794 places 24 houses in Chowringhee between Dhurrumtolla and Brijitolla, the Circular Road and the Maidan. Lord Cornwallis in his day found few houses in Chowringhee and one-third of the Company's territories were jungle, inhabited only by wild beasts.

Dhurrumtolla derives its name from a great mosque, since pulled down, which was on the site of Messrs. Cook & Co.'s stables. "The ground belonged, with all the neighbouring land, to Jafer, the Jemader of Warren Hastings, a zealous Mussalman. The Karballa, a famous Mussalman assemblage of tens of thousands of people, which now meets in the Circular Road, used then to congregate there, and by its local sanctity, gave the name to the street "Dhurrumtolla" or "holy street." Garden Reach is one of the old places. General Martin described it in 1760 as containing 15 residences. Sir W. Jones lived in a bungalow at Garden Reach.

Kidderpur is called after Colonel Kyd. Lall Bazar, during Holwell's time, was noted as a famous bazar. In 1768 Mrs. Kindersley describes it to be the best street in Calcutta. It then stretched from the Customs House to Boytakhana.

Previous to 1757 Shovabazar and Pathuria Ghata were full of jungle. Maharaja Nubkissen Bahadur, the Tagores

* Sir Elijah Impey's Park has been thus described: It stretched to Chowringhee Road in the West and Park Street in the North, an avenue of trees leading through what is now Middleton Street, into Park Street from his house; it was surrounded by a fine wall, a large tank was in front and plenty of room for deer; a guard of Sepahis was allowed to patrol about the house and grounds at night, occasionally firing off their muskets to keep off the dacoits.

and other ancient families made these localities habitable. Raja Nubkissen's street was constructed at his own expense and presented to the Government. He also constructed a road 32 miles long, from Behalla to Kulpi.

The native part of the town east of Chitpur Road is said to be of recent origin. "Tiretta Bazar" is from a Frenchman named Tiretta. He established the bazar in 1788; its monthly income was Rs. 38,000; it was then valued at Rs. 2,00,000. Tiretta was superintendent of streets and buildings. Having become bankrupt, his properties were sold up in a lottery.

Rope-walk, now known as Mission Row, was a scene of hard fighting during the siege of Calcutta in 1757. It was named after the Mission Church. During the siege, the Nabob's troops demolished the Church, but in 1767 it was again rebuilt. Kiernander, the first Protestant Missionary, erected this church. *Old Court House Street* is called after the Old Court House or Town Hall. This house was erected about the time 1725-27 by Mr. Bourchier, a merchant, afterwards appointed Governor of Bombay in succession to Mr. Law in 1734. It was formerly a lower-roomed house and was said to belong to the charity school. Another version states that about the year 1767, with the aid of public subscription, Mr. Bourchier succeeded in erecting this Court House, the upper portion of which was also built by subscription. Stavorinus, writing in 1770, says :— "Over the Court House are two handsome assembly rooms. In one of these are hung up the portraits of the King of France and of the late Queen, as large as life, which were brought up by the

English from Chandernagore, when they took that place." The Court House was conveyed to the Government in 1792, and in the same year it was razed to the ground owing to dilapidated conditions. Mr. Orme, speaking of it in 1756 terms it "a very spacious house of one floor in which the Mayor's Court and assizes used to be held." How it became the property of the Old Calcutta Charity Fund is unknown.

Baboo Ghat was constructed by Baboo Raj Chundra Das, a millionaire of Calcutta. The Nimtola Ghat Street owes its name to a Nim tree. Clive Street was once a grand theatre of business, and Lord Clive's residence stood where now stands the Oriental Bank. Bagbazar or Bachbazar, Shambazar, Hatkhola, Janbazar and Bortola were mentioned even in 1749. Matsya Bazar or Machooa Bazar was famous as a mart for fish in the last century.

The Barabazar is mentioned in the very early history of Calcutta as a seat of trade. Chitpur Road is named after the goddess Chitteswari, whose shrine still stands at Chitpur. In early days human sacrifices were offered here. Her sanctity is so deep-rooted among all classes of the native population that even now vows are made and pujas offered for the attainment of cherished objects. This is the oldest road in Calcutta, forming a continuation of the road between Murshidabad and Kalighat. Mention is made in 1742 of Simla and Mirjapur. The sites were covered by paddy fields and stagnant tanks, which emitted noxious gas, very injurious to health. Simla was notorious as a rendezvous of thieves and rogues. As late as 1826, it is stated that in Simla "no native for love or money could be got to go this way after sun-set. It was once the abode of the weavers, and the produce of their loom was used by the fashionable native gentry. The site of the Cornwallis Square and of the Circular Canal was long noted for the murders committed there.

Baitakhana Street, now the Bow Bazar and the Baitakhana Street, derived its name "from the famous old tree that stood here and formed a Baitakhana or resting place for the merchants who traded to Calcutta and whose caravans rested under its shade."

Maniktollah is named after Mussulman Pir "Manik." Loudon Street is from the Countess of Loudon, Russel Street from Mr. Justice Russel, and Barretto Street from the Portuguese merchant Joseph Barretto. In an account given by Mr. Holwell in 1752, are mentioned Doubapara, Baniapukur, Tangra, Dolland, &c.

There are localities in Calcutta named after the trade practised by the residents there; such as Kumartuli (from potters), Suriparah (from liquor-vendors), Kansariparah (from braziers), Chutarparah (from carpenters), Jeliaparah (from fishermen), &c., &c. These traders not only carried on their respective vocations, but also belonged to different castes, and their social usages impressed their surroundings. Now-a-days events succeed each other so rapidly, and the minds of the people are engrossed in so many ways, that they no longer think of holding congregations of fellow-castemen. Thus few of the localities and streets now bear any association with the inhabitants. The houses in the northern part of the town have sprung up in quite an irregular way without any method or consistency, and with very little regard for even sanitary necessities. It was Mr. Warren Hastings who practically applied his taste for architecture. Mr. William Hodges, R. A., says: "For its (Calcutta) magnificence, however, it is indebted solely to the liberal spirit and excellent taste of the late Governor-General; and it must be confessed that the first house was raised by Mr. Hastings, which deserves the name of a piece of architecture; in fact it is even in a purer style than any that has been built since, although it is on a smaller scale than many others."* Mrs. Fay in 1780 thus speaks of Warren Hastings's house, Belvedere: "The house is a perfect bijou, most superbly fitted up with all that unbounded affluence can display; * * * * * * the grounds are said to be most tastefully laid out." Further on he built another house called "The Hastings House." His Excellency Lord Curzon of Kedleston has lately purchased this house and has furnished it as a guest house for the native feudatory chiefs. Mr. Hastings also built another house at a watering place Suk Sagor. There was also the Retreat at Baraset, the favourite abode of Governor Cartier so far back as 1763. Lord Clive had a resting place at Dum-Dum.

Eminent native gentlemen began to build houses in and around Calcutta. The Ray Rayan Maharaja Raj Bullabha Bahadur resided at Sutanooti. Ray Rayan Maharaja Gooroodas, son of Maharaja Nundkumar, lived at Charakdanga in Sutanooti. Dewan Ram Charan, Banian of Governor Vansittart and founder of the Andul Raj, lived at Pathuriaghata. Dewan Gonga Govinda Sing's residence was at Jorasanko. Canta Babu, the Banian of Warren Hastings,

* Travels in India during the years 1780 83, by William Hodges, R. A.

also lived at Jorasanko. Darpanarain Tagore, the Dewan to Mr. Wheeler, lived at Pathuriaghata. Munshi Sadaruddin, the Persian teacher of Richard Barwell, lived at Machua Bazar. Raja Petambar Mitter, the ancestor of Raja Rajendra Lala Mitter, also lived at Machua Bazar. Madan Mohan Dutt, the son of Ram Krishna Dutt, lived at Nimtola in Sutanooti. Banamali Sarkar, Dewan to the Commercial Resident at Patna and his deputy lived at Kumartuli. Govindaram Mitter, Dewan to the Zemindar of Calcutta, lived also at Kumartuli. He built a Navaratna or nine steepled temple on the Chitpore Road, the highest pinnacle of which is higher than the Ochterlony Monument. The main building and the highest steeple were blown down by the great cyclone which occurred in 1737. Omichand, the well-known millionaire and banker, lived in Calcutta in more than regal magnificence. His house was divided into various departments like a palace. Most of the best houses in Calcutta belonged to him. Omichand's famous garden, now called Halsi Bagan, was the head-quarters of Siraz-ud-doula during his siege of Calcutta in 1757. Maharaja Nubkissen's two dwelling houses in Sobhabazar were famous for their grandeur and style. According to Dr. Sambhu Chandra Mukherjee, they are in Oriental estimation the only two specimens of palatial buildings in a city styled the City of Palaces.* Nawab Mahammad Reza Khan, the Naib Dewan of Bengal, had a house in Chitpore. The Mysore family settled in Tallygunj in the beginning of the 19th century; and the Oudh family settled in Metiabruj (south of Kidderpur) in the middle of the century. Raja Ram Mohon Roy lived at Amherst Street. Dewan Kasinath lived somewhere

* Mukherjee's Magazine, 1861.

near Barabazar. Babu Baisnab Charan Seth, noted as a wealthy person and an honest merchant, lived in Barabazar. Gouri Sen, who lived in Barabazar, was famous for his open-handed liberality. He used to spend large sums of money in liberating prisoners confined for debts, and to pay fines for people who fought for a good cause. Hence his name is remembered in an adage " লাগে টাকা দেবে গৌরী সেন "—Gouri Sen will supply money, if required. Babu Sobharam Basack, noted as a very wealthy merchant, lived in Barabazar.

The ancient and wealthy Mullick families of Barabazar and Chorebagan, the ancestors of Raja Sukhomoy Roy, Ramdulal Dey, Moti Lal Seal, the ancestors of Kali Prosonno Sing, Gocul Mittra of Bagbazar and several other noted families, settled in Calcutta previous to the English settlement and after the battle of Plassey.

The old fort, called Fort William, was built in 1692; and it served like the feudal castles, " to form the nucleus of the town (as in England all those towns whose names end in Caster, were originally Roman camps,) the natives meeting with protection, and enjoying privileges in trade, soon settled down in Sutanooti and Govindpore."* Sir John Goldsborough selected the site of the old fort in *Dhee Collecotta* (Calcutta), it lay north of the burial ground, where Charnock and Goldsborough were buried, and south of the Barabazar which supplied provisions to the British settlement. Hamilton says the Governor's mansion (in the Fort) was an imposing structure, and the best and most regular piece of architecture. Inside the fort were also situated the old Zemindar's Kachary, a good hospital and barracks

* Vide *Calcutta Review*, Vol. XVIII.

for soldiers, and a church raised by the Company and public subscription; it was named after St. Anne.* The present Fort William was commenced by Lord Clive in 1757 at a short distance lower down the River Hughli than the old one; it was not finished till 1773. It cost £2,000,000. "It is of an octagon form, five of the faces are regular, while the forms of the other three, which front the river, are according to the fancy of the Engineer."

A ditch goes round the entire building. "The ditch is dry, with a cunette in the middle which receives the water of the river by means of two sluices that are commanded by the fort..The fort contains only such buildings as are necessary, such as the residence of the Commandant, quarters for the officers and troops, and the arsenal............................Each gate has a house over it, destined for the residence of a Major."† The valuation of the "fort and its interior buildings" was "Rs. 120,000," as was estimated jointly by the Engineer of the Fort, the Master Attendant and the Surveyor, in January 1757.‡ "In 1849, according to Major Ralph Smith, it mounted 619 guns, had a powder magazine big enough to contain 5,100 barrels of powder of 100 lbs. each, an arsenal containing 40 to 50 thousand stands of arms, besides pistols and swords. There were three to four thousand pieces of iron and brass ordnance of various calibre with shot and shell in proportion, amounting to nearly two million rounds exclusive of case and grapeshot. It was then capable of containing 15,000 men....................................the buildings

* Mr. A. K. Roy's Census of India, Vol. VII.

† Vide Oriental Commerce by William Milburn, Vol. II.

‡ A. K. Roy's Census of India, Vol. VII.

and arrangements have been steadily improved since 1857."*

The present Government House stands on the northern end of the Maidan. It was commenced by the Marquis of Wellesley in 1799 and was finished in 1804. The total cost amounted to about £150,000; for the grounds £8,000, for the building £130,000, and for the first furnishing £5,000. The grounds occupy about 6 acres and the design was adopted from Lord Scarsdale's seat of Keddleston Hall, Derbyshire, built by Robert Adam. Besides the apartments for the Viceroy and his staff, the building contains a Council Chamber in which the Supreme Legislative Council holds its sittings. The paintings, statues and other decorations that have been secured for it from time to time contribute greatly to the splendour of the mansion and are all interesting studies, and some of them of great historical importance.

The High Court is situated west of the Government House and close to the river. It was built in 1872 on the site of the Old Supreme Court. Its style is Florid Gothic, and the design was suggested by the Town Hall at *Ypres.*

The Town Hall also stands west of the Government House, between it and the High Court. It is of Doric style and was built in 1804 by the citizens of Calcutta at a cost of about Rs. 700,000. Among many interesting pieces of Art, it contains a marble statue of Warren Hastings, and that of Maharaja Roma Nath Tagore.

There are other public buildings, such as—The Bank of Bengal on the Strand, the Central Telegraph Office, the General Post Office, the new Secretariat of the Government of Bengal called the Writers' Buildings, etc. The

* Vide A. K. Roy.

Maidan has not only been called the lungs of Calcutta, but it is also celebrated for its monuments. From the statue of the great Sovereign, Her Majesty the Empress Victoria, it contains the statues of many Viceroys and Governors-General, Commanders-in-Chief and other high and distinguished officials. They are most of them excellent pieces of sculpture.

CHAPTER V.

RELIGIOUS, CHARITABLE AND EDUCATIONAL INSTITUTIONS.

A generous writer has borne the following testimony to the character of our fellow citizens, such as it was in those early days: "The inhabitants of Calcutta are distinguished for liberality which unquestionably cannot be paralleled among the nations of the universe ; a sober retrospect of them in their collective body will exhibit this unshaken truth : I speak not only from study and long observation, but from personal experience."* It has been the good fortune of the people endowed with such generous instincts to be guided by philanthropic Englishmen, of whom there was an abundance in those days. History affords striking evidence of the many sterling qualities of the head and heart which impelled Englishmen to be associated with works whose humanising influences have done so much to contribute not only to the happiness, but to the high moral standard of the people. Let me transcribe here very briefly the account given by this writer of Mr. Charles Weston, son of a Recorder of the Mayor's Court, who was born at Calcutta in 1731. Holwell was his friend and associate, and he carried arms as a

* A Compendious Ecclesiastical, Chronological and Historical Sketch of Bengal. Printed at Calcutta in 1818.

militia-man when Calcutta was attacked in 1756. By industry he rose to opulence. Of him it can be said that fortune never smiled upon a worthier favourite. It would be difficult to chronicle every act of his piety. To relieve the distresses of the indigent he made for regular provision. "Those who have seen better days, on whom fortune has ceased to smile, are comforted by Charles Weston." To his friends, associates and comrades he was always helpful in the seasons of their need. He was rightly nicknamed the "General Friend of Man."* Colonel Stewart's piety and humility of soul won all hearts. He was surnamed "Hindu Stewart." He looked with equal veneration upon Krishna and Christ. It is not necessary nor possible to enumerate in detail all the instances of individual piety of good men of different nationalities. It is enough to mention a few. Mr. Kiernander, the first Protestant Missionary in Calcutta, came out in 1758. He built a Protestant Church on the 27th May 1767 at a cost of more than 60,000 Sicca Rupees. About this time his Mission School came into existence, and "the following year 175 children had been received by him, 37 of which number he has provided for." The East India Company for a time lent a house for his school and church, and ultimately they were removed and he built houses for them in the present Mission Street. Colonel and Mrs. Robert Clive and Mr. and Mrs. Watts were among his valued friends. The Emperor of Delhi commissioned him to translate the religious works of the Christians into Arabic. He did so, and transmitted the same to his Imperial Majesty at Allahabad. Kiernander married twice. His second wife bequeathed her effects to her husband's church and school,

* Vide "A Compendious, Ecclesiastical, &c., &c."

and out of the sale proceeds of her estate he added a large room to his mission school building, capable of containing 250 children. Sir Eyre Coote and his lady evinced a great interest in this mission, and Lady Coote received sacrament here. In 1783, Kiernander's son gave Rs. 3,000, and he himself Rs. 1,000, and Sir Eyre Coote Rs. 500 to this mission. During his lifetime he gave away £12,000 in aid of it. In his later years he met with reverses of fortune, and his church and school did not escape from the clutches of law. Grant stepped forward and paid Rs. 10,000 to save the temple. In 1787 this church and school became public, and were transferred to the hands of the three trustees. Kiernander died in 1799. He was born on the 21st Nov. 1711 at Akstad in Sweden. His noble efforts to benefit his race—the Portuguese—were most conspicuous. His church was known among the common classes as Lall Girja. The Portuguese and English languages were taught in his school. The Armenian and Bengalee boys were also allowed to receive instruction there. It was his too sanguine expectation that the Hindu students would be converted to Christianity, but he was cruelly disappointed there.*

In Calcutta all religions are tolerated. It does not appear when the first church was built. There was a Christian church at Agra about the year 1600 built by the permission of the Emperor Akbar. Captain Hamilton, who was in this country from 1688 to 1723, published an account of his travels in 1727. He states therein: "About fifty yards from Fort William stands the church built by the pious charity of merchants residing there, and the Christian

* A Compendious Ecclesiastical and Historical Sketch of Bengal and the *Calcutta Review*, Vol. XVIII.

benevolence of sea-faring men, whose affairs called them to trade there; but Ministers of the Gospel being subject to mortality, very often young merchants are obliged to officiate and have a salary of 50 pounds per annum added to what the Company allowed them for their pains in reading prayers and a sermon on Sundays." In 1709 the Bishop of London christened it the church of "St. Anne." "This edifice, distinguished by its five lofty towers and spire, stood where the octagon now is at the west end of Writers' Buildings, and was ruined by the Nabob Siraj-ud-doula's army in 1756. In the great cyclone of 1737 the spire was blown down...

As soon as Calcutta began to enjoy repose from the troubles of 1756, the erection of a new church became an object of general desire." For a time the Portuguese church of Our Lady of the Rosary was taken for the Presidency church, but this proving damp and unwholesome, it was restored to the Portuguese. In July 1760, a temporary place of worship was erected within the battered walls of the Old Fort and named "St. John's Chapel." It was complained in 1774 that Calcutta had a noble play-house and no church. It was not, however, until the year 1782 that the inhabitants of Calcutta seriously determined to erect an edifice for public worship suitable to the capital of the Indian Empire. In 1782 a Church Committee was organised. Warren Hastings and his Council were its patrons. It was proposed to erect a church after the model of St. Stephen, Walbrooke, in London. As the model was determined on, one plan of St. Stephen's was executed by Colonel Polier and another by Colonel Fortnam. The first meeting of the Building Committee met on 1st December 1783, and Rs. 35,950 was subscribed and Rs. 25,592 was raised by lottery. The Maharaja Nubkissen Bahadur presented six bighas of land then valued at Rs. 30,000. The Company gave 3 per cent. from its revenue. Interest in the matter was so aroused that on the day when the foundation stone was laid, the Governor-General gave a public breakfast. The chief Government servants proceeded with great ceremony to the scene. Charles Grant despoiled Gour of some of its marble and loose stones of great length. Mr. Davis undertook ornamenting the church. A barrister, Mr. Hall, drew up the contract gratuitously. Wilkins, the great Orientalist, superintended the moulding of the stones prepared at Benares. Earl Cornwallis gave 3,000 sicca rupees. Zoffani, the great artist, painted the altar-piece gratis. It took 3 years to build the new church, and it was opened on the 24th of June 1787 by Earl of Cornwallis. Amongst others, the tombs of the following are preserved here—Hamilton, Charnock and his Hindu widow, and Watson.*

In 1839, on the southern corner of the Maidan, the building of St. Paul's Cathedral was commenced. The design and the plan were prepared by Major Forbes of the Bengal Engineers. The Cathedral was consecrated on the 8th October 1847. About £75,000 was raised for its construction, and of this amount the Bishop gave £20,000, one-half for the building and the other half for the endowment. The East India Company gave the site and £15,000. A sum of £12,000 was raised by public subscription in India, and £28,000 was subscribed in England. The cost of con-

* A Compendious Ecclesiastical, Chronological and Historical Account of Bengal, *Calcutta Review*, Vol., XVIII, and Hand book to Calcutta by Messrs. Newman & Co.

struction of the building was £50,000. The subscription raised in England represented a grant of £5,000 from the Society for the Propagation of the Gospel, also a grant of £5,000 from the Society for the Promotion of Christian Knowledge, and lastly a gift of £4,000 from an individual, Mr. Thomas Natt of London. The late Bishop Wilson's pious efforts raised this Temple of God. Now-a-days the Viceroy and Governor-General of India and other high personages attend the services held here, which are conducted by the Lord Bishop of Calcutta. Calcutta at present boasts of several churches belonging to the Roman Catholics, the Protestants, the Presbyterians, and the Methodists. The Armenians have had their places of worship so far back as the year 1689, but in 1720 an Armenian, Mr. Phanoos, purchased land for the Church, and in 1724 Aga Nazor took the land and by public subscription an Armenian Church named St. Nazareth was built. There is a story that in 1734 Hoozuri Mull, brother-in-law and executor of Omichand, the great banker, bore the cost of a steeple of St. Nazareth. There are also the prayer halls of the Chinese, the Jews, the Parsis, the Greeks and other nationalities.

The Mahommedans have their Musjids in the town of Calcutta, Tallygunj and Chitpore—486 in number—of which 376 Musjids are for the Sunnis, and 110 for the Shias. Prominent amongst them are the following:—

(*a*) Sinduriapati Musjid, at 98 Lower Chitpore Road, was founded by Hafiz Samaruddin Shaheb. Its present owner is Hafiz Abdul Aziz. A free boarding-house is attached to it for the maintenance of the indigent Mahommedan students.

(*b*) Haji Jakeria Mahommad's Musjid at Lower Chitpore was built by Haji Jakeria Mahommad. Its present owner is Haji Nur Mahommad Jakeria. A large number of students is provided with free board and lodging at the Musjid.

(*c*) Dhurumtolla Musjid, commonly called Tippoo Sultan's Musjid, was built and endowed in 1842 by Prince Golam Mahommad in gratitude to God and in commemoration of the Court of Directors granting him the arrears of his stipend in 1840.

(*d*) The Musjid at Machuabazar Street was founded by Fatu Kanjuria, an inhabitant of Cuttack. Mahommad Ghayasuddin is its present owner. As usual, a free boarding for a limited number of students is provided.

(*e*) A cobbler named Dina Chamrawallah built a Musjid at Harrison Road. Here also a free boarding is attached.

The Mahommedans worship in all those Musjids mentioned above, as well as in others; and in every Musjid there is an Imam or preceptor or priest for praying before God. These Musjids are situated on rent-free lands, and are exempted from Municipal rates and taxes.*

The Brahmo Somaj, or the Theistic Church, has three places of worship in Calcutta, one built at the instance of the late Babu Keshab Chandra Sen, situated in Machuabazar Street and known as the New Dispensation Church; another on Cornwallis Street, the well-known Sadharan Brahmo

* I am indebted to Syed Jafferalli for this list of Musjids. My thanks are also due to Khan Bahadur A. F. M. Abdur Rahaman, Judge, Small Causes Court, and Munshi Vilayet Hossein.

Somaj, but the first Brahmo Somaj in Calcutta was the Adi Somaj, founded by Babu Devendra Nath Tagore, son of the famous Dwaraka Nath Tagore. The Adi Somaj belongs to Babu Devendra Nath Tagore alone, but is open to all the Brahmos. The Brahmo Somaj was founded by Raja Ram Mohan Roy.

Kalighat, or Kalikshetra, is reckoned by the Hindus as one of the holiest places of worship in Hindustan. In the golden age, when the good King Daksha ruled, four toes of the right foot of the dead body of the great Sati, another name for Durga, were cut off and thrown over this locality by the Chakra of Vishnu, (the God of Preservation) of the Hindu Trinity. The sanctity of the place thus owes its origin to this divine association. To a Hindu, whatever sect he may belong to, be he a Saiva, a Sakta, or a Ganapatya, this place is very dear. From remote times, vows have been made here for the attainment of objects, and it is on record that in many instances the objects have been realised. Yogis and Sannyasis and saintly Hindus congregate at this place, and after quietly performing their worship of the great goddess go their own way. When the Feudatory Hindu Chiefs of the northern parts of India happen to be in Calcutta, they regard it as obligatory on them to offer Puja to Mother Kali before they return to their territories. The holiness of the temple has come to be known far and wide, and veneration for it is so deep-rooted in the minds of the Hindus that it may be compared to that of the temple of Bisweswar at Benares. It is said that the East India Company in their early days used to offer Puja to the Deity at

Kalighat. On the occasion of their Punnahas they participated in the ceremony, which they solemnised.*

It is unnecessary here to dwell at length on the origin and history of the shrine. In Markandiya Puran, and in the Tantrasar and several other purans and tantras, that subject has been fully discussed. It is said that formerly the temple of the great Goddess was on the very bank or ghat. It has therefore been quietly assumed that the present name of Kalighat is derived from the following circumstances. There is a tradition which is mentioned at Brihannil tantra (a spiritual book of the Hindus) that at a much anterior period this goddess Kali was only known to few devotees. Allusions to the shrine are found from the period when the celebrated Hindu King Ballal Sen flourished down to the period when Akbar ruled and the immortal poet Kabikankan composed his devotional hymns in honour of Chandi. It is stated that in 1809, Sontosh Roy of Barisa near Calcutta erected the present shrine. In his views of the History, &c., of the Hindus, Rev. Ward says: "At Kalighat near Calcutta is a celebrated image of this goddess whom (in the opinion of the Hindus) all Asia and the whole world worshippeth. The daily offerings to this goddess are astonishingly numerous; on days when the weather is very unfavourable not less than 320 pounds of rice, twenty-four of sugar, forty of sweetmeats, twelve of clarified butter, ten of flour, ten quarts of milk, a peck of peas, eight

* "Last week, a deputation from the Government went in procession to Kalighat and made a thank-offering to this goddess of the Hindus, in the name of the Company, for the success which the English have lately obtained in this country. Five thousand rupees were offered. Several thousand natives witnessed the English presenting their offerings to this idol. We have been much grieved at this act, in which the natives exult over us." [Life and Times of Carey, Marshman and Ward, by Marshman, Vol. I.]

hundred plantains and other things (the price of which may amount to five shillings) are offered, and eight or ten goats sacrificed. On common days, of all these things three times the quantity; and at great festivals, or when a rich man comes to worship, ten, twenty or forty times this quantity; and as many as forty or fifty buffaloes and a thousand goats are slain.

"Raja Nabakrishna of Calcutta, about fifty years ago, when on a visit to Kalighat, expended, it is said, not less than 1,00,000 rupees on the worship of this goddess. Amongst the offerings was a gold necklace valued at 10,000 rupees, a rich bed, silver plates, dishes and basins; sweet-meat and other food sufficient for the entertainment of a thousand persons; and trifling presents of money to nearly two thousand of the poor.

"About twenty years ago Jaya Narayan Ghoshal of Kidderpore near Calcutta expended twenty thousand rupees at this place, where he sacrificed twenty-five buffaloes, one hundred and eight goats, and five sheep, and presented to the goddess four silver arms, two gold eyes and many gold and silver ornaments.

"About ten years ago, a merchant from East Bengal expended five thousand rupees on the worship of this goddess, besides the price of a thousand goats which were slaughtered.

"In the year 1810, a Brahmin from East Bengal expended on this idol about 4,000 rupees, with part of which he bought a golden necklace, the beads of which were in the shape of giants' skulls.

"In the year 1811, Gopee Mohan, a Brahmin of Calcutta, expended 10,000 rupees on the worship of this goddess, but, being a Vaishnava, he did not offer any bloody sacrifices. The Hindus, it seems, are not the only persons who worship this black stone: I have received accounts several times of Europeans, or their native mistresses, going to this temple and expending thousands of rupees in offerings. The Brahmin with whom I wrote this account declares that when he was a student at Varisa near Kalighat, he several times saw the wives of Europeans come in palanquins with offerings; though I suppose these ladies were born in India. But the proprietors of the temple positively assured this Brahmin (as he says) that very frequently European men presented offerings, soliciting some favour at the hands of the goddess; and that very lately a gentleman in the Hon'ble Company's service, who had gained a cause at law, presented thank-offerings to Kali which cost two or three thousand rupees............................It is further affirmed that many Mussalmans (four or five hundred) present offerings monthly to Kali." Rev. Ward further on says:— "The village of Kalighat owes the greater part of its population to this temple; from which near two hundred persons derive their subsistence, exclusive of the proprietors, who amount to about thirty families. Some proprietors have a day in turn, others half a day, and others two or three hours, to whom all the offerings presented in the portion of time thus apportioned belong." The monthly expenses for the worship of the deity under all heads amounted, as Rev. Ward says, to sicca rupees 6,000, or Rs. 72,000 a year. At the present day Kalighat and its neighbourhood are included in the town of Calcutta, and persons of all denominations have settled there, and it has grown up into a populous suburb of Calcutta. The number of proprietors or shebaits has, since Rev. Ward wrote, much multiplied. There are at the shrine two other deities known as Sree Sree Nukuleswar and Sam Roy, who are also held in great reverence and worshipped by the Hindus. Sree Sree Govindaji was removed to Kalighat from Govindapore, where now stands the present Fort William. The belief is deep-rooted that the sanctity of Kalighat as a holy place has been further enhanced by the presence of Nukuleswar Bhairab—one of the Hindu Trinity.

As an instance of the religious nature of the Hindus, Rev. Ward says that Raja Ramkrishna of Krishnagore "spent a lakh of rupees in setting up the image of goddess Sree Sree Kali at Baranagore." His endowments for the maintenance of Brahmins and the poor are quite befitting the position of the Nuddea Raj family. I have already alluded to Babu Govinda Ram Mitra's nine steepled Temple. The goddess Sidhcswari on the Upper Chitpore Road in Baghbazar was also established by him. All classes of Hindus offer worship to the goddess. Babu Gocul Chand Mitra of Baghbazar established images of Madan Mohan, another name of Lord Sree Sree Krishna, and built a fine temple which he endowed and which is commonly known as "Madan Mohan's house." There is a tradition that this image originally belonged to the Raja of Bishnupore in Bankura, who pledged this for a considerable amount to the pious Babu Gocul. When, however, the Raja wanted back the image, Gocul felt much distressed and was reluctant to part with the deity, and in the meanwhile the Bishnupore Raja was advised in a dream not to press the matter on Gocul, and so the Raja desisted in demanding from Babu Gocul Chandra Mitra the return of the image.

Rev. Ward publishes the following account of the Lord Sree Sree Gopinathjee installed at his residence by Maharaja Nubkissen Deb Bahadur :—

"Two religious mendicants, since become famous among the followers of Krishna—Chaitanya and Nityananda—sent their disciple Goshu Thakura, who did not relish an austere life, to Agradwipa, and directed him to take a certain stone with him and make an image of Gopinathjea, which he should set up there and worship. Goshu Thakura obeyed the spiritual guides, took the stone on his head, set it up as a god, the gift of Chaitanya and Nityananda, and began to worship it in public daily."

How the divine image came into the possession of the pious Maharaja is thus narrated by Rev. Ward :—

"Raja Nubkissen of Calcutta once seized this image (Gopeenath of Agradwipa) for a debt of three lakhs of rupees due to him from the owner, Raja Krishna Chandra Roy (of Krishnagore)."*

Maharaja Nubkissen built two spacious Thakurbaries or mansions dedicated to gods, and also presented jewellery, gold plate, &c., to the deities. The present value of the property cannot be less than four lakhs of rupees. These two Thakurbaries, even at the present day, are looked upon as the grandest buildings dedicated to the gods in Calcutta.

* Ward's "View of the Hindus."

The Jain temple is situated on the outskirts of Maniktola and Halsibagan Road. The grounds attached to the temple are adorned with walks, flowers, statuary, fountains and lovely houses for feasting and amusements. The temple is handsomely built. The Marwaris generally belong to the Jain sect; their annual procession from Barabazar to the temple is the richest and grandest among those that pass through the streets of Calcutta. Pareshnath, Mohabeer and Adinath were the founders and reformers of Jainism. Its followers also worship such saints as Tirthankaras or Jinas. The Jainas like the Buddhists have great respect for animal life, and Pinjrapoles or asylums for invalid animals have been opened through their agency at differrent places in and around Calcutta. This interesting community is well known as the intelligent commercial class in Barabazar, dealing specially in cloths and jewellery. A new sect has arisen under the influence and teaching of Ramkrishna Paramahansa, looked upon by his followers as a saint. Swami Vivekananda was his notable disciple, and through his exertions a Matha or convent has been raised at Bellur on the other side of the river. Many of the followers of this new creed have identified themselves with varied works of piety. Numbers of Hindus flock to the annual festivals held at this place in honour of the celebrated founder.

Calcutta is noted for its charities. It would be difficult to estimate the liberality of the individual citizens. Acts of charity are as conspicuous now as they were in the early days. The good Edward Ives, the physician and friend of Admiral Watson, thus describes the spirit of charity prevalent in Calcutta in his time (1756-57).

"It is not possible to point out a part of the world where the spirit of charity is more nobly exerted than in our East India Company's settlements. Numerous instances may be mentioned where princely subscriptions have in a few hours been raised and applied to the effectual relief of many unfortunate families."* I shall endeavour to give in a brief compass an outline, which I fear must be an imperfect one, of several institutions of charity in Calcutta. It is well known that in several religious institutions in Calcutta, there are provisions made to look after the distress of the poor. Among the Hindus and Mussalmans it is necessary to feed and help the poor after the performance of any religious rites and ceremonies. Despite all the so-called changes and the cruel apathy and indifference to the distresses of the needy and helpless, that are so constantly laid at the door of the people of Calcutta, it is refreshing to find that their sympathy with the poor has been increasing. I shall mention some of the leading institutions of charity.

1. *The District Charitable Society.*—Bishop Turner, with the co-operation of private individuals, both European and Native, established the Society at Lall Bazar in 1830. An Alms House and a Leper Asylum in Amherst Street are attached to this institution. Government contributed handsomely to its funds, and Babu Dwaraka Nath Tagore of Jorasanko paid a lakh of rupees to this institution.

* "Sketches of Calcutta."

The Presidency Hospital.—According to Mr. Hamilton it came into existence in 1709. It is situated to the south of the present Presidency Jail and is open only to Europeans.

3. *The Mayo Native Hospital.*—Its original name was the Native Hospital. It owes its origin mainly to Rev. John Owen. It was established on the 13th September 1792, and was situated on Chitpore Road. It is open to the native population of Calcutta, particularly to the labouring class. Raja Baidyanath contributed Rs. 30,000 towards its funds. In 1796, some say 1798, the Hospital was removed to "the open and airy road of Dharamtolla." The Government grant was Rs. 600 per mensem, and the public subscribed Rs. 54,000. Lord Cornwallis gave Rs. 3,000, each Member of the Council Rs. 4,500, and the Nabob Vizier gave Rs. 3,000. The Government raised its grant afterwards to Rs. 2,000 per mensem. In 1871, removal to its present site was determined upon, and the surplus of the Mayo Memorial Fund, which amounted to Rs. 50,000, was transferred to the Hospital. Since then it came to be denominated as the Mayo Native Hospital. D'Souza contributed Rs. 10,000 for building purposes, and a portion of the Dharamtolla property was sold for Rs. 79,000. The building has 3 stories with out-door patients' rooms and quarters for the Resident Medical Officer. An out-door dispensary was retained in the old Hospital at Dharamtolla and three other dispensaries attached to the Hospital are in Park Street, Chitpore Road and Sukea's Street. This Hospital now stands on the Strand Road (North).

The Medical College Hospital—Is situated in College Street. It was built in 1848 during the administration of the Marquis of Dalhousie. From the funds of the Old and New Fever Hospitals, the balance of the fund of the Lottery Committee, and a splendid donation of Rs. 50,000 from the Raja Protap Chandra Singh of Paikpara, the Hospital was erected. A new Eye Infirmary has been erected to the north-east of the Hospital and has been named after Babu Shama Charan Laha who provided funds for its construction. A ward for the treatment of the Jews has been built at the sole expense of Mrs. Ezra and is attached to the main Hospital building; and in July 1882 the Eden Hospital for women and children was set up to meet a long-felt want in Calcutta. It was opened by the late Sir Ashley Eden. A writer makes this remark: "The Eden Hospital is now probably one of the most perfect Hospitals in the world........ ...." The subsidiary buildings include two large blocks for the residence of the two Hospital nurses.................. The liberality of the Seal family of Colootollah has greatly added to its usefulness, and Chunilal Seal's Out-door Dispensary is a noble instance of the benefactions of the benevolent donor.*

* It is said that a gun was fired from the ramparts of Fort William in honour of the performance of the dissection of the human bodies by the Hindu student, Babu Madhu Sudan Gupta, whose portrait is still to be seen in the Medical College Theatre. Mr. J. W. Kaye writes:—

"When Lord Bentinck first arrived in India, men of sound judgment and long experience shook their heads and said that the natives of India, to whom the touch of a corpse is the deadliest contamination, could never be brought to face the science of anatomy as European students face it in the dissecting-room. But the experiment under his auspices was tried. It was tried and succeeded. The Medical College of Calcutta was founded; and Hindus of the highest casts learnt their lessons in anatomy, not from models of wax or wood, but from the human subject. The beginning was small; but the progressive advancement was striking. In 1837—the first year of which a record was kept—sixty bodies were dissected before the students. In the next year it was precisely doubled. In 1844 the number had risen to upwards of 500. The College was highly popular. There was evidently a strong desire on the part of the native youths for medical and surgical knowledge..............."

5. *The Campbell Hospital*—Was originally known as a Pauper Hospital. It is maintained by the Government and the Calcutta Municipality.

6. *The Albert-Victor Hospital.*—This Hospital owes its origin to the Calcutta Medical School, established some 15 or 16 years before, mainly through the efforts of Dr. R. G. Kar, its present worthy Secretary, and other eminent physicians of the town. A portion of the fund of the Prince Albert-Victor Hospital represented the balance of the Albert-Victor Permanent Memorial Fund.*

7. *The Calcutta Society for the Prevention of Cruelty to Animals.*—Lord Elgin established this institution in the year 1862, after the model of the Royal Society of London. For a long time the want of an institution of this nature was greatly felt in Calcutta. In 1869, through the efforts of Babu Peary Chand Mitter, an enthusiastic member, an Act for the prevention of cruelty to animals was passed by the Bengal Legislature. The Society is supported partly by public subscriptions and partly by the dues allowed by the Government.

"In 1844, that liberal and enlightened native gentleman, Dwarka Nath Tagore, offered to take to England and to educate at his own expense two students of the Medical College. Dr. Goodeve, one of the professors of the college, offered to take a third pupil at his own expense, and raised an additional sum, by private subscription, which enabled him to take a fourth. The four pupils who accompanied the professor, and started in the steamer *Bentinck* on the 8th of March, were Bhola Nath Bose, a pupil of Lord Auckland's school at Barrackpur, who was supported at the Medical College by His Lordship for five years, and was considered by the late Mr. Griffith the most promising Botanical pupil in the school—Gopal Chundra Seal, Dwarka Nath Bose, a native Christian, educated in General Assembly's Institution, and employed for some time as assistant in the Museum, together with Surjee Comar Chuckerbutty, a Brahmin, native of Comilla, a junior pupil, and a lad of much spirit and promise."

* The College of Surgeons and Physicians, started by Indian medical gentlemen, has since been amalgamated with it.

8. *The Calcutta Deaf and Dumb School.*—Principally through the efforts of Babus Umesh Chandra Datta, B.A., Principal, City College, Jamini Nath Banerji, Srinath Singha and Mohini Mohan Mazumdar, this philanthropic institution came into existence. It is now in a most flourishing condition, and has a building of its own on Circular Road, and all classes of people, both official and non-official, take interest in its blessed work.

9. *National Association for Supplying Female Medical Aid to the Women of India.*—The Countess of Dufferin is the founder of this noble institution. It has branches scattered all over India. The management of its affairs is under the control of a Central Committee.

10. *The National Association* (Bengal Branch).—Its object is the promotion of social intercourse between Indians and Europeans and the dissemination of female education among respectable classes. Miss Mary Carpenter was the founder of this institution.

11. *The Indian Association for the Cultivation of Science.*—This Association was established in 1876, and is located in a spacious and magnificent building in Bow Bazar Street. To the single-minded devotion of the late eminent Dr. Mahendra Lal Sircar, M.D., D.L., C.I.E., it owes its origin and present prosperity. Since 1876, every succeeding Viceroy and Governor-General of India has been its patron, and the rulers of Bengal and several other personages have evinced a great interest in the institution.

12. *The Sovabazar Benevolent Society*—Was established in 1883-84. The Maharaja Komal Krishna Deb

Bahadur was its first patron and early supporter. His second son, Raja Binaya Krishna Deb Bahadur, is the founder. Its object is to relieve the distress of poor students, helpless widows and invalids, irrespectively of caste and creed. On occasions of famine, flood and other calamitous events, it bestirs itself to espouse the cause of the sufferers. The rulers of Bengal and other high personages take interest in its welfare. It is located at 106-1, Grey Street.

13. Maharaja Bahadur Sir Jotendra Mohan Tagore, K.C.S.I., has made an endowment in the name of his venerable mother and placed it under Government control for the relief of Hindu widows. This blessed work has been carried on by a committee appointed by the Government and the munificent donor.

14. *The Calcutta Orphanage.*—Babu Pran Krishna Datta is its founder. This institution has derived a valuable support through the kind interest of the large-hearted Kumar Manmatha Nath Mittra, Rai Bahadur, the grandson of the late Raja Digambar Mittra, Bahadur, C.S.I. The institution will soon have a building of its own, owing to the praiseworthy efforts of the enlightened Kumar.

There are the Anath-Bandhu-Samiti, the Bhawanipur Sahayya-Samiti, and the Palli-Samiti, in Ward No. 1, in the northern part of Calcutta, whose benevolent work to help the needy has deservedly gained them a local reputation.

I pass on now to notice the Educational Institutions. The English company of merchants, missionaries and other enlightened persons, did their part well in making an attempt to introduce education after a European model. It is quite natural that when the East India Company was merely a body of commercial adventurers, and was subject to Mahomedan laws and regulations, their efforts in this direction should be of a very meagre character. Even in England education was then entirely left to private and clerical enterprise. The Government hardly then stepped in to take up national education as one of its serious concerns. In the days of the Mahomedans, education was not neglected. Arabic, Persian and Urdu were taught among all classes of people. At the same time Vernacular instruction was given in the different provinces. From the earliest times the Hindus were noted for their love of learning. Here was developed a literature which is unsurpassed in its beauty and the intellectual subtlety of its contents. When Buddhism was prevalent, the Buddhist monks gave instruction to the students at several of their notable centres; and it is stated that the number of students at some of these centres was five to ten thousand. The *Pandits* have their *Toles, Chatuspaties* or Seminaries for giving instruction. In them the medium of instruction is both Bengali and Sanskrit, and grammar, rhetoric, law, astronomy, logic, metaphysics, and light literature, such as drama, fiction, &c., are the subjects taught. Some of these seminaries are endowed, but the great bulk of them subsists on the free gifts made on the occasions of marriage, *Sradh, Pooja* and other festivals; and the presiding *Pandits* also receive annual stipends known as *Barshika* from opulent Hindu families. The disinterestedness of the *Pandits* in affording gratuitous instruction, food and even clothing to their pupils, and the privations to which the latter subject themselves in the prosecution of learning, are alike honourable to both, and evince a love of knowledge and desire for its diffusion.

It is said that 20 charity children were provided for at an annual sum of about Rs. 2,400, and they were lodged and fed at the Old Court House or Town Hall. This fund came into existence in or about the year 1734. There is a conflicting opinion about the great banker Omichand's contribution of 30,000 rupees in aid of this fund. In 1734 A.D., Mr. Bruchier gave the Old Court House to the authorities "on condition of their paying Rs. 4,000 annually to support a charity school." The fund was further augmented as the restitution money was appropriated to this charity which the Company received as compensation for the English Church pulled down by the Moors in 1756.

We read the following accounts of the sources from which the Old Calcutta Charity Fund arose.*

1st.—The original subscription made before or about the year 1732.

2nd.—Church collection.

3rd.—The restitution money for the demolition of the Old Church made by the Nabob Meer Jaffer Alli Khan. The amount is unascertained.

4th.—The donation of Omichand by himself or his Almoner after his demise. He died in Calcutta in 1763. The amount and particulars are unascertained.

5th.—Seven thousand current rupees (or less) paid in the year 1773-74 by Mr. Charles Weston, as executor to the estate of Lawrence Constantius, an opulent Portuguese, deceased.

* Sketches of Calcutta.

To the above must be added 800 rupees per month, paid by the Company to the fund, as rent for the Mayor's Court or Town Hall, afterwards called the Old Court House. When afterwards the Old Court House had to be pulled down, the Government "agreed with the Church Wardens to pay that sum (Rs. 800) perpetually." There is every probability that the Warden and Chaplains had the direct management of the above fund, but the sole control was vested in the Hon'ble Company. In 1788, Dr. Bell delivered a series of lectures on experimental philosophy in this school, where lectures were also provided. In 1790 the property of the Old Calcutta Charity amounted to current Rs. 2,45,897. The Free School Society associated itself with the Old Calcutta Charity. Its fund in 1790 was Rs. 58,062. The two institutions were amalgamated and known as the Free School. The united value of the two was Rs. 3,03,989. It will not be amiss here to say something about the Free School Society. It came into existence on the 21st December, 1789. To meet the deficiency of a public charitable institution on a large scale in this great capital was among its objects. The Marquis of Cornwallis, the Governor of Chinsurah, warmly sympathised with its objects.*

About 1780, one Mr. Hodges advertised a Government School near the Armenian Church for teaching reading, writing and needle-work. Another advertised "a boys' boarding school beyond Chitpore Bridge, opposite the avenue leading to the Nawab's garden, reading, writing and arithmetic taught, Rs. 50 monthly, at the master's table, at a separate one Rs. 30; he does not intend to take more than 14

* A compendious Ecclesiastical, Chronological, and Historical Sketch of Bengal since the foundation of Calcutta, and *Calcutta Review*, Vol. XVIII.

boys unless he gets an assistant." In 1781, Mr. Griffith had a boarding school in his garden house near the Baitakkhanah, where "young gentlemen are genteelly boarded, tenderly treated and expeditiously taught." *

Mr. Archer, in 1800, opened a school for boys. His success attracted others to the field. In those days the office of school-master was recklessly adopted by all kinds and classes of men, who, instead of taking to the occupation of a lacquey or shoe-maker, found the office of a pedagogue more congenial to their taste. Thus a "broken-down soldier, a bankrupt merchant and a ruined spendthrift betook themselves to this profession. They looked upon it as one of the sources of income. It is said that an individual named Andiram Dass set up a school in his house, where a number of young Hindus used to attend daily upon him for hours and to wait his pleasure and convenience to get some scraps from his book. This pious philanthropist used to give out five or six words every day for their study."† It is stated that with the establishment of the Supreme Court in 1773-74 English education began to spread in a systematic way. One, Ramram Misra, and more especially his pupil Ram Narayan Misra, were then looked upon as English scholars of attainment. He kept a school in which a number of Hindu youths received their training, the fee ranging from Rs. 4 to Rs. 16. Previous to this period, Maharaja Nubkissen Deb Bahadur and Babu Nilmani Dutt, an ancestor of Mr. Romesh Chandra Dutt, C.I.E.,‡ were conversant with the English language; but it is not known how they learnt it. Perhaps

* Transactions of the Bengal Social Science Association, Vol. I.

† Ram Kamal Sen's Preface to his Dictionary.

‡ *Vide* Clive's Deposition. (Memoirs of Maharaja Nubkissen, page 70, and Marquis of Cornwallis's deposition anent the impeachment of Warren Hastings.)

the Maharaja learnt the language from Mr. Warren Hastings, whose Persian and Bengali teacher he was.

Mr. Archer's school was not the only one at the time. Farrell's Seminary and the Dhurumtolla Academy were its rivals. Messrs. Halifax, Lindstedt, and Draper also opened their schools about this time. In all these, a plain English education was given; and the principles of navigation and book-keeping were also objects of study. Mr. Drummond, himself a student of these institutions, writes:—

"He was the first person who introduced the study of grammar and the use of the globes in the Dhurumtolla Academy............................In truth, people looked for no higher qualification than *that comprised* in the three 'Rs.' —reading, writing, arithmetic." Mr. Drummond did a great deal to raise the standard of education to a higher level. It was at his instance the annual examinations were held. As at present, so was it formerly, a grand day for boys. It was a day of fear, of trembling and of joy. The prospect of a defeat—a discomfiture—was appalling to the lads; while the uncertain prospect of a prize and the too certain prospect of the joyful holidays were indeed soul-enlivening and soul-thrilling. To him alone is to be attributed the introduction in those days into his school of the study of English literature and the Latin classics. At this Academy, Derozio, afterwards the famous teacher of the Hindu School, received his early training. We have already spoken of Mr. Kiernander's Mission School. Mr. Canning had an Academy where the late Raja Sir Radha Kant Deb Bahadur, K.C.S.I., was educated. At Mr. Sherburn's School Dwarkanath Tagore received his education; and the Union School at Bhawanipur was the *Alma Mater* of Babu Harish Chandra Mukerji, Editor of the *Hindu Patriot*. Raja Dr. Rajendra Lala Mittra was a student of Khem Bose's School at Pathuriaghata. There were other schools conducted by Ram Mohan Napit, Kristo Mohan Bose, Bhubon Dutt, Shibu Dutt, Arratoon Peters and others. Raja Ram Mohun Roy also established a school under the title of the Indian Academy. It was popularly called Ram Mohun Roy's Hindoo School, and situated at Manicktolla Street. There were other private institutions, of which I mention the following:—

Indian Free School ...	... Morning	125	pupils.
Seal's Free College ...	... Day	300	,,
Patriotic College ...	... Day	110	,,
Oriental Seminary (A.D. 1823)	... Day	585	,,
Anglo-Indian School ...	... Morning	100	,,
Union School (A.D. 1793)	... Day	100	,,
Hindu Benevolent Institution	... Day	100	,,
Literary Seminary ...	... Day	50	,,
Charitable Morning School	... Morning	80	,,

Of these educational institutions, the Oriental Seminary deserves prominent notice. Such distinguished persons as the late Justice Shambhu Nath Pandit, the late Babu Akshay Kumar Datta, the eminent Bengali writer, and Mr. W. C. Bonnerjee, the eminent Calcutta Barrister, were among its early students. Its founder was Babu Gour Mohan Addy. A writer in the *Calcutta Review** thus writes about him:—

"At the age of 27, finding that he had no other resources, he opened a school for his countrymen, and for a number of years perseveringly laboured until he could number about 200 pupils. He then entered into partnership with one Mr. Turnbull, and found his school make great progress.

* Vol. XIII.

After the death of his colleague, until the day of his own death, he conducted the school under his own superintendence. Fortunately he picked up one Mr. Herman Geoffry, a Barrister and child of misfortune, and, under his able tuition, Gour Mohan saw his school rise to great importance. ....He was a very pious-looking man, and so candid as to tell his pupils of the first class, that he could not superintend their lessons. In him was no false pride. What he knew, he could communicate better than any other native. He was exceedingly good-tempered; and it was matter of surprise to us to see how well he steered his course through the variety of temper and dispositions with which he had to deal, and on no occasion did he give offence. He was very popular among his pupils, and though a strict disciplinarian, and having to do with boys whose attendance is dependent on their own will, he commanded the respect of all, and was beloved by many."

The Seal's Free College cannot be passed over without a short notice. It came into existence by the benefaction of the noble Mati Lal Seal. This is the only institution in Calcutta which imparts education to the poor native students free of charge. Some of the boys get free boarding. Babu Mati Lal Seal rose from very indigent circumstances to great opulence. He was highly distinguished for his piety and unlimited charity. He was a large-hearted philanthropist, and was the founder of the Kalootolla Seal family.

I have hitherto briefly noticed the efforts of private individuals in establishing educational institutions in Calcutta. I shall now briefly mention the services of the missionaries and other bodies of men towards this end. To enter into the subject at once, I shall speak first of the "*Mahapathshala*, or the Hindu College of Calcutta." A preliminary meeting of respectable Hindus was held at the residence of the Chief Justice (Sir E. Hyde East) on the morning of the 4th May, 1816,* for the purpose of subscribing and forming an establishment for the liberal education of their children. The Chief Justice opened the business, dilating on the advantages of the establishment of an educational institution, and urged the audience to move in the matter. The proposal was cordially supported by the Hindu gentlemen, including the eminent *Pandits*, and a decent amount † was subscribed on the spot. And at this preliminary meeting Messrs. W. C. Blaquiere and J. W. Croft were appointed provisional treasurers to receive subscriptions. A public meeting was held on the 21st, at which the Governor-General and his councillors were appointed patrons, the Chief Justice, Sir E. Hyde East, President, J. H. Harington, Esq., Chief Judge of the Sudder Dewani and Nizamat Adalat, Vice-President, eight Europeans, five eminent *Pandits* and fifteen other native gentlemen, members of the Committee. And at the meeting of the 27th, Mr. Joseph Barretto was appointed Treasurer and Lieut. Francis Irvine, English Secretary, and Dewan Baidya Nath Mukerjee‡ was appointed as Native Secretary to assist the English Secretary in his work, and a Sub-Committee, consisting of Mr. W. C. Blaquiere, Ram Gopal Mullick, Gopee Mohan Deb and Hari Mohan Tagore, was formed to take measures

* Some writers have put it 14th May. I have derived my information from the copy of the proceedings found in the archives of the late Raja Sir Radha Kanta Deb Bahadur, K. C. S. I. who was Governor of the Hindu School, and whose father was one of its founders.

† Upwards of £6,000 was raised. *Vide* I. W. Kenye's Administration of the East India Company.

‡ Whose grandson was the famous Hon'ble Justice Anukul Chandra Mukerjee.

for providing a proper place for the site of the intended college, as also to procure a temporary building for the location of the institution. The object of the institution declared in this meeting was as follows:—

"That the primary object of the institution is the tuition of the sons of the respectable Hindus in the English and Indian languages, and in the literature and science of Europe." On the 11th June next, English gentlemen of the Committee desired to relinquish their right of voting, and the President and the Vice-President also desired that they should be considered as mere private friends of the institution. Hitherto all the sittings of the Committee were held at the house of the Chief Justice. Perhaps it would be interesting to the readers to know the names of the teaching staff and their salaries:—

NAMES.	SALARIES.
Mr. James Isaac De Anselme, Head School Master of English Department	Rs. 200 per month and Rs. 100 as outfit ... on entering the service.
Mr. Nicholas Willard, Monitor ...	„ 36
„ Peter Emneer, Monitor ...	„ 36
„ Henry Ward, Monitor ...	„ 16
Moulavi Mâh. A. Bukshee, Teacher of Persian ...	„

Lieut. Francis Irvine's pay as Secretary was Rs. 300, and Dewan Baidya Nath Mukerjee's pay as Native Secretary, Superintendent and Accountant was Rs. 100 per mensem.

The Hindu College was opened on Monday, the 20th January, 1817, at the house of Babu Gora Chand Bysack, paying a monthly rent of Rs. 80. The renting was necessary as Babu Haronath Kumar was unwilling to place his Chitpore house, situated on the west side, in the hands of the Committee. Such men as the late Mr. David Hare and Horace Hayman Wilson evinced great interest in the institution. The services of the late David Hare, for ameliorating the condition of the Indians, have deservedly made his name honoured and respected. It was on his lands, which he made over to the Government, that the Hindu and Sanskrit Colleges were built at a cost of Rs. 1,24,000. His efforts to make the Medical College of Calcutta useful and popular in its early days of struggle are matters of high praise. Although he may not be called an educated man in the common acceptation of the term, his absorbing interest in education and his idea of spreading Western education in the land of the East, entitle him to be regarded as an educationist of a high order. There were few men, European or Indian, who did so much for the Hindu College, as David Hare. He was a great philanthropist and a friend of the poor. He came to this city in 1800, as watch-maker, and after following that profession for some time, he gave it up and devoted his time and fortune to the education of the natives. We find him closely associated in all progressive movements then started for the good of the country. His zeal and energy for the introduction of trial by jury into Civil Courts, the emancipation of the Press, and his strenuous opposition to the cooly trade are only a few instances of his many-sided activity. The *Friend of India*, in a handsome obituary notice, said nothing but the truth when it observed: "No individual in India has ever pursued so remarkable a career as the late David Hare.........Mr. Hare affords the remarkable, and in India the solitary instance of an individual without any refinement of education, without intellectual endowments, without place or power or wealth, acquiring and retaining for a long series of years one of the most important and influential positions in native society, simply by a constant endeavour to promote the improvement of the rising generation. He died on the 1st of June, 1842, and a tomb was immediately erected by a rupee subscription. The inscription on the tomb is as follows:—"He was a native of Scotland and came to this City in the year 1800, and died 1st June, 1842, aged 67, after acquiring a competence by probity and industry in his calling, as a watch-maker. He adopted for his own the country of his sojourn, and cheerfully devoted the remainder of his life with *unwearying* zeal and benevolence to one pervading and darling object on which he spared no personal trouble, money or influence, *viz.*, the education and moral improvement of the Natives of Bengal, thousands of whom regarded him in life with filial love and reverence, and lament him in death, as their best and most disinterested friend, who was to them even as a father."

On the 17th June, 1841, under the auspices of the late Raja Kissen Nath Roy, ancestor of Maharaja Monindra Chandra Nandi, a public meeting of the Hindu Community was organised at the theatre of the Medical College for the purpose of determining on the most suitable testimonial to be voted to the memory of David Hare. A full-length statue was determined on, which can be seen between the Presidency College and Hare School. The inscription on the pedestal is as follows :—

"In honour of David Hare, who by steady industry having

acquired an ample competence, cheerfully relinquished the prospect of returning to enjoy it in his native land, in order to promote the welfare of that of his adoption."

At the instance of the late Babu Kisori Chand Mitter, the Hare Anniversary Committee was formed with himself as secretary and the late Rev. Dr. K. M. Banerjee, D.L., as its president. A speech or essay on some point connected with the intellectual and moral improvement of the Indians is delivered at every anniversary of his death; and a Hare Prize Fund was also opened for the encouragement of the Bengali language.

The subsequent history of the Hindu College can be told in a few words. The Hindu College building was completed in 1825, but the failure of Joseph Barretto and Sons, who acted as treasurers, caused the loss of all the funded property that was with them. The Managing Committee applied to the Government for help, and the Government readily came forward and desired that the Committee of Public Instruction should henceforth exercise control over its management. There was a difference among the members about the Government proposal. Ultimately it came to a happy settlement by the selection of Dr. H. H. Wilson* and David Hare to represent the contending parties. About

* The following sketch of Professor Wilson's varied accomplishments is really not overcharged. It is written by one who differs widely from him on many essential points, and is uninfluenced by personal friendship:—" Perhaps no man, since the days of the admirable Crichton, has united in himself such varied, accurate and apparently opposite talents and accomplishments. A profound Sanskrit scholar, a grammarian, a philosopher and a poet, he was at the same time the life of society and a practical clear-headed man of business. On the stage as an amateur, or in the professor's chair as the first Orientalist of our time, he seemed always to be in his place; he has written on the antiquities, the numismatology, on the history, literature, chronology and ethnology of Hindustan; and on all these subjects not even Colebrooke himself has written so much and so well. His works show all the erudition of the German school, without its heaviness, pedantry and conceit; and his style is the best of all styles—the style of an accomplished English gentleman."—*(Calcutta Review)* Kay's History of the Administration of the E. I. Company.

this time, Raja Buddinath, Harinath Roy, son of Kanto Baboo, and Kalisanker Ghoshal gave Rs. 50,000, Rs. 20,000 and Rs.20,000 respectively, which amounts were appropriated to the establishment of scholarships to induce students to prolong their academic career. The old Hindu College is now known as the Hindu School and is a Government institution.

The Hare School—Is named after the sacred memory of David Hare. It is a Government institution.

La Martinière College—Was founded by General Martin, who bequeathed two lakhs of rupees for a school for the Christians, and a further sum of one lakh and fifty thousand rupees "to add to the permanency of the school." The College has two departments—one for boys and the other for girls—affiliated to the B. A. standard of the Calcutta University. This is one of the most wealthy institutions in Calcutta.

Claude Martin was a native of Lyons in France. He fought under Count Lally in India. Subsequently he was in the service of the East India Company, where he rose to the rank of Major-General. The school was opened on the 1st March, 1836, and according to General Martin's Will, it was named "La Martinière." My esteemed friend, Mr. S. C. Hill, B.Sc., late of the Imperial Library of the Government of India, has recently written a valuable biography of Claude Martin.

St. Xavier's College—Is located at 10 and 11 Park Street, and was established by members of the Society of Jesus, who in 1834 were sent by His Holiness the Pope to support the cause of religion in Calcutta. To the generosity of the two residents—one vacated his house for the location of the College, and the other contributed liberally for its support—it owes its existence. In 1844 the Right Rev. Dr. Carew purchased the present building originally intended for the Sans Souci Theatre. It was then named St. John's College, and since the advent of the Belgian Jesuits, its management has been made more efficient and the present name given.

The London Missionary Society's Institution.—This is the outcome of the London Missionary Society's educational work in Bengal, which began in 1798. In 1854 it was transferred to a larger and commodious building at Bhawanipur, consisting of a fine library, halls, class rooms, &c.

The General Assembly's Institution.—This institution was established by the active help of the General Assembly of the Church of Scotland. Dr. Alexander Duff, in 1830, not only established this institution, but imparted sound Christian instruction through the medium of the English language, instead of the vernacular, which was used by the earlier missionaries. For several years the school was held in various hired premises. At length in 1838, when the new building was completed, it was transferred to its present site in Cornwallis Square. The situation is perhaps the best that could have been selected.

In 1844, the institution was temporarily closed in consequence of the missionaries having joined the Free Church. It was re-opened in 1846 by the Church of Scotland under the superintendence of the Rev. Dr. Ogilvie.

It has two departments—the School and the College.

Free Church of Scotland Institution and Duff College.—This institution traces its origin to the labours of Rev. Alexander Duff, D.D., in connection with the General Assembly of the Church of Scotland, before the disruption in 1834. On the disruption taking place, the General Assembly's Institution was temporarily closed, and Dr. Duff had to leave the building with his valueable library. Teachers, pupils, and converts followed Dr. Duff and the other missionaries; and the institution was removed to a hired house at Nimtolla. The present building was completed with the aid of the funds raised by Dr. Duff in Scotland, England and India in 1857, when the institution was removed there. It has School and College Departments.

Dr. Duff used to live first at 22 Mirzapur Street and then at 2 Cornwallis Square. At his first residence, he delivered lectures on the evidences of Christianity, which resulted in the conversion of the late Rev. Dr. K. M. Banerjee, D.L., C.I.E.

Dr. Duff also opened an Orphanage, a Hindu Girls' School and a Normal School.

Bishop's College.—Bishop Middleton, with the enthusiastic co-operation of the Society for the Propagation of the Gospel, laid the foundation stone of the College on the 15th December 1820. It was founded with the object of propagating the benefits of Scriptural as well as general education, as also of translating the Scriptures and other religious works, and of affording residence to European missionaries on their arrival in India. The College had a boarding house attached to it and was endowed with several scholarships—the holders of which were allowed board and education free of cost. This College was formerly located at the present Sibpur Government Engineering College building. Thence it was removed to 233 Circular Road, and subsequently to 224 Lower Circular Road.

From the foregoing hasty sketch, it would be difficult to charge the inhabitants of Calcutta with cruel apathy and indifference to education. It would seem that in those days they displayed a warm and active interest in the moral and intellectual training of the rising generation; nor were the Government and the officials slow to recognise their own responsibilities. The enlightened mind of Warren Hastings anticipated one of the needs of the country by founding the *Calcutta Madrasa* in the year 1780, on the European model. The object of this institution was to impart instruction in Arabic, and also in Persian, then the Court language of the country. This institution came into existence from the handsome donation of Rs. 3,00,000 made by Maharaja Nobokissen Bahadur.* Warren Hastings also extended his patronage to Hindu Pandits, and about this time, through his encouragement and assistance, translation of Hindu and Moslem works was commenced. His efforts to translate Moslem and Hindu codes have extorted well-deserved admiration from various quarters, for his sympathy and appreciation for the Oriental races.† Through his zeal and activity the Asiatic Society of Bengal was founded, with Sir

* *Vide* Memoirs of Maharaja Nubkissen Bahadur.
† Malleson's Warren Hastings.

William Jones as its president. According to Lord Teignmouth, it was due to Warren Hastings' endeavour that Europeans began to make an attempt to learn the Oriental languages.* To Lord Wellesley belongs the credit of founding the College at Fort William for the English officials; and the Marquis of Hastings felt the supreme necessity of public education, for we read in his Minute on the Judicial Administrations of the Presidency of Fort William, Bengal, dated the 2nd October 1815: "In looking for a remedy to these evils, the moral and intellectual improvement of the natives will necessarily form a prominent feature of any plan which may arise from the above suggestions, and I have therefore not failed to turn my most solicitous attention to the important object of public education." His Lordship desired also to establish a Sanskrit College, but it was not till Lord Amherst became Governor-General that the Calcutta Sanskrit College was founded in 1824, with an annual income of Rs. 30,000. Previous to this, in 1791, the Benares Sanskrit College, and in 1823, the Agra College, were established. Lord Hardinge was also anxious for the spread of education—especially of vernacular education—in the country. A writer dealing with this topic remarks that it was in Hughli the seeds of English education were first sown; and one Robert May, dissenting missionary, residing in Chinsura, opened in his dwelling-house, in July 1814, a school with 16 boys on the Lancastrian plan. The Government afterwards extended its patronage by paying monthly Rs. 600 to this institution. The munificent Maharaj Adhiraj Tej Chand of Burdwan exhibited a great desire to spread English education in the country. The efforts of the mis-

* *Vide* Sir John Shore's Notes on Warren Hastings.

sionaries, in the field of vernacular education, have been strenuous. With no encouragement from the authorities, and under fear of deportation by the Company, they not only devoted themselves with zeal to their work of conversion, but they were also the first among the Europeans to study the vernacular dialects. Sir William Hunter writes:—"About 1810, the Baptist Mission at Serampore, above Calcutta, raised Bengali to the rank of a literary prose dialect. The interest of the missionaries in education, which has never ceased to the present day, although now comparatively overshadowed by Government activity, had two distinct aspects: they studied the vernacular in order to preach to the people and to translate the Bible; they also taught English as the channel of Western knowledge.* It is said that previous to 1817 David Hare, in conjunction with the late Raja Sir Radha Kanta Deb Bahadur, K.C.S.I., employed much time in improving the vernacular schools. A student belonging to David Hare's Vernacular School thus describes his efforts:—" Mr. Hare's educational efforts were directed in the first place towards the encouragement of the vernacular. He supplemented the deficiencies of numerous Guru Patshalas by the employment of inspecting Pandits and the grant of printed books. Periodical examinations were also held at Raja Sir Radha Kanta Deb Bahadur's garden house, and prizes given. He then established a sort of central vernacular school directly under the School Society. This was a large institution and numbered about 200 boys. It was the best vernacular school of the day. For the encouragement of regular attendance, each child got eight annas a month if he was not absent a single day during that

* Hunter's Imperial Gazetteer, Vol. VI, page 422.

month. If absent only one day he got six annas, if two days four annas, and if he was absent for more than two days then he got nothing. Distinguished lads from the vernacular schools were sent to the Hindu College, in which the Society always maintained 30 boys. An English school was afterwards established adjoining the central vernacular—a number of select boys of the vernacular school would attend the English classes also. It was thus from sunrise till 9 A.M., Vernacular; from 10½ A. M. to 2½ P.M, English; from 3½ P.M. to sunset, Vernacular again."*

In 1838, Adam published his reports at a cost of three lakhs of rupees borne by the Government, surveying the vernacular education throughout Bengal and Behar, which brought into prominence the efforts of the missionaries, private individuals and the part played by Government. Lord Dalhousie and the Hon'ble Mr. Halliday did much for the promotion of vernacular education. But Lord William Bentinck's administration is marked by the encouragement and promotion of the study of English in the school. During his rule (1833) the Charter of the East India Company was renewed and a Law Member was appointed to the Governor-General's Council, who might not be a servant of the Company. Thomas Babington Macaulay (afterwards Lord Macaulay) was the first Law Member of the Council. His advent at this juncture proved an incalculable support to the advocates of English education in this country. His celebrated Minute, dated the 2nd February 1835, was a vigorous protest against the Orientalists. Lord Macaulay in summing up his views stated:—

* Adam's Report on Vernacular Education in Bengal and Behar.

"I think it is clear that we are not fettered by the Act of Parliament of 1813; that we are not fettered by any pledges expressed or implied; that we are free to employ our funds as we choose; that we ought to employ them in teaching what is best worth knowing; that English is better worth knowing than Sanskrit or Arabic; that the natives are desirous to be taught English, and are not desirous to be taught Sanskrit or Arabic; that neither as the language of law, nor as the language of religion, has the Sanskrit or Arabic any peculiar claim on our encouragement; that it is possible to make the natives of this country thoroughly good English scholars; that to this end our efforts ought to be directed."*

The modern system of education was based upon a comprehensive despatch sent out by Lord Halifax. And during the administration of Lord Dalhousie the old Hindu College was transformed into the Presidency College. Moral and Mental Philosophy, Logic, Natural Science, &c., were included in the curriculum. In 1857, the Calcutta University was established in imitation of the London University. It is merely an examining body, with the privilege of conferring degrees in Arts, Law, Medicine and Civil Engineering. It consists of a Chancellor, a Vice-Chancellor and a Senate. Its governing body is called the Syndicate, composed of the Vice-Chancellor and a few members elected by the different Faculties. In 1882-83, the noble Lord Ripon appointed an Education Commission, which aimed to complete the scheme inaugurated in 1854. The late Sir William Hunter, the President of the Commission, observed :-

* The late Raja Ram Mohun Roy made similar advocacy for English Read his Memorial to Lord Amherst, published in the Biography of David Hare by Peary Chand Mitter in 1877.

"Female education and the instruction of certain backward classes of the community, such as the Mahommedans, received special attention. The general effect of the Commission's recommendations is to develop the Department of Public Instruction into a system of truly national education for India, conducted and supervised in an increasing degree by the people themselves."

During the Viceroyalty of Lord Curzon, an Education Commission upon a wider basis was appointed, which went about from province to province taking evidence of expert educationists and other leading persons. Its purpose was to probe the present system with a view to bringing to light its defects and shortcomings, and finding out the means for their remedy. I cannot do better than refer to the Resolution published in March 1904, issued from the Home Department of the Government of India, for a comprehensive statement of the educational policy of the Government. At present, in Calcutta, more than a dozen first grade Colleges exist, owned by the Government, the missionary bodies and private individuals. I have already mentioned some of these Colleges. Among the Native first grade Colleges, the Metropolitan Institution founded by the late Pandit Iswar Chandra Vidyasagar and affiliated in 1879, the City College, belonging to the Sadharan Brahmo Somaj, affiliated in 1881, the Ripon College, founded by Babu Surendranath Banerji, and affiliated in 1884, the Central College, founded by Babu Khudiram Bose, and affiliated in 1896, and the Bangabasi College, affiliated in 1887 as a second grade College, and in 1896 as a first grade College, may be mentioned.

Pandit Iswar Chandra Vidyasagar was the eldest son of Pandit Thakurdas Banerji and was born in 1820 in the village Birsinha in the District of Midnapore. He was admitted into the Sanskrit College on the 1st June, 1829, and prosecuted his studies there till 1841. From 1841-42 to 1858, he served the Government on a salary ranging from Rs. 50 to Rs. 500 in various capacities, such as Head Pandit and Head Clerk of the Fort William College, Professor and then Principal of the Sanskrit College, and at last Inspector of Schools in the districts of Burdwan, Nuddea, Hughli and Midnapur. He died in July 1891. A writer has justly stated that "to Iswar Chandra, the present able Principal (Sanskrit College), animated by the spirit of a Bacon and a Bopp, are we indebted for making the institution, besides the mental training given in it by Sanskrit, a philological one, a royal academy for Bengali, a fount for purity of style, a training school for able philological teachers. He has taken the noble Sanskrit away from being the weapon of superstition and Brahminical enthralment to be the lever for giving dignity to the language of the masses. What Whateley has done for popularising logic, or Socrates philosophy, Iswar Chandra has done for facilitating the study of Sanskrit Grammar, rendering a study hitherto so abstruse as easy as Greek. His Grammar and easy Reading Lessons in Sanskrit are now the class books in various English Schools, where the pupils learn the Bengali Sadhu Bhàshà by his system—and professor Wilson's statement is verified, that a native can be taught Sanskrit in three or four years. Instead of youths being "four or five years engaged on the study of Sanskrit Grammar, and not advanced beyond its simplest rudiments, they, after three months' study of the declensions and conjugations, begin reading simple Sanskrit sentences, and then study the Belles Lettres and poetic works, thus liberalising the mind. For an account of Iswar's improved system, see Report of the Committee of Public Instruction for 1852. His elementary Sanskrit Grammar and Reader have been introduced into the course of study of the chief Missionary Institutions in Calcutta, and into various mofussil schools, as being the best means of grounding pupils thoroughly into the Bengali idiom and in etymology and in making them familiar with technical terms. The Mugdabodha is being gradually displaced by the natives themselves. Iswar's name will go down to posterity with those of Wilkinson of Sehore and of Dr. Ballantyne who has made Bacon intelligible to the Pandits of Benares—men who have done so much for enlisting the learned and influential classes of this country in a course of diffusing enlightened ideas."

Sitting at his feet and reflecting on his career, one realises that in no other case is it more aptly illustrated, that an honest man is the noblest work of God, than in the life of the venerable Pandit. Here was a person born of poor parents, but of the highest caste, and belonging to a class that realises in actual life the high ideal of "plain living and high thinking." His talents and energy, his purse and influence—nay, he himself—were all dedicated to the service of humanity. The movement that he started for the re-marriage of Hindu child-widows shows the breadth of his sympathies. It was characteristic of him that what he did he did with his whole heart. As to his philanthropy, a remarkable writer, Mr. N. N. Ghose, has well said "that when Vidyasagar died, charity shrieked." His detestation of all kinds of sham hypocrisy and artificialities of life is

* *Calcutta Review*, Vol. XXII.

striking. He never bartered his conscience for any worldly prospects. His efforts to establish educational institutions—and more especially his Metropolitan Institution—at a time when everybody considered that they would prove abortive, were really a marvel. Single-handed, and without any extraneous help whatsoever, he managed his institution wholly officered by the children of the soil.

The Calcutta Sanskrit College was founded by Lord Amherst, as has been already observed, in 1824. A Committee was appointed for the management of the institution. Several endowments were assigned for the payment of stipends to the pupils. Stipends were formerly allowed to Brahmin students only, and the College was originally open to them alone. That restriction has now been removed, and Hindu students of all castes are admitted there. A medical department with a dissection class was also attached to the institution, but it was abolished owing to the incompetence of the teaching staff. A valuable Sanskrit library is attached to the College.

The Calcutta School Book Society was founded in 1817. The following Circular was issued in 1817, May 7 :—

To

Baboo Gopee Mohan Deb.

Calcutta, 7th May 1817.

Dear Sir,

Will you let me have the pleasure of seeing you to-morrow to request your permission for your son to attend a meeting to be held under the auspices of Mr. Bayley for the encouragement of school learning by providing proper books for the purpose. It is hoped that the object will be equally desirable for, and promoted by, Hindus and Musalmans as well as by the English gentlemen, being intended to promote moral education amongst all of us. The meeting on Tuesday next will be merely preparatory, in order to settle the general resolutions, which have been directed to be translated into Bengali and Persian, for the better understanding of them by the native gentlemen, and when approved by the Committee, they will be made public and the subscription book opened to receive contribution of the well-disposed of every description. The subscriptions are intended to be on a moderate rate, so that our friends need not be alarmed for the amount. I hope that yourself and our friends in general, to whom I wish to mention the subject, will find this object worthy of your zealous approbation and support, as it will be found very useful, if well executed, for our own College, in supplying us with good books.

I am,
Dear Sir,
Yours faithfully,
(Sd.) E. H. East.

In May 1821, this Society received from the Government a donation of Rs. 7,000, and a monthly subscription of Rs. 500, to be continued "while its concerns are so judiciously administered." This Society did an important service to vernacular education by publishing a number of valuable works in Bengali on Geography, Natural History, &c.

The Calcutta School Society was established in the year 1818, under the patronage of the Marquis of Hastings, with the object of helping the existing vernacular schools, establishing others, and preparing students of superior merit for becoming teachers and translators. In 1821 it had under its control 115 vernacular schools and 3,828 students. In 1823 its monthly grant from Government was Rs. 500. David Hare was its European Secretary and Raja Sir Radhakant Deb Bahadur, K.C.S.I., its Native Secretary. Men like Sir Antony Butler, J. Harrington and others used to take much interest in it.

I cannot close my brief and somewhat incomplete description of the Educational Institutions without recording the efforts of many pious workers in the field of female education. One Mrs. Pitt* is said to have been its earliest supporter. Mrs. Durel's Seminary for Girls attained in those days much celebrity; and Rev. Mr. Lawson has been reputed for his cleverness in composing sweet poems and as being a good sculptor, painter and musician. His female school was in a very good condition; and he paid special attention to English composition. The Military Orphan Society concerned itself in imparting practical lessons to girls. Mr. Thomson, much moved by the destitute condition of the offspring of European soldiers, established the Female Orphan Asylum at the Circular Road. The Government subscribed Rs. 200 per month to this institution.

* Rainey, however, in his Historical and Topographical Sketch of Calcutta, says :—

"A Girl's school was established about the year 1760 by Mrs. Hedges (probably the first school for young ladies in Calcutta) in which dancing and French were then professed to be taught * * * * . The Kidderpur School was not then in existence, and Mrs. Hedges was able to retire in 1780 with a snug fortune. We are told that the pupils at Mrs. Hedge's school were 'childish, vain, imperious, crafty, vulgar and wanton.'"

Rev. Mr. Hovendon founded another orphan society for the training of ladies.

In 1819 the Calcutta Female Juvenile Society was founded for the support of the Bengali Female Schools. This Society first succeeded in establishing a school containing 32 girls, to which within one year 8 more girls were admitted. Reading, writing and needle-work were taught here. In 1822, this institution was incorporated with the Bengal Christian School Society. In the same year the Ladies' Society for native female education was established. Miss Cook (afterwards Mrs. Wilson) did much for the success of this institution.

The late Hon'ble J. E. Drinkwater Bethune gave a real start to female education in Bengal. In November 1850, a girls' school called after the name of that gentleman was established in Cornwallis Street. To this school is attached a boarding house for the Lady Principal and the students. The school has now been raised to the standard of a first grade College, teaching up to M.A. course of the Calcutta University. The late Raja Sir Radhakant Deb Bahadur, K.C.S.I., rendered invaluable service to the cause of female education. Drinkwater Bethune spoke of him in the following terms:—

"I am anxious to give you the credit which justly belongs to you, of having been the first native in India who in modern times has pointed out the folly and wickedness of allowing the girls to grow up in utter ignorance, and that this is neither enjoined nor countenanced by the Hindu Sastras." Raja Sir Radhakant's efforts for the spread of female education were in consonance with the views entertained by his distinguished ancestors. Rev. Ward has stated that the wives of Raja Nubkissen were famed for their learning. There were other noted Indians whose services in this cause are of considerable importance. Such men as the late Pandit Iswar Chandra Vidyasagaro, Babus Peary Chand Mitter, Peary Charan Sarkar, and several others, identified themselves with the cause of female education. It is impossible to ignore the important services rendered by the missionaries. Their Infant and Girls' Schools all over Calcutta and its surroundings, held at the private residences of Hindu inhabitants, are a valuable medium for the diffusion of female education. The special feature, in the course of studies in these schools, was that in the colloquial vernacular Biblical lessons were imparted. In recent years, the Hindu Mahakali Pathsala, with its several branches in and around Calcutta, has been established with the object of imparting education to Hindu girls on national lines. Moral and religious instruction has been the chief characteristic of this institution. To Mataji Maharani Tapashwini belongs the rare credit of founding this institution. The Hindu public have warmly seconded the noble effort of this philanthropic lady, and this institution has become popular among all sections of the community. I have not described various other educational institutions for females. The zeal of the Brahmos in this connection deserves much praise; and schools and colleges for European girls are now conducted in Calcutta in an efficient manner. Among Mahommedans, also, female education has found its way, and several Moslem girls' institutions have lately sprung up, and Maharaja Manindra Chandra Nandi Bahadur of Cassimbazar has made a large contribution in aid of one of them.

The Rev. Long narrates* that there was a public library in the Old Fort as early as 1770. In the *Oriental Commerce*, an interesting account of the list of books imported from Europe is given. A Mr. Andrew, who had a circulating library, complained in 1780 of the loss he sustained owing to "gentlemen going away, and in their hurry not recollecting their being subscribers to the library or having any books belonging thereto." In those days books only came once a year from England; printing charges were 500 per cent. higher than now: we have seen a book (Asiaticus) of 142 pages, 12mo, printed in Calcutta in 1803, and sold to non-subscribers at Rs. 24 a copy.† The Old Harkara circulating library stood many years.‡

The Calcutta Public Library was founded in 1835 as a library of reference and circulation. It was first located in Dr. E. P. Strong's residence on the Esplanade free of charge. In 1841 it was removed to the Fort William College building, and finally in 1844 it was transferred to its present building and was named after the beneficent Lord Metcalfe. Both Europeans and Natives were its early subscribers and life members. In 1890-91 the Calcutta Municipality used to contribute for the support of the institution and began to exercise its control over it along with the life members. In 1903, the Government of India amalgamated this institution with the Imperial Library. The consent of the proprietors or life members was obtained before the Government assumed its sole control. Among the indigenous libraries started in the northern or native part of the town are the Bagbazar Public Library and Reading Room, the Kambuliatolla

* Rev. Long's Peeps into the Social Life in Calcutta.
† Transactions of the Bengal Social Science.
‡ *Calcutta Review*, Vol. XXXV.

Boys' Reading Club, the Chaitanya Library, the Cornwallis Square Library and Reading Room. &c.* They are supplying mental food to all classes of people, both male and female. Some of them have their own houses, others are located in rented houses or in the houses of private persons. These bodies render useful services to the community. They organise lectures, publish pamphlets, and sometimes issue magazines. As a rule they eschew politics. Europeans and Indians of rank take interest in these institutions.

Among literary and scientific institutions, the Asiatic Society of Bengal is not only the earliest of its kind in Calcutta, but the most useful body in India. It was established on the 15th of January 1784, with the object of investigating whatever is performed by man or produced by nature in all parts of Asia. Warren Hastings was its first Patron and made Sir William Jones its first President. It is not a light task to convey, in a few sentences, an adequate idea of the many and varied valuable services of this institution. In the field of research its services have been invaluable. The revival of Sanskrit learning and the assignment to it of its proper place in the republic of letters have been in a large measure due to it. Perhaps Sanskrit works would have been a sealed book to European *Savants*, had not this body interested itself in publishing and distributing them in the civilised world. The Theosophical and several other kindred bodies derive material assistance from its numerous and valuable publications. Such men as the late Dr. Horace Hayman Wilson, Thomas Colebrooke, James Prinsep and last, but not the least, Raja Dr. Rajendralala Mittra, D.L., C.I.E., were among its distinguished members. The Society has

* The first two libraries have been lately amalgamated.

attached to it a museum containing a large and varied collection of Geological and Ethnological specimens; besides, there are many Archæological relics and statues, coins, rare portraits, copper sunnuds, busts, pictures, &c. It has a splendid library attached to it, containing, among other things, Sanskrit, Arabic, Persian, Hindustani, Burmese and Nepalese manuscripts. The building of the Museum is a massive and imposing one on the Chowringhee Road. The building of the Asiatic Society is located at 57, Park Street.

The Agri-Horticultural Society of India.—This Institution owes its origin to the support of the Baptist Missionary James Carey, and its meetings are held on the ground floor of the Calcutta Public Library known as the Metcalfe Hall. In its early days, such Indians as Raja Sir Radhakant Deb Bahadur and Babu Dwarkanath Tagore took an active interest in its welfare. The Society has a nursery garden at Alipur, where all species of plants and flowers are grown for sale to the public and for distribution amongst its members. Annually a Flower Show is held there.

The School of Arts.—This school was founded in the year 1854 by a number of gentlemen, under the name, "The Society for the Promotion of Industrial Arts," which originated at a meeting held at the house of Mr. Hodgson Pratt in the early part of that year. The object of this institution is to impart instruction in drawing, etching, engraving, and moulding. Monsieur Rigaud — a French Plaster-coat maker—was its first teacher. In 1864 the Bengal Government took charge of this school. The school is now under a European Principal and is open to all comers. A fine picture gallery is attached to the school. Formerly it was located in Bowbazar Street, but it has, of late, been transferred to its present building near the Indian Museum.

The Bethune Society—Was established to create a taste for literary and scientific pursuits, and to promote an intellectual intercourse between the Europeans and Indians. Such men as the late Hon'ble Mr. Justice Phear, Colonel Malleson, Rev. K. M. Banerjee, Mr. Monomohan Ghosh, Barrister-at-law, Babu Prosonna Kumar Sarvadhikari and others took warm interest in its proceedings, read discourses and delivered lectures under its auspices.

The Bengal Social Science Association—Came into existence in 1867, through the efforts of Miss Mary Carpenter and under the advocacy of the Hon'ble Messrs. Justices Phear, and Beverley, Rev. J. Long, Nawab Abdul Lateef Khan Bahadur, C.I.E., and others. The object of the Association was to promote social progress in the presidency of Bengal, by uniting Europeans and Natives of all classes in the collection of facts bearing on the social, intellectual and moral condition of the people. Many interesting and important lectures were given on subjects relating to Law, Education, Health and Trade, in its connection. Unfortunately this Association and also the Bethune Society have now ceased to exist.

The Mahommedan Literary Society—Was established in 1863, and its popularity and success among all sections of the community were mainly attributed to the untiring zeal and industry of the late Nawab Bahadur Abdul Lateef, C.I.E. Indeed the late Nawab Bahadur was looked upon as a leader of the Indian community, and it was through his efforts that several Viceroys, Commander-in-Chief and Lieutenant-Governors honoured the Society with their presence at its annual conversazione, held at the Town Hall. This Society has been founded with a view to promoting social feeling and literary activity amongst all classes, and especially among the Mahommedans.

The Society for the Higher Training of Young Men, or the Calcutta University Institute.—This Institution is the outcome of the earnest desire of Sir Charles Elliot, the late Lieutenant-Governor of Bengal, to develop the mental, moral and physical condition of the students of Bengal. Babu Protap Chandra Mozumdar, an eminent writer and orator, Mahamahopadhyaya Mahesh Chandra Nyayaratna, C.I.E., late Principal of the Sanskrit College, Raja Binaya Krishna, Rai Bahadur Bankim Chandra Chatterji, B.A., Sir Dr. Gurudass Banerji and several other eminent Indians were associated with its early growth.

Babu Protap Chandra Mozumdar became its Secretary and Raja Binaya Krishna its Treasurer. Lectures were provided, and social re-unions, innocent and healthy sports and entertainments were organised, at which the rulers of Bengal freely mixed with the student community. The late lamented Mr. C. R. Wilson, M.A., subsequently became its secretary, and the present name "Calcutta University Institute" was given. It is located on the east wing of the Sanskrit College and has a splendid library attached to it. The Marcus Square Recreation Ground is the outcome of this institution, where healthy sports, for the students of the Calcutta Colleges, are arranged. Sir Charles Elliot started this institution from the contribution of Raja Binaya

Krishna, which he placed at the disposal of the Bengal Government. A Committee has been appointed to look after its affairs.

The Bengal Academy of Literature or the Bangiya Sahitya Parishad—Was inaugurated at the residence and under the auspices of Raja Binaya Krishna Bahadur. Mr. L. Liotard, the late Babu Kshetrapal Chakravarty and the Raja were its founders. Its original object, among others, was to make the Bengali language known among the Western *savants* and to arouse their interest in it. The business was at first conducted in English. The Right Hon'ble Professor F. Max Müller and the late John Beames began to take interest in the Academy, but owing to the strong opinion of almost all the eminent Bengali authors, the use of the English language was discontinued in its proceedings. The present name, the Bangiya Sahitya Parishad, was given by the late Pandit Umesh Chandra Batabyal, M.A., at the instance of the Raja. The institution is now a self-supporting one and is located in Cornwallis Street. It will soon have a building of its own.

The Sahitya Sava.—Another organisation has been established under the active support and help of Raja Binaya Krishna Bahadur. Its projectors were Rai Rajendra Chandra Sashtri Bahadur, M.A., Maharaj-Kumar Sailendra Krishna, Deb Bahadur, the Hon'ble Justice Sarada Charan Mitter, the late Dr. Mohendra Lal Sarkar, M.D., D.L., C.I.E., Mahamahopadhyaya Kamakshya Nath Tarkabagis, Pandit Kali Prasanna Kavyavisarad, Rai Bahadur Dr. Chuni Lal Bose, Rai Bahadur Dr. Surjakumar Sarvadhikari, Babu Soshi Bhusan Chatterji, F.R.G.S., Babu Amrita Lal Bose,

Babu Norendra Nath Sen, Pandit Mahendra Nath Vidyanidhi and others. Among others, its object is the cultivation of History, Geography, Sociology, Mathematics, Natural Science, Philosophy (both Eastern and Western) and other branches of knowledge. Its special feature lies in its attitude of respect and sympathy towards the Pandit class without whose aid and co-operation the resuscitation of Sanskrit literature would be impossible. It has also got a monthly journal of its own, which has been highly spoken of in the Parliamentary Blue Book, relating to the material and moral progress of India. The late Lieutenant-Governor, Sir John Woodburn, K.C.S.I., appreciating its work, became its patron.

His Honour the Lieutenant-Governor of Bengal has kindly accepted the post of its Patron, and many leading officials have shown their kind sympathy to it by heartily joining the institution.

CHAPTER VI.

TRADE AND COMMERCE.

Commerce plays an important part in modern history. It is one-half of politics. For in the first place the importance of a nation greatly depends on its wealth, and its wealth greatly depends on commerce. A desire to expand commerce, rather than a merely scientific curiosity, has been the mainspring of adventures in quest of new lands. The same spirit has often lain at the root of military expeditions. Conquest and annexation have been inspired, in modern times, not so much by a love of authority, as by a love of wealth. No Power cares to assert supremacy over a bleak and barren territory. The character of an individual is said to be known by his company. With equal truth it may be said that the condition of a nation is known by its wealth. It may not have been so in ancient India, Greece or Rome. It is so to-day. The importance of nations as Powers, is measured, according to European standards, by their fighting capacity, but that itself is very largely an affair of wealth, as money, they say, is the sinews of War. Commerce has been a great factor in the development of Calcutta—possibly the greatest—and some account of it as effects this town must be attempted. It may be left to antiquarians to determine when the inhabitants of Bengal first had commercial intercourse with other nations and countries. Heeren, Macpherson and other authoritative writers have thrown considerable light upon this subject. Sir William Hunter, in his work on Orissa,* has written that the ruin of Tamluk as a seat of maritime commerce, affords an explanation of how the Bengalees ceased to be a sea-going people. In the Buddhist era they sent warlike fleets to the east and the west, and colonised the islands of the Archipelago. The adage *Banijye basatir Lakshmyah*—or the seat of the goddess of wealth is on commerce—still lingers on among the Hindus.

Mr. Walter Hamilton estimates† that "seldom less than one million sterling in cloths belonging to native merchants was deposited in Calcutta for sale, and every other species of merchandise in an equal proportion."

"The total capital belonging to the native monied and commercial interests has been estimated to exceed 16 million sterling, which is employed by them in the Government Funds, loans and discounts to individuals, internal and external trade, and in various other ways * * * * In September 1808, the Calcutta Government Bank was established with a capital of 50 lacs of rupees, of which Government had 10 lacks and individuals the remainder. The notes issued are not less than 10 rupees or more than 10,000."‡

* Vol. I, page 314-15.

† The East India Gazetteer, published in 1815.

‡ In *Oriental Commerce* the following account of the establishment of the Bank is given:—

A bank was established in Bengal and incorporated by charter on the 2nd January, 1809. The capital stock amounts to 5,000.000 Rs. and is divided into 500 shares of 10,000

The following table, taken from W. Hamilton's *East India Gazetteer*, shows the state of trade about a century ago in this country. Trade from 1st June, 1811 to 30th April, 1812 (11 months):—

IMPORTS.

Merchandise ...	...	...	1,13,38,692.
Treasure ...	...	...	67,85,698.
	Sicca Rupees	...	1,81,24,390.
			or
			£22,65,549.

EXPORTS.

Merchandise ...	...	...	3,40,03,009.
Treasure ...	...	...	6,14,673.
	Sicca Rupees	...	3,46,17,682.
			or
			£43,27,210.
Total ...	...	Rs.	5,27,42,072.
			or
			£65,92,759.

The ships and vessels arrived at Calcutta in 1811-12:—

			Tonnage.
Under English colours	193	...	78,504.
Under Portuguese colours	11	...	4,180.
Under American colours	8	...	2,313.

Rs. each; of which shares 100 belong to the Government and 400 to individuals. All persons in the service of the Company, and the Judges in the several courts, as well as others may hold shares in the Bank. The affairs are managed by nine Directors, of whom three are nominated by the Government and six by the proprietors. The bank is prohibited from engaging in trade or any kind of agency, and the business is confined as far as possible to discounting negotiable private securities, keeping cash accounts, receiving deposits and circulating cash notes; and they are at liberty to receive in deposits, and for safe custody, bullion, treasure, jewels, plate and other articles of value, not liable to spoil or waste, on such terms as they may deem reasonable.

Under Indian colours, including donies	389	66,227.
	601	1,51,224.

Ships and vessels departed from Calcutta in 1811-12:—

		Tonnage.
Under English colours ...	194	... 77,072.
Under Portuguese colours ...	10	... 4,020.
Under Spanish colours ...	1	... 650.
Under American colours, ...	8	... 2,369.
Under Indian colours, including donies	386	... 65,650.
	599	1,49,761

Much valuable information can be obtained from Milburn's *Oriental Commerce*,* a few extracts from which will be interesting.

COMMERCE WITH LONDON.

The following is a statement of the merchandise and treasure imported into Bengal from London, exclusive of the East India Company's, in the years 1802 to 1806 inclusive; likewise of the merchandise and treasure exported from Bengal to London during the same period; together with a list of the articles of which the imports and exports consisted in 1805.

* *Oriental Commerce* contains a geographical description of the principal places in the East Indies, China and Japan, with their produce, manufactures and trade, &c. By William Milburn, Esq. Published in 1813 (London).

IMPORTS INTO BENGAL FROM LONDON.

Years.	Merchandise.	Treasure.	Total.
	Sicca rupees.	Sicca rupees.	Sicca rupees.
1802	35,90,683	12,63,387	48,54,070
1803	30,55,400	9,85,601	40,41,001
1804	29,34,485	7,97,680	37,32.165
1805	36,28,301	8,69,576	44,97,877
1806	59,12,500	5,68,921	64,81,421
Total.	1,91,21,369	44,85,165	2,36,06,534

EXPORTS FROM BENGAL TO LONDON.

Years.	Merchandise.	Treasure.	Total.
1802	1,11,45,261	......	1,11,45,261
1803	1,08,15,545	......	1,08,15,545
1804	89,16,168	......	89,16,168
1805	60,99,065	......	60,99,065
1806	90,34,869	......	90,34,869
Total.	4,60,10,908	......	4,60,10,908

ARTICLES OF IMPORT IN 1805.

	Sicca Rs.
Books	90,656.
Boots and Shoes	54,735.
Cutlery and Hardware	1,39,144.
Copper	135.
Carriages	1,16,218.
Cordage	14,178.
Glass and Looking-glasses	2,79,575.
Hosiery	1,06,794.
Haberdashery	95,448.

ARTICLES OF IMPORT IN 1805.—*contd.*

Hats	80,629.
Jewellery	28,630.
Ironmongery	65,907.
Millinery	97,746.
Malt Liquors	1,35,212.
Oilman's Stores	1,67,763.
Perfumery	63,624.
Provisions	16,444.
Plate and Platedware ...	56,591.
Piece-goods	67,792.
Saddlery	1,32,827.
Wines and Spirits	7,87,265.
Metals	1,03,775.
Naval Stores	55,693.
Stationery	61,487.
Woollens	1,15,580.
Sundries	6,94,453.
Treasure	8,69,576.
Total ...	44,97,877.

ARTICLES OF EXPORT IN 1805.

	Sicca Rs.
Piece-goods	3,31,582.
Indigo	45,23,124.
Sugar	54,478.
Raw Silk	7,87,106.
Cotton	1,18,912.
Elephant Teeth	9,278.

ARTICLES OF EXPORT IN 1805.—*contd.*

Gums	24,160.
Ginger	2,750.
Cossumba	4,815.
Sal Ammoniac	2,680.
Cutch	1,025.
Shell-lac	12,139.
Sundries	9,466.
IMPORTS RE-EXPORTED, *viz.*—	
Wines and Liquors	55,176.
Camphor	72,009.
Spices	20,366.
Cassia	24,983.
Books	14,354.
Coculus Indicus	5,571.
Coffee	4,676.
Galls	2,520.
Sundries	17,895.
Total ...	60,99,065.

Merchandise imported from London, in 1802 to 1806 inclusive. Sicca Rs.	1,91,21,369.
Merchandise exported to London	4,60,13,908.
Exports exceed the Imports ...	2,68,92,539.
Treasure imported into Bengal from London during the same period ...	44,85,165.

Balance in favour of Bengal in 5 years, 3,13,77,704, which, at 2*s.* 6*d.* per rupee, is £3,922,213; on an average of 5 years £784,442 12*s.* per annum.

From the statement of the merchandise and treasure imported into Bengal from London as well as of the merchandise exported from Bengal to London, in the years previous to 1802—from 1795 to 1801 inclusive—we find that the imports into Bengal amounted to Sicca Rs. 1,64,03,175; and the amount of merchandise exported was Sicca Rs. 5,30,43,579 Evidently then the exports exceeded the imports by 3,66,40,404, and when we take into account the amount of treasure imported into Bengal from London, during the same period, which was Sicca Rs. 82,23,924, we find that the balance in favour of Bengal was Sicca Rs. 4,48,64,328, which, at 2*s*. 6*d*. per rupee, is £5,608,041; on an average of seven years £8,011,485. 12*s*. 6*d*. per annum. Thus we find that the average of balance per annum in favour of Bengal in the seven years previous to 1802 (from 1795 to 1801) exceeded the average per annum in the five years, from 1802 to 1806 by £16,706. 0*s*. 6*d*. per annum.

According to Milburn, in 1715 the superior skill of the English in navigation induced all classes of merchants in the province of Bengal to freight most of the goods which they exported to foreign markets on the shipping belonging to the colony, which in ten years after the Embassy amounted to 10,000 tons, by which many private fortunes were acquired, without injuring the Company's trade, or subjecting their property to disputes with Government; and people of all denominations in Calcutta enjoyed a degree of independence and freedom unknown to the other inhabitants of Bengal, who were subject to the oppressions of the Nabob. About the year 1795, the East India Company appointed a Reporter of External Commerce for this Presidency, and particular instructions were given as to the mode of keeping the accounts; since which period a clear and comprehensive statement of the amount of the merchandise and treasure imported into, and exported from Bengal, has been annually made up and transmitted to Europe, together with a list of the articles of which the imports and exports consisted.

The commerce of this Presidency is arranged under the following heads, *viz.*—

I. To and from London (exclusive of the East India Company's trade) comprehending the investments of the commanders and officers of the Company's ships; the goods shipped by individuals on the tonnage allowed by the Act 33, Geo. III, chap. 52; and the cargoes of such country ships as have been permitted to proceed from Bengal to England, and return laden with European commodities.

II. To and from other parts of Europe, under the denomination of Foreign Europe, comprising Denmark, Hamburg, Lisbon, Madeira, Cadiz, &c.

III. To and from the United States of America.

IV. To and from British Asia, which comprehended, in 1801, the under-mentioned places; and notwithstanding the acquisitions which have since taken place, is continued under the same arrangement:—

1. Coast of Malabar, which includes the whole of the western side of the Peninsula.

2. Coast of Coromandel, which includes the whole of the eastern coast.

3. Island of Ceylon.
4. Coast of Sumatra.

V. That to and from the under-mentioned places comprehended in 1801, under the head of Foreign Asia; and though some of the places have since been added to the British possessions the same arrangement is continued.

1. Arabian and Persian Gulf.
2. Pegu.
3. Penang, and places to the eastward.
4. Malacca.
5. Batavia.
6. Manilla.
7. China.
8. Various places.

Under the head of various places are comprehended the Maldive and Laccadive Islands, Mozambique, and other ports on the east coast of Africa, New South Wales, Cape of Good Hope, St. Helena, &c.

The whole of the commerce from port to port in India, commonly called the country trade, is in the hands of individuals, the East India Company never interfering; and from the various statements, it will be seen that there is no place of commercial note from the eastward of the Cape of Good Hope, to which a trade is not driven by the British or native merchants resident in the Company's territories, except Japan, to which country the East India Company, in the infancy of their establishment, made several unsuccessful attempts to establish a trade. For a long period, all European nations, except the Dutch, have been forbidden visiting Japan; notwithstanding which a ship has recently been sent from Calcutta, but was unable to obtain permission to trade.* Until the passing of the Act in the year 1793, the East India Company had almost a monopoly of trade between India and China. No private person was permitted to trade on his own account. If any person or body of persons without the express permission of the Company carried on trade, they were liable to deportation and were called Interlopers. A writer † remarks:—

"Calcutta possesses the advantage of an excellent inland navigation, foreign imports being transported with great facility on the Ganges, and its subsidiary streams, to the northern nations of Hindoosthan, while the valuable productions of the interior are received by the same channels. But with the construction of the Hughli Bridge and opening of the East Indian Railway, the trade and commerce have been developed to an unprecedented degree. The East Indian Railway has connection with many other Railways since constructed. The Hughli Bridge is made on the cantilever system, and will form an interesting example of that principle. Of the three spans of which the bridge consists, the central cantilever span rests on two strong piers in the middle of the river; while the second and third spans, which project from either bank, rest upon the opposite ends of the middle cantilever span, instead of on separate piers of their own. Thus the two extremities are supported on solid masonry works on either bank and the two massive middle piers supply the rest of the support to the entire structure. Each of the two central piers is sunk to a depth

* Milburn's *Oriental Commerce*, Vol. II.
† Walter Hamilton in his *East India Gazetteer*.

of 100 feet below mean sea-level, or 73 feet below the river-bed. These piers have been forced down through 64 feet of sand and silt, followed by 1 foot of wave gravel, and 8 feet of hard yellow clay. The bridge is 36½ feet high above the highest water mark, and thus there is ample space for the steamers and native cargo boats to pass under the bridge. The bridge is 1,200 feet in length, having two spans of 420 feet each projecting from the banks and one central canti-lever span of 360 feet. The cost of construction has been estimated at about £900,000, or ninety lacs of rupees."

According to Mr. A. K. Ray * the trade of the English in Bengal first began from Balasore, and their first ship, the *Falcon*, ventured to sail up the river penetrating inland to Hughli conveying a cargo of bullion and goods valued at over £40,000. In 1704, the port dues were said to be Rs. 500. Tonnage pass-money was Rs. 384 and was realised from various vessels bound from Madras and Europe. For every tonnage, the charge fixed was only a rupee. The Company did not allow their pilots to attend ships other than their own. As the services of the pilots were clandestinely availed of by others, the Company was strict. But the Hon'ble Court of Directors made liberal provision for the recruitment and enlistment of young men in the pilot service with a view to giving facility to loading and unloading goods on the banks of the river. The first wharf was constructed in or about 1710. At one time saltpetre was in great demand from this country. Mr. A. K. Ray writes :—"The war in Europe, in the time of Queen Anne, created a great demand for saltpetre, and it was therefore jealously guarded by the

* Census of India, Vol. VII., Part I, by A. K. Ray.

Company's troops on its way down the river from Patna. The demand for saltpetre abated by the year 1720."* A writer in the *Calcutta Review* is responsible for the following :—

Ship-building began to be brisk after 1770, teakwood being chiefly used; we have an account of the launch of a ship built by Captain Watson at his dockyard, Kidderpur. Warren Hastings and his lady were present at the launch and subsequent entertainment. After this, Indian ship-building was viewed with enormous jealousy in London by all the dockyard men and shipwrights connected with Leadenhall Street. Even as late as 1813, a writer in England asks :— "Is it not a matter to be deplored that the Company should employ the natives of India in building their ships, to the actual injury and positive loss of this nation, from which they received their charter ?" Mistaken as the Company have been in this particular, it is not very difficult to divine what will take place if an unrestrained commerce shall be permitted : if British capital shall be carried to India by British speculators, we may expect a vast increase of dock-yards in that country, and a proportional increase of detriment to the artificers of Britain.† A large dock was also situated by the river-side at Tittagarh near Barrackpore, where a large ship of 5,000 tons burthen was launched, and its launching was enviously looked upon by ship-builders at Liverpool. The ship-building establishment of Gilbert stood on the site of the Old Mint.‡

In 1762 money was first coined in Calcutta, and it is

* A Short History of Calcutta, by A. K. Ray, M.A.
† *Calcutta Review*, Vol. XXXV.
‡ *Calcutta Review*, Vol. XV.

mentioned that as late as 1770 no copper coin was issued. Pice were then hardly in use. Cowries (a kind of shell) were then in extensive use. As early as 1680, a Mr. Smith was sent out from England as Assay-Master, on an annual salary of £60. The Old Mint was situated west of St. John's Church, where the Company coined its rupees for 1179tom 1832. The New Mint on the Strand Road was opened in 1832. Previous to 1791 the coinage was executed by contracts; the copper coin chiefly by Mr. Prinsep (father of the late James Prinsep) who conducted an establishment at Fulta. Coining their own names (though with the Moghuls" head and a Persian inscription) was an object of early ambition with the English and other European Powers.*

If English commerce made Calcutta what it is, it is also true that it benefited English capitalists no less by a rich return. But there were men in England who were jealous of it. "There was a strong party in England opposed to trade with India, who raised clamourous complaint loud and general."† At the end of the eighteenth century trade was opened with many countries, notably with America, China, &c.‡ In 1789 European commodities were offered to the Indian markets almost at a half-price of their original cost. It is said that in consequence of the market being overstocked, such a course was adopted. The commanders and officers of the Company's ships experienced very heavy losses; and after the authorities being satisfied with their hardships complained of, the payment of the Company's duties on their outward investments was remitted.

* *Calcutta Review*, Vol. XV.
† *Calcutta Review*, Vol. XXXV.
‡ *Oriental Commerce*, by W. Milburn.

In the "Gentleman's Magazine" for 1784 the following appeared :—

"There is no branch of European commerce that has made so rapid a progress as that to the East Indies. The whole number of ships sent to Asia by all the maritime powers of Europe at the beginning of the present century did not amount to fifty sail, of which England sent 14, France 5, Holland 11, the Venetians and Genoese together 9, Spain 3, and all the rest of Europe only 6; neither the Russians nor Imperialists at that period sent any. In the year 1744, the English increased their number of ships to 27, the Venetians and Genoese sent only 4, and the rest of Europe about 9. At this period 300 sails of European ships belonging to the several powers are employed in the East India traffic, of which England alone sends 68, being the whole of the East India Company's shipping. The French, last year, employed 9, the Portuguese 18, the Russians and Spaniards make up the remainder. But neither the Venetians nor Genoese now send a single ship to India." In those days trade was also carried on by the officers of the Company on their own private and personal account; and not infrequently the interests of the master clashed with those of the servant, and the consequences can better be imagined than described. According to Mr. Bolts, a private Company was formed in Calcutta among the servants of the Hon'ble Company to carry on trade in salt, betel-nut and tobacco. The Company existed for two years, and it is stated that the shareholders had a net profit of Rs. 10,74,002. The Directors at home put a stop to this private trade, as it clashed with that of the Hon'ble Company. It consisted of 60 shares.*

* Evidence of our Transactions in the East Indies and Bolts' Consideration of the Indian Affairs.

In *Oriental Commerce* it is stated that "the sole amount of the private trade of the commanders and officers at the Company's sales in London, during the above period (from 1784 to 1791), amounted to the undermentioned sums, including the goods imported from China, which may be estimated to be at least £250,000 per annum of the amount :—

	£
1785-86	611,205.
1786-87	547,337.
1787-88	918,389.
1788-89	810,516.
1789-90	838,484.
1790-91	930,930.
1791-92	709,450.
1792-93	703,578.

Making in the period of eight years £6,069,889, which, after deducting the estimated amount of China goods, tea, nankeen, china-ware, drugs, &c., £250,000 per annum, leaves £4,069,889 for the sale value of Indian goods. This amount includes duties, as at this period the whole of the duties, whether on goods exported, or used at home were paid by the Company, and drawn back on exportation." According to Milburn "the trade carried on by foreigners from Europe is very beneficial, as the greater part of their import consists of treasure......... their returns are made in the manufactures of the country ....and that the balance of this trade in favour of Bengal has, upon an average of twelve years, amounted nearly to half a million sterling per annum, exclusive of duties, &c., and the benefits arising to the British merchants resident at Calcutta, who are the principal agents in the transactions of all foreign business."* A writer,† commenting on European mercantile morality, cites a Dutch authority, Mossel, who thus speaks about the Dutch East India Company :—" For a series of years they have been *guilty* of the greatest enormities, and the foulest dishonesty ; they have looked upon the Company's effects confided to them as a booty thrown open to their depredations; they have most shamefully and arbitrarily falsified the invoice prices." Nor was the fault solely the want of principle on the part of merchants; it arose very largely from laziness. Grand Pre writes of Madras what applies to Calcutta also :—" The trade of Madras is still more completely in the hands of the Blacks than that of Pondicherry, the concerns being more extensive and lucrative and the sales more brisk. The European merchant entirely neglects the minute details, and looks only at the abstract of the accounts given him by his *dobachi* : a negligence perfectly suited to the manners in which he lives, at a distance from the spot where his affairs are conducted, which he visits only once a day, and that not regularly, and bestows upon them two or three hours' attention."

Atkinson, in his " City of Palaces," thus alludes to this state of things :—

"Calcutta ! nurse of opulence and vice,
Thou Architect of European fame
And fortune, fancied beyond earthly price,
Envy of sovereigns, and constant aim,
Of kin adventures, Art thou not the same,
As other sinks where manhood rots in state ?
Sparkling with phospher brightness,
There stood proud cities once, of ancient date,
Close parallels to thee, denounced by angry Fate."

* W. Milburn's *Oriental Commerce*, &c., Vol. II.
† *Calcutta Review*, Vol. XXXV.

Nor was civilian morality higher. Clive, Sumner and Verelst, appointed Commissioners of Inquiry into the conduct of civilians, thus report to the Court in 1765: "Referring to their conduct, their transactions seem to demonstrate that every spring of the Government was tainted with corruption, that principles of rapacity and oppression universally prevailed, that every spark and sentiment of public spirit was lost and extinguished in the abandoned lust of universal wealth." It is also recorded that there were persons who, after being employed in the services of the Company, came out to this country and opened business concerns on their own account and then resigned their service. Mr. William Bolts is a striking instance in point. He was of German extraction and arrived in India as one of the Company's servants. Having resigned the service, he commenced to trade for eight years, and during that period he amassed a fortune of nine lakhs of rupees.* According to the Rev. Long, Mr. William Bolts was the first among the Europeans who were conversant with the Bengali language, and he wrote a valuable book, "Consideration of the Indian Affairs." He was subsequently deported for his turbulent spirit and questionable conduct. From a very early period, Barrobazar was the nucleus of trade. The Armenians, Marwaris and other nationalities had their business concerns perhaps previous to Job Charnock's coming to Calcutta. The Setts and Bysacks were also early traders. From the town duties much curious information can be gathered of the several kinds of articles that were offered for sale. Among others, the following † may be mentioned upon which or from whom the duties were then levied:—

* H. Blochman's Calcutta During Last Century.
† R. C. Sterndale's Historical Account of the Calcutta Collectorate.

Retailers of cowries.	Paddy.
Cotton thread.	Chunam shops.
Apothecaries' shops.	Tobacco shops.
Oil shops.	Firewood shops.
Hardware.	Straw shops.
Tyar.	Mats.
Milk.	Bamboos.
Jaggree.	Braziers.
Sweetmeat.	Betel-nut.
Smiths.	Greens.
Silver-smiths.	Sugarcanes.
Betel.	Plantain.
Cucumbers.	Tamarind.
Trees.	Fishmongers.
Weavers.	Roasted rice.
Salt.	Potters.
Rice.	Cloth.
Venison.	Shoemakers.

From Holwell's account, the following appeared to have been the principal firms :—

The glass-maker's firm, which dates from	...	1738
,, vermilion shops ,, ,,	...	1738
,, caulker's firm ,, ,,	...	1738
,, tobacco shops ,, ,,	...	1740
,, bhang ... ,, ,,	...	1738
,, chest-maker's firm ,,	...	1748
,, red lead and lapis tutiæ (vitriol)	...	1746
,, dammer and oakum ...	...	1746
Dee Calcutta and Govindpur's burdened oxen	....	1738
Dee Calcutta and Bazar Calcutta's ferry boats	...	1738

The fireworks firm, which dates from	...	1738
„ chinnams „ ...	„ ...	1752
„ timbers „ ...	„ ...	1752
Old iron, tea cattys and old nails	„ ...	1751

Besides this, there was a duty on—

Piece-goods at	2 per cent.
Sale of boats and sloops at ...	5 „
Sale of slaves	Rs. 4-4 each.
Grant of pottahs	Rs. 4-4 each.
Arbitration bonds, salistnameh ...	20 *punds* of cowries.
Commission on recovery of debts...	(not stated)
General releases	Annas 8.
Mortgage bonds	Rs. 5 per cent.
Marriages	Sicca rupees 3.
Russey salammy (measurement of holdings)	Re. 1.
Salammy on new-built sloops ...	Rs. 50 to 100 (according to burden).

Mooriannoes.—

Duty on export liquors ...	Rs. 2-4 per leager.
License for a treat ...	Not fixed.
Order for beat of drum ...	one *cowand* & one *pund* of cowries.
Duty on export on rice ...	1 *seer* 8 *chittacks* per maund.

Mr. Sterndale writes that "in May, 1795, the Calcutta town duties were abolished, but with certain exceptions they were re-established in May, 1801." By regulation X of 1810, they were again abolished. They were, however, again re-established to be finally abolished by Regulation XIV of 1836, which repealed all regulations prescribing the levy of town duties. Grain appears in later years to have been exempted from duty or charges other than the "*coyally*," for, by an advertisement of the 19th February, 1773, it was declared that "all liquors, provisions and other necessaries of life (except grain) shall pay the duties in like manner with other merchandise as has been heretofore customary at this presidency," but it was also declared that no grain shall be landed within the limits of the city of Calcutta under permit from the Custom Master specifying the quality, and no grain shall be sold, but in presence of the *coyalls* or officers of the Custom House, who shall be authorised to receive their established *coyally dustoor* agreeably to the ancient and immemorial usage of the settlement.* In 1765 the Collector, Mr. George Gray, levied certain duties on the women of the town, which Lord Clive disapproved, and they were in consequence abolished. From Mr. Gray's explanation, it would appear that it was customary for the *demi-monde* to present a *nuzzerana* or salammy and he desired to collect the dues and from the proceeds to erect and maintain what would in these days be called a "Lock Hospital"—an institution he considered very necessary in the interests both of the women themselves and the inhabitants of the settlement.

It would be tedious to detail here the various town duties which were collected by the Company upon several articles. They were charged not only on all goods imported or exported into or from the town, but on all sorts of trades, manufactures and sales of articles.

Mr. Sterndale says that "before the sack of Calcutta—

* Colebrooke.

but in what year I have not been able to discover—an attempt was made to levy as town duty a commission of 5 per centum on all sales of European houses. The European inhabitants, however, resisted this impost, and with such success that in 1757, the Court of Directors ordered its relinquishment, 'assuring all the inhabitants of Calcutta that we have a tender regard for their ease, and do therefore consent that the said duty be laid aside.' It was, however, still levied from Natives, Armenians and Portuguese, as appears from the records. The Hampden who took the most prominent part in resisting this task was a Captain Durand, whose insolent behaviour the Directors considered tended to such a contempt of our authority as ought never to be borne, and whose resistance called forth an order to deport him with ships of the season."

According to Bolts, "town duties included a duty on licenses to marry at the rate of 3 Sicca rupees per party," but I have failed to trace the issue of any such licenses in the records of the office; also a percentage on the sale of "slaves" and "sloops and boats." He also states that "all grain brought into the *gunges* or public granaries, as well as every necessary of life and many other articles brought to the *bazars* or public markets in Calcutta, pay a duty upon importation, the collection of which is superintended by the Collector. The privilege of exercising many handicraft trades is likewise farmed out by the Collector to farmers, who collect from some certain sums for the license of exercising their respective trades, and from others even a part of their daily wages." *

* Sterndale's Historical Account of the Calcutta Collectorate.

The several kinds of articles that find extensive sale represent in no small degree the tastes and idiosyncracies of the people, and the so-called necessaries of life are sometimes those articles that gratify our vanities or our hobbies. As an instance in point, the following may be mentioned. :—

"To Ramessore Samroot Gope. From any person or persons that are willing to mark their bulls for the use of their funeral ceremonies, you are to receive your customary fees, provided it should not be taken by force, and demanding any improper or superfluous fees on pain of punishment and immediate dismissal from this occupation. 1st April, 1765."

"To Nemoy Churn Dass Brojobassy, Fukeer. You are to receive one *cowrie* per diem on each shop within the town and districts of Calcutta as an alms for the maintenance of the beggars. Calcutta, 31st July, 1765."

"A *pottah* is hereby granted unto Shake Nuncoo, an inhabitant of the town of Calcutta, for the exclusive privilege of purchasing all the saltpetre water which is used in cooling the liquors of the gentlemen and others residing in the town of Calcutta and the 15 dhees, that by reboiling the same he may extract from it the saltpetre. In consideration of such privilege he is to pay the annual sum of Sicca rupees 101 to the Company. The term of this *pottah* is for three years, during which time it will continue in force.

Calcutta Committee of Revenue, the 1st March, 1774. Phillip M. Dacres."*

* Sterndale's Historical Account of the Calcutta Collectorate.

According to Nabob Mahammed Reza Cawn, merchants and traders of former times used to export, after extensive local consumption, various indigenous and manufactured articles to different parts of the world. In his opinion there was then a large number of monied people whose importance and influence in the country were not viewed with jealousy. The Moghul Government made it their special object to encourage native trade, but during Mir Jaffer's regime, all this was changed, and native merchants, instead of being encouraged, were fleeced. Merchants then carried on banking business and Rajas and Zemindars were accommodated by them to pay off the Government dues. By that, Reza Cawn thinks the money of the merchants was increased, and when tenants and cultivating classes experienced privations and hardships, the products of their labours were purchased at the usual price by the said merchants. By the above means, the interests of neither classes were allowed to suffer. Reza Cawn further goes on to state that if the strong oppressed the weak and complaints were made, the hakims or judges at once looked into the matter and brought to book the offender. A reference may be made to Muhammed Reza Cawn's description of the former and present state of the country, the causes of its decline, and the way there is of recovering and bringing it again into a flourishing condition. This valuable document was written at the instance of Sir Philip Francis and others and was delivered to them. It is to be found among the records of the Government of India in the Home Department.

Apropos of Indian trade, Forster in his travels in 1782-83 says that he met with a hundred Hindu merchants at Herat, carrying on a brisk commerce, another hundred men at Tarshish, and others settled at Baku Mushid, Tezd, and along parts of the Caspian and Persian Gulfs. Mr. Forster met at Baku a Sanyasi, recommended by some Hindus to their agents in Russia. He was willing to go even to England. Hindus have been settled at Astrachan as at Calcutta without their families.*

It is necessary to say something in a general manner about the trade carried on by the several European nations in this country. From remote ages Europeans have carried on their trade with India through the Persian Gulf and the Red Sea. Since the days of Alexander the Great to those of Vasco da Gama, European travellers appeared in the Indian horizon and brought back to their countries stories of fabulous wealth, unparalleled magnificence and richness of the Indian soil. Not only the land and sea routes presented a natural barrier, but the warlike tribes inhabiting those tracts that lay between, made it very difficult to carry on regular and systematic trade. Commerce indeed struggled over-land and *via* the Red Sea, being carried on chiefly by the Italian cities on the Mediterranean which traded to the ports of the Levant.† It was due to Vasco da Gama's discovery of maritime passage to India round the Cape of Good Hope. It facilitated to an immense extent the rapid success of European commerce. For over a century it was the Portuguese who had a complete monopoly of the Oriental commerce. I have discussed in a previous chapter ‡ the rise of the Portuguese and the causes of their downfall. The Dutch may be said to have first broken the Portuguese monopoly. William Barents and others attempted to come

* *Calcutta Review*, Vol. XXXV.
† Imperial Gazetteer of India, Vol. VI.
‡ Chapter IV.

to India by sailing round the northern coast of Europe and Asia. But Cornelius Houtman was the first Dutchman who doubled the Cape of Good Hope and reached Sumatra and Bantum in 1596. From 1600 to 1700 A.D., the Dutch were the foremost maritime power, not only in the Eastern Seas, but in all other parts of the world. The memorable massacre of the English by the Dutch at Amboyana in 1623, drove the English Company from the Indian Archipelago to the Indian peninsula, and the Dutch became masters there. About this period they also forced the Portuguese to retire from place to place, and at last wrested almost all their territorial possessions. From 1635 to 1669 their campaigns were directed against the Portuguese. But Clive sounded the death-knell of Dutch supremacy in India. And in the wars conducted between the English and the French from 1793 to 1811, the English wrested from Holland every one of her possessions. But subsequently Java and Malacca were given and Sumatra taken.* Sir William Hunter's observation as to the failure of the Europeans to obtain a footing in Indian trade is very valuable and suggestive. According to him, the Portuguese failed because they made an impossible task of taking the Bible in one hand and the sword in the other,† or in other words, to make a conquest and conversion of India. The Dutch failed because their trade was based upon a grinding monopoly which must ultimately go down. In spite of the genius and brilliancy of the French people, their fickleness, want of mutual confidence and co-operation decided their destiny in India. Although Germany and Austria had never any territorial footing, they have always had a trade in this country.

* Imperial Gazetteer, Vol, VI,
† Do. Do.

Even now they play an important part in the commerce of Calcutta. German mercantile agents are to be seen in the rice districts, jute districts and cotton districts.

The desire of Englishmen to come to India dated so far back as the time of Henry VII. In 1553, Sir Hugh Willoughby made a move along the north of Europe and Asia, but it was reserved to his second in command, a Swedish servant, Chancellor, to open a passage through the good graces of the Grand Duke of Moscow, and he thus laid the foundation of the Russia Company for carrying on the overland trade between India, Persia, Bokhara and Moscow. From 1576 to 1616 many infructuous attempts were made to find out a north-east passage to the East Indies. Such persons as Forbisher, Davies, Hudson and Baffin have left on modern maps their imperishable mark. And it is well known that Sir Fancis Drake, who circumnavigated the globe, came to the port at Ternate, one of the Malaccas, the king of which island agreed to supply the English with cloves. The causes of the success of the English have thus been described by Sir William Hunter:—

"England emerged the prize-winner from the long contest of the European nations for India. Her success was partly the good gift of fortune, but chiefly the result of four elements in the national character. There was—first, a marvellous patience and self-restraint in refusing to enter on territorial conquests or projects of Indian aggrandizement, until she had gathered strength enough to succeed. Second, an indomitable persistence in those projects once they were entered on, and a total incapacity on the part of her servants in India of being stopped by defeat. Third, an admirable mutual confidence of the Company's servants in each other in times of trouble. Fourth, and chief of all, the resolute support of the English nation at home. England has never doubted that she must retrieve, at whatever strain to herself, every disaster which may befall Englishmen in India; and she has never sacrificed the work of her Indian servants to the exigencies of her diplomacy in Europe. She was the only European power which consciously, but absolutely, carried out these two principles of policy. The result of that policy, pursued during two and a half centuries, is the British India of to-day." *

In regard to the modern trade of Calcutta, it is not possible to do more in this place than to indicate its character and extent by a few statistical tables.

The aggregate sea-borne trade of Calcutta with foreign countries and with other ports for the past five years is shown in the subjoined statements:—

	1898-99.	1899-1900.	1900-01.	1901-02.	1902-03.	Increase or decrease in 1902-03 as compared with 1901-02.	Percentage of difference.
(I). FOREIGN TRADE	Rs. Lakhs.	Rs. Lakhs.	Rs. Lakhs.	Rs. Lakhs.	Rs. Lakhs.	Rs. Lakhs.	
Imports.							
Merchandise ...	2,965·22	3,221·34	3,382·20	3,613·04	3,588·80	—24·24	—·67
Gold	233·83	370·70	452·39	311·35	403·66	+93·31	+29·64
Silver	128·38	198·86	206·23	245·35	169·28	—76·07	—31·00
Total Imports ...	3,327·43	3,781·90	4,041·32	4,169·74	4,161·74	—8·00	—·19

Exports. Foreign merchandise	20·56	22·00	23·99	20·28	19·05	—1·23	—6·06
Indian ,,	4,431·21	4,941·67	5,419·82	5.360·75	5,199·31	—161·44	—3·01
Gold	·01	·05	9·10	151·43	19·01	—132·42	—87·45
Silver	75·13	39·63	53·63	53·56	64·61	+11·05	+25·63
Total Exports ...	4,576·91	5,003·35	5,506·54	5,586·02	5,301·98	—284·04	—5·08
Aggregate foreign trade ...	7,904·34	8,735·25	9,547·86	9.755 76	9,463·72	—292·04	—2·99
(II). Coasting Trade.							
Imports.							
Indian produce ...	370·26	366·27	428·12	454·40	453·32	—1·08	—0·24
Foreign merchandise	39·25	46·75	53 31	33·75	38·87	+5·12	+15·17
Gold	·75	·28	·37	·54	·62	+·08	+14·81
Silver	23·79	82·41	247·38	99·18	44·45	—54·73	—55·18
Total Imports ...	434·05	495·71	729·18	587·87	537·26	—50·61	—8·61

* Imperial Gazetteer of India, Vol. VI.

	1898-99.	1899-1900.	190-001.	1901-02.	1902-03.	Increase or decrease in 1902-03 as compared with 1901-02.	Percentage of difference.
	Rs.	Rs.	Rs.	Rs.	Rs.	Rs.	
Exports.	Lakhs.	Lakhs.	Lakhs.	Lakhs.	Lakhs.	Lakhs.	
Indian produce ...	545·62	639·27	671·05	571·90	572·31	+·41	+·07
Foreign merchandise	129·77	113·36	88·12	84·18	92·72	+8·54	+10·14
Gold	1·35	·04	·47	·64	·04	—·60	—93·75
Silver	54·85	156·03	123·65	81·16	117·91	+36·75	+45·28
Total Exports ...	731·59	908·70	883·29	737·88	782·98	+45·10	+6·11
Aggregate Coasting trade ...	1,165·64	1,404·41	1,612·47	1,325·	1,320·24	—5·51	—·41
Aggregate Trade ...	9,069·98	10,189·66	11,160·33	11,081·51	10,783·96	—297·55	—2·68

FOREIGN TRADE.

1902-1903.

Imports.		Exports.	
Cotton goods ...	16,03,35,219	Jute, raw ...	10,41,95,315
Metals ...	3,77,73,739	Jute manufactures	8,98,18,317
Oils	1,67,24,640	Tea ...	6,01,51,769
Sugar ...	1.48,35,817	Opium ...	5,50,75.605
Machinery and Mill-work ...	1,21,47,007	Oil-seeds ...	4,68,18,448
Hardwares and Cutlery ...	76,78,531	Grain & Pulse ...	4,60,35,241
Jewellery ...	65,40,228	Hides & Skins ...	4,56,36,511
Liquors ...	53,77,156	Lac ...	1,82,33,836
Woollen goods ...	50,50,150	Cotton, raw ...	75,35,438
Salt ...	49,31,607	Indigo ...	65,97,903
Apparel ...	47,82,450	Silk, raw ...	51,98,936
Railway materials	47,55,006	Cotton twist and yarn ...	48,89,449
Drugs & Narcotics	47,09,290	Saltpetre ...	42,68,942
Provisions ...	34,78,206	Coal & Coke ...	38,50,579
Spices ...	34,32,036	Oils ...	33,42,861
Glass & Glassware	30,11,049	Provisions ...	18,09,459
Instruments and Appliances ...	26,16,522	Hemp, raw ...	13,42,456
Chemicals ...	21,81,296	Manures ...	12,80,175
Animals ...	19,38,358	Apparel ...	11,67,599
Paints & Colours	17 04,569	Woollen manufactures ...	11,32,511
Matches ...	13,67,852	Mica ...	10,23,032
Paper & Pasteboard	13,36,562	Fodder, bran ...	9,52,243
Carriages, Carts, &c.	12,15,090	Wool, raw ...	9,03,871
Silk manufactures	11,92,821	Silk manufactures ...	7,23,954
Dyeing materials	10,82,837	Fibres & Bristles	6,02,632
Tea chests ...	10,57,532	Wood ...	5,60,205
Stationery ...	10,15,350	Drugs, Narcotics (including tobacco)	5,83,089
Earthenware and Porcelain ...	9,20,631	Cordage, rope ...	4,84,025
Flax and flax manufactures...	9,23,369	Dyeing materials other than indigo	5,13,758
Books and printed matter ...	9,00,093	Horns ...	4,43,234
Wood & manufactures thereof ...	8,76,067	Spices ...	2,85,064
Building materials	8,69,065	Wax (including candle) ...	2,55,177
Toys ...	7,92,444	Coir ...	2,54,058
		Animals ...	2,33,429

FOREIGN TRADE.—*contd.*

1902-1903.

Imports.		Exports.	
Leather & manufactures thereof ...	7,74,173	Cotton manufactures ...	2,42,834
Arms and Ammunition ...	6,19,703	Metals ...	1,81,177
Soap ...	5,79,555	Borax ...	1,09,701
Corals ...	5,33,943	Caoutchouc, raw	91,321
Clocks & Watches	5,20,385	All other articles	14,85,423
Hemp and manufactures thereof	4,16,836		
Pitch, Tar, and Dammer ...	3,91,243		
Umbrellas ...	3,69,161		
Cabinet-ware ...	3,12,328		
Hides and Skins	2,37,881		
Caoutchouc ...	2,27,525		
Gums & Resins ...	1,87,302		
Ships, parts of ...	1,60,032		
Fruits and Vegetables ...	93,537		
Grain and Pulse	19,383		
All other articles	36,03,801		
TOTAL MERCHANDISE	32,65,99,348	TOTAL MERCHANDISE	51,85,64,406
Treasures.		*Treasures.*	
Gold ...	4,03,66,201	Gold ...	19,01,334
Silver ...	1,69,27,628	Silver ...	64,60,646
TOTAL TREASURES	5,72,93,829	TOTAL TREASURES	83,61,980
GRAND TOTAL ...	38,38,93,177	GRAND TOTAL ...	52,69,26,386

DISTRIBUTION OF FOREIGN TRADES OF CALCUTTA BY COUNTRIES.

	IMPORTS.			EXPORTS.			Percentage which the total of each country bears to the whole.	
	1900-01	1901-02	1902-03	1900-01	1901-02	1902-03	In 1901-1902	In 1902-1903
	Rs. Lakhs.	Rs. Lakhs.	Rs. Lakhs.	Rs. Lakhs.	Rs. Lakhs.	Rs. Lakhs.		
Europe.								
United Kingdom ...	2527·04	2592·63	2636·04	1887·77	1768·18	1635·03	47·42	46·80
Germany	100·59	120·86	73·34	625·71	569·03	576·64	7·52	7·13
France	18·49	24·98	33·78	246·79	270·23	278·99	3·20	3·41
Austria-Hungary ...	86·86	94·35	58·76	134·75	116·24	119·19	2·30	1·95
Belgium	90·05	105·50	99·57	42·38	32·24	45·25	1·50	1·59
Russia	115·26	152·52	115·77	9·26	11·80	25·84	1·79	1·56
Italy	29·82	28·93	25·47	120·17	95·85	100·16	1·36	1·38
Other Countries ...	1·87	3·93	4 85	76·07	56·95	61·72	0·63	0·73
TOTAL EUROPE ...	2969·98	3123·72	3047·58	3142·90	2920.52	2842·82	65·72	64·56
Africa.								
Mauritius	41·70	34·79	42 53	95·25	81·46	87·98	1·26	1·44
Natal	0·30	0·30	30·08	32·36	45·04	57·35	0·49	0·95
Egypt	8·32	14·30	18·40	39·10	71·53	61·25	0·93	0·87
Cape Colony	0·05	0·04	0·14	27·17	31·42	45·40	0·34	0·49
Other countries in Africa ...	1·16	1·09	1·18	14·44	14·08	12·34	0·18	0·15
TOTAL AFRICA ...	51.53	50·52	92·33	208 32	243·53	264·32	3·11	3·91

DISTRIBUTION OF FOREIGN TRADES OF CALCUTTA BY COUNTRIES.—*contd.*

	IMPORTS.			EXPORTS.			Percentage which the total of each country be ars to the whole.	
	1900-01.	1901-02.	1902-03	1900-01	1901-02	1902-03	In 1901-1902	In 1902-1903
	Rs. Lakhs.	Rs. Lakhs.	Rs. Lakhs.	Rs. Lakhs.	Rs. Lakhs.	Rs. Lakhs.		
America.								
United States	56·71	51·14	38·12	613·96	695·59	729·69	8·12	8·39
South America	...	...	...	77·63	89·42	118·50	0·97	1·30
Other countries in America	0·02	2·17	0·09	26·15	43·70	63·64	0·50	0·63
TOTAL AMERICA ...	56·73	53·31	38·21	717·74	828·71	909·83	9·59	10·38
Asia.								
China	102·49	99·48	113·10	456·98	574·39	517·03	7·33	6·91
Strait Settlements ...	84·78	84·48	89·37	337·34	308·54	293·77	4·27	4·20
Ceylon	138·19	92·06	64·87	287·26	189·33	178·05	3·06	2·66
Arabia	17·12	23·67	20·02	50·94	55·85	55·78	0·86	0·80
Java	22·39	27·80	42·15	11·12	14·04	11·25	0·46	0·59
Turkey in Asia	0·25	0·09	0·06	30·13	28·80	30·40	0·31	0·31
Japan	80·76	4·81	8·33	16·52	25·72	12·18	0·33	0·23
Oher countries in Asia ...	4·32	7·68	8 79	40·14	37·77	37·09	0·50	0·51
TOTAL ASIA	450·30	340·07	346·69	1230·43	1234·34	1135·55	17·12	16·24
Australasia	225·83	213·01	314·12	185·73	189·58	134·81	4·37	4·92
GRAND TOTAL ...	3754·37	3780·63	3838·93	5485·12	5461·68	5287·33	100·00	100·00

The Licenses for Professions, Trades and Callings issued uring the year 1902-1903, may be thus classified :—

Class I. Companies with paid up capitals amounting to 10 lakhs of rupees or upwards ... 156.

Class II. (*a*) Companies whose paid up capital is less than 10 lakhs ... ... 352.

(*b*) Merchants, Agents, Wholesale Traders, Builders and Auctioneers whose places of business are assessed at Rs. 350 a month or upwards ... . 123.

Class III. (*a*) Surgeons and Physicians ... 25.

(*b*) Practising Barristers, Attorneys and Pleaders of High Court ... ... 284.

Owners of markets and bazars valued at Rs. 100 a month or upwards ... ... 25.

Merchants, Agents, Wholesale Traders, Builders, Auctioneers and Keepers of Hotels, Boarding-Houses and other Traders and Shop-keepers whose places of business are assessed at Rs. 100 a month or upwards, but at less than Rs. 350 ... ... 1,257.

Class IV. Pleaders of Subordinate Courts, Muktears and Law Agents ... ... 221.

Practising Licentiates of Medicine and Veterinary Surgeons ... ... 147.

Brokers and Dealers in precious stones ... 249.

Pawn-brokers and Money-lenders ... 175.

Owners of Cargo-boats ... ... 16.

Keepers of Hotels, Boarding-houses, Traders and Shop-keepers whose places of business are assessed at or above Rs. 25, but at less than Rs. 100 a month ... 2,428.

Class V. Native Doctors, Kavirajes and Hakims 201.
Poddars and Money-changers ... 181.

Coolie-suppliers, Shipping-agents, Order-suppliers, Boat-suppliers and Dalals other than those included in class IV, and Midwives ... ... 264.

Keepers of permanent stalls at a daily public market or bazar and miscellaneous Shop-keepers whose places of business are assessed at or above Rs. 10 a month, but less than Rs. 25 4,496

Class VI. Miscellaneous Shop-keepers whose places of business are assessed at less than Rs. 10 a month ... ...14,321.

Class VII. Itinerant dealers selling goods in baskets or trays ... ... 187.

Traders whose places of business are offensive or dangerous ... ... 432.

25,540.

Traders, Shop-keepers and others who were defaulters in the previous year ... 4,697.

Total ... 30,237.

It is very difficult to form an accurate estimate of the entire body of modern trade which has multiplied itself so enormously since its commencement in Calcutta over two and a half centuries ago. It is only the trade and commerce that have made Calcutta the centre of so many interests and activities. All the nations of the civilised world are vitally interested in its affairs. The motley group of mankind that inhabit the countries between China and Peru, are to be seen here carrying on a brisk commerce and amassing fortunes that would excite the envy of a prince. Consuls are sent from almost all parts of the world to safeguard the interests of the particular class of people they represent. Canals and roads have been opened, jungles cleared, and the whole country now wears the appearance of a smiling garden. Railway lines and telegraph wires now connect Calcutta with all parts of India. The whole commercial gain has had fascination enough even for the quiet Hindu. He is now to be seen running to and fro, deeply immersed in trade, pursuing no other thought than his present avocation. Pre-eminently the West has captured the East in this respect. The impetus given in this direction cannot be exaggerated. The mills, dock-yards, press-houses and factories have raised the people of the lower classes to a life of ease and plenty. Even the women and juvenile population have been attracted by this new call of industry. Their wages have been increased, and now-a-days it is not easy to get servants, and specially women servants, for private employment; indeed quite a new problem now confronts the economist and the legislator. Human progress means more than a surplus of advantages over evils. It is idle to deny that numbers of men are well provided by the growth of modern industry and commerce. And despite many fluctuations in trade and commerce, the wages of this vastly increased population have been gradually rising; at the same time, the multiplication and diversity of employments has been of incalculable benefit to the poorer population.

The present is pre-eminently a commercial epoch. In agriculture, the improvements introduced have been of manifold good to the poor cultivators. Banks have been introduced and other remedial measures adopted to rescue them from unmerited ruin at the hands of the money-lender. Methods have thus been devised so that capital, skill and energy are now easily introduced into the home of the peasant. Cheap clothing, cheap implements, and cheap and speedy means of transporting products by railways or steamers to distant markets and convenient places are among the many blessings that machinery has conferred upon the agricultural poor. At the same time great centres of intellectual energy have multiplied upon the land and they diffuse their moral and intellectual influence to the remotest district. The establishment of Insurance Companies is a new feature of the era of commercial activity. Its wholesome and stimulating influence upon the progress of commerce has been very considerable. While dilating upon this pleasant aspect of the growth of commerce and the new feature of the manufacturing industry, let us also boldly face its darker side. The evils accompanying the sudden growth of manufactures were most serious. Its baneful effect in destroying the hand-loom industries has done immense injury to the weavers and other classes of skilled labourers and artisans. The woollen hand-industry has also received a deathblow, and the social evils that have arisen, such as intemperance, extravagance and other vices, are too serious to be lightly regarded. The danger that menaces us in the near future should by all means be a question among questions demanding the attention and taxing the highest powers of the statesman and the economist.

CHAPTER VII.

THE HISTORY OF CIVIL AND CRIMINAL JUDICATURE UNDER BRITISH RULE.

VOLTAIRE has observed "there never was a perfect Government, for men are always influenced by passions, and if they had no passions, they would need no Government."* In the case of meting out justice between man and man, and by men, the cogency of the above remark cannot be questioned. In primitive days it is said that Might was Right. When the first man enclosed lands for his own purposes and appropriated them by force, he became, so to speak, by his own right and title, the proprietor and lord of the soil. Hence originated his title. In modern civilized countries, the proceedings of the Ecclesiastical Courts form a very strange chapter. The treatment of the Catholics by the Protestants, and of the Protestants by the Catholics, discloses how passions overshadow the sense of justice. Alas! the persecution did not end here. The wrath of the Divinity was invoked for the eternal damnation of the sinners. It is futile to expect perfect justice, so long as mankind is governed by passions and sentiments. Rousseau's pronouncement touching the effect of human vanity, contains a truth which it is impossible to deny. "If we explore the original source of the disorders of society, we shall find that all the

* History of England in the 18th Century, by W. G. H. Lecky, Vol. V.

evils from which men suffer come to them through error, much more through ignorance, and that what we do not know at all injures us much less than what we think we know."*

It is the fashion of some writers to denounce the justice administered by the Mahommedans in the 17th and 18th centuries. In that period, in France and in other parts of Europe, both the Civil and Criminal laws were so harsh, and embodied principles, some of which were so absurd, that Mahommedan laws and institutions could be favourably compared to them.†

Nabob Mahammad Reza Cawn says that there existed two kinds of courts of justice during the Moslem rule: One was called Adalut—that is, Alia or the Nabob's own Court—and the other called Khalsa Cutchery, where questions of land revenue, debts and other causes wereheard and decided. In this Court judgment was given under the signature of the presiding Officer or Hakim. In the Adalut or Nabob's own Court, criminal cases, such as those of murder, robbery and other high crimes, were heard and decided. This Court was composed of a number of judges, and the final verdict rested with the Nabob himself. The presiding judge waited upon him, explained the whole case, and the Nabob put his signature if all the judges concurred in their finding. The punishment was meted out according to the religion and personal law of the accused.‡ According to the late Mr. Justice C. D. Field, "under the Mahommedan Government

* *Life of Voltaire*, by James Parton, Vol. II. Rousseau's Letter to Voltaire.

† Lecky's History of England in the 18th Century, Vol. V.

‡ Mahammad Reza Cawn's description of the former and present state of the country, the causes of its decline, and the way there is of recovering and bringing it again into a flourishing condition.

justice was distributed by two distinct classes of tribunals, *viz.* (1) those of the Kazis, who administered the elaborate system of Mahommedan law; and (2) those of the Officers of Government whose authority was regulated by no fixed rules, but was generally exercised with a view to their own interest, more especially when the litigants were aliens in race and creed. The King occasionally inquired into petitions; but the calls of war or the other cares of State or the pleasures of the harem, left little leisure for taking any regular or systematic share in the administration of justice. In the provinces, or subahs, the same two classes of tribunals existed. When the Kazi was a man of celebrity and individual importance, his power and influence upon the distribution of justice were great in proportion; but it commonly happened that the Governors and their Officers assumed the disposal of all the more important cases, while the Kazi became merely an Officer for registering deeds and performing marriages. The following are the judicial authorities which we found in existence at Murshidabad immediately after the grant of the Dewani:—

I. The Nazim, who, as Supreme Magistrate, presided personally at the trial of capital offenders.

II. The Diwan, who was supposed to decide cases relating to real estate or property in land, but who seldom exercised this jurisdiction in person.

III. The Darogah-Adalut-al-Alica or Deputy of the Nazim in the Criminal Court, who took cognizance of quarrels, frays and abuse, and also of all matters of property excepting claims of land and inheritance.

IV. The Darogah-i-Adalut-Diwani, or Deputy of the Diwan in the Civil Court.

V. The Foujdar or Officer of Police and Judge of all crimes not capital.

VI. The Kazi who decided claims of inheritance or succession.

VII. The Muktasib, who had cognizance of drunkenness, the vending of spirituous liquors and intoxicating drugs, and the examination of false weights and measures.

VIII. The Mufti, who expounded the law for the Kazi, who, if he agreed, decided accordingly. If he disagreed, a reference was made to the Nazim, who called a council of the jurisconsults.

IX. The Kanungos or Registrars of the land, to whom cases connected with land were occasionally referred for decision: and

X. The Kotwal or Peace-officer of the Night, subordinate to the Foujdar."*

In the *Ayin-Akbari*, it is mentioned that the officers employed in the administration of justice and in police duties are the Mir-i-Adl or Lord Justice, who seems to have been superior to the Kazi, whose judgments required his sanction: the Foujdar for making the peace and maintaining the police: and the Kotwal or Head Constable of the town. The Foujdar exercised jurisdiction in criminal cases.† During the closing years of the Moslem rule, the administration of

* Introduction to the Regulations of the Bengal Code by C. D. Field.

† See foot-note, Field's Introduction to the Regulations of the Bengal Code.

justice greatly deteriorated. The law courts became an engine and instrument of oppression to the innocent people. Even the petty zemindars set up a court of their own. Authority and power were transferred to the hands of military adventurers, who pillaged the rich and the wealthy in order to uphold and maintain their authority. No wonder that the *Ayin-Akbari* and the latest *Fetawii Alemgiri* of the great Emperor Alamgir or Aurangzeb were set at naught. They were of little service then. The canons of justice were enunciated by adventurers, by bandits and robbers. That was a period when everybody became somebody. In the meantime the Europeans appeared on the scene. Their mutual rivalries and quarrels touching their trade and commerce contributed greatly to the disordered state of the time.

I have not said anything about the way in which justice was administered by the Hindus. The scope of my book precludes me from entering into a full discussion of it. From the institutes of Manu and several other law-books (Smritis),* a comprehensive view can be formed of the Hindu law courts respecting civil, criminal, municipal, fiscal and other matters. I recommend to my readers a close examination and study of the ancient laws of the Hindus, some of which have now been rendered into English. In the early days of English rule, a Hindu Court called Caste Cutchery or the Jatimala Cutchery existed. Alluding to it Warren Hastings says: "The Court of Caste, commonly called Jatimala Cutchery, is of as ancient institution as the Government itself; and the proceedings of it are as regular as those of any of the Courts of justice in the country."† We gather

* The Chapter dealing with these topics in Manu and other ancient writers is called Vyavahara.

† Sir John Strachey's Hastings and Rohilla War.

also from the remarks of Warren Hastings that this Court "has cognisance of the disputes among the lower kinds of people."* It appears from the proceedings that the Banians of the Governor-General generally happened to be its presiding officers in the place of the Governor himself.

In or about the year 1698 (1699), Calcutta was raised to the rank of a Presidency. The name given to the Presidency was "Fort William in Bengal." A President and a Council composed of the undermentioned officers were appointed. They were:— (1) The Accountant; (2) The Warehouse-keeper; (3) The Marine Purser and (4) Receiver of Revenue or Collector of Calcutta.† The first President of the Council was Mr. John Beard. All kinds of business—in fact the whole administration—were in the hands of the President and Council. No law courts had then been instituted.

From a charter of Queen Elizabeth, bearing date 1601 A. D., the Company of Merchants derived their power, which is clearly defined. Among others the following conditions are given:—"To make, ordain, and constitute such and so many reasonable laws, constitutions, orders and ordinances, as to them, or the greater part of them, being then and there present, shall seem necessary and convenient for the good government of the said Company and of all factors, masters mariners, and other officers employed or to be employed in any of their voyages, and for the better advancement and continuance of their trade and traffic." They were also empowered to put in use and execute such laws, "and at their pleasure to revoke and alter the same, or any of them, as

* Selections from the State Papers and Despatches, by G. W. Forrest, Vol. II.
† An Historical Account of the Calcutta Collectorate, by R. C. Sterndale.

occasion shall require," and to provide such pains and penalties by imprisonment or fine as might seem to them necessary to secure their due observance.* The year 1618 was most favourable to the interests of the English. Sir Thomas Roe, the famous ambassador of King James I. of England, came to the Mogul Court at Delhi in 1615 to represent his Sovereign. He so far ingratiated himself with the Mogul Emperor, Jehangir, that he was able to obtain important privileges for his countrymen who traded in India. According to Mr. Cowell, the Mogul granted the privilege that disputes between the English should be decided only by themselves. The East India Company, before the end of the 17th century, had obtained and made use of the permission to build fortifications at Madras and Calcutta, and thus established and defended their own authority within their own factories. Under these fortifications natives built houses as well as Europeans. And when the Nabob on that account was about to send a Kazi or Judge to administer justice to the natives, the Company's servants bribed him to abstain from this proceeding.†

The charter of 1601 was renewed in 1609 and 1661. But in 1698, under the award of Lord Godolphin, the two Companies that existed were amalgamated and came to be known as the East India Company. The charter also vested the Company with the government of all their forts, factories and plantations—only the sovereign power was reserved for the Crown. Courts of Judicature were established as before, but nothing was then said about a power of legislation.‡

* Cowell's History and Constitution of the Courts, &c.
† Do. do. do.
‡ Do. do. do.

In or about the year 1720, some of the functions of administration were delegated to the "Zemindar" of Calcutta. Generally a Member of the Council, who was also a servant of the Honorable Company, filled the post. The name of the Court was the Fouzdari Court. From its first establishment in 1720 to 1756, Babu Govindram Mitter acted as Deputy or Dewan to the Zemindar. According to Mr. Sterndale, one Mr. Freke was the first Zemindar.* The principal or head Cutchery of the Zemindar was situated in Calcutta, where he farmed out lands and punished the tenants who were backward in their payments, by way of confinement and whipping, independently of other Courts then in existence. The functions of the Zemindar have been thus stated by Mr. Holwell. He had two capacities, quite distinct and independent of each other. He was the Superintendent and Collector, and also Judge or the Presiding Officer of the Court or Zemindari Cutchery. The salary attached to the post was Rs. 2,000 per mensem. But Holwell says that it was nothing in comparison with the perquisites he received. It is said that "the bulk of the receipts from the firms appears to have gone into his pocket. Besides which, he was largely engaged in private trade, from which he derived a large income . . . . . Many substantial windfalls came in his way, when the traditionary pagoda tree was shaken by stormy political winds of the time." It is mentioned that the Zemindar tried all criminal cases where the natives did not apply to the English Courts of Justice. He used to decide all suits of any amounts amongst the natives. In cases of capital punishment only he was allowed to give judgment,

* It was only Mr. Sterndale's conjecture.

but only the approbation of the President and Council was taken "when the lash was inflicted till death."* I shall proceed to give an account of the life of the famous Zemindar, John Zephaniah Holwell, who was of Irish extraction. He assumed the office of Zemindar in 1752 and remained in the post till 1756. His first visit to Calcutta was as a sergeant's mate of an East Indiaman in 1732. In 1736 he was appointed as one of the aldermen of the Mayor's Court, and in 1748 he returned to Europe. He prepared a plan for reforming abuses in connection with the Zemindar's Cutchery and submitted the same to the Court of Directors, who were so pleased with him that they made him the permanent Zemindar of Calcutta and twelfth in the Council. In 1760 he succeeded Clive for a few months as Governor. He was once offered by some unknown party as a bribe the sum of a lakh of rupees to induce him to drop the prosecution which he was about to institute in connection with the erection of the present Fort William building. He, instead of appropriating the amount, handed it over to the Company. He published the valuable tracts known as the Holwell India tracts, which contain much important information regarding Calcutta. He returned to England about 1760 and died in 1798.†

* "The ancient Moguls and Nawabs would not permit any of the professors of Islam to be hanged according to the English custom, esteeming that too ignominious a death for a Mahommedan to suffer; therefore, in such cases as were deemed capital, only the lash was permitted to be inflicted until death on the Mogul's subjects, Mahommedans and Gentoos, but the officers of the Court called *Chawbuck Swars* or lash-bearers are sometimes so dexterous as to be able to kill a man with two or three strokes of the Indian Chawbuck." *See* R. C. Sterndale's "Historical Account of the Calcutta Collectorate."

† The Zemindar's Court has been written by consulting such books as—Rainey's Topographical Sketch, &c., R.C. Sterndale's Historical Account of the Calcutta Collectorate, *Calcutta Review*, Vol. XVIII., Cowell's Tagore Law-lectures, 1872, and Blochman's Calcutta During Last Century, a lecture.

The establishment of the Mayor's Court in Calcutta in the year 1726 (Rev. Long says 1724) calls up many associations and reminiscences. It was on the representation of the Court of Directors that it came into existence. Amongst others, the Directors made the following representation that "there was great want at Madras, Fort William and Bombay of a proper and competent power and authority for the more speedy and effectual administering of justice in civil causes, and for the trying and punishing of capital and other criminal offences and misdemeanors." It was composed of a Mayor and nine Aldermen, seven of whom with the Mayor were required to be natural born British subjects. The remaining two might be foreign Protestants, the subjects of any State or Prince in amity with Great Britain. The appointment of the Mayor and Aldermen was vested in the Governor or President of the Council. According to Rainey,* the Mayor was elected annually by the Aldermen. The post of Alderman was for life, but the Governor and Council could, upon any reasonable ground, remove any Alderman. This court was declared to be a Court of Record, and was empowered to try and determine all civil suits, actions and pleas between party and party. It had also the authority to grant probates of will and letters of administration to the effects of intestates.

The remuneration of the Mayor and Aldermen was Rs. 20-22 per month. Rainey says the Mayor and Aldermen donned their official garbs. The former used to be seated on a velvet cushion, and the latter appeared in red

the Topographical and Historical Sketches of Calcutta, by Rainey.

taffety for gowns. The Mayor's Court had jurisdiction in criminal and civil matters only over Europeans; but with the consent of the parties, suits between the natives were allowed to be entertained. At last it was declared that suits between natives would be decided amongst themselves, and the Mayor's Court would have no jurisdiction over them. Mr. Bourchier erected the Mayor's Court at Calcutta. It was then known as Court House and situated in Old Court House Street. Some writers, speaking about its proceedings, amuse the readers with its queer judgments. A writer in the *Calcutta Review* publishes the following anecdote:—

A gentleman of the Council of Calcutta, who happened also to be a Zemindar, was indebted to one William Wilson, a sail-maker, for a petty sum amounting to Rs. 75 9as. 7p. for a job done for him. The sail-maker sent over the bill with receipt annexed to the gentleman for payment, which he considered to be exorbitant, and as such withheld payment and kept back the bill with receipt annexed. On this the sail-maker brought the matter to the notice of the Mayor's Court, and the gentleman, for fear of being exposed publicly, agreed to compromise the suit by paying the bill in full with the costs of suit. The complainant's attorney had to send his Banian, a Hindu "black merchant of Calcutta," who held a high position in society, repeatedly to receive the amount of the bill. Without getting any payment at all, on the last occasion the Banian got enraged and said to the gentleman that if it was not paid some bad consequences might ensue; which being told, the gentleman, who was a Zemindar as well, grew angry and ordered the black merchant to be seized and carried to the Cutchery, where he was without an inquiry tied up and flogged and beat on his head with his own slippers.

Another, on the authority of Governor Verelst, is reproduced :—

"In the year 1762, a native detected one of his women in an act of infidelity. Throughout the East women are wholly subject to the will of their masters, and every husband is the avenger of his own wrongs. The man, therefore, satisfied of her guilt, proceeded to punishment by cutting off her nose. He was arraigned at the Calcutta Sessions. He confessed the fact, but urged that he had done nothing to offend the laws and customs in which he had been educated, that the woman was his property, and that by such customs he had a right to set a mark upon her for her infamy; that he had never heard of the laws by which they tried him, but desired to put one question to the Bench—Did they believe that if he had known the punishment to be death, he would ever have committed what they now called a crime? The man, notwithstanding this defence, was condemned and hanged—for if the Court possess jurisdiction, they must proceed according to the English laws."

The case of Radhachuran Mitter, who was also sentenced to be executed for a forgery, but whose punishment was remitted on the presentation of a petition, dated March 1765, by the inhabitants of Calcutta, is too well known to need any detailed statement here. Indeed, it was stated by a writer in a Magazine* that the Mayor's Court was under the thumb of

* *Calcutta Review*, Vol. XVIII.

the Government, "cases having occurred where trials were superseded at the dictum of the Governor, who by his patronage greatly influenced the members."*

I have endeavoured in the foregoing account to trace, step by step, the development of the law courts and the history of the administration of justice introduced into this country by Englishmen. Although cases can be multiplied illustrating the freaks or the incompetency of the individuals in administering justice, it can never be for a moment doubted that these law courts rendered useful services in those days. The beneficial consequences upon society were obvious.

The Court of Request was founded in 1753, consisting of 24 Commissioners selected by the Governor and Council from among the inhabitants of Calcutta, who determined all suits "where the debt, duty or matter in dispute should not exceed 5 pagodas, or 40 shillings." Complaints were heard on every Thursday, and the three members formed the bench or Court. Native inhabitants were at first chosen to be Commissioners, but ultimately only the European traders were selected for its members. *The Court of Quarter Sessions* took cognisance of offenders accused only of high crimes such as "murder," "treason," &c. It is also stated that there existed three other Courts in Calcutta under the authority of the Moguls. The original object of these Courts was the preservation of good order and better government within the limits of the Company's land and factory.

* The History of the Mayor's Court has been based upon Cowell's Tagore Law Lectures, 1872; Rainey's Historical and Topographical Sketch; Kaye's Administration of the E I. Company; Blochmann's "Calcutta a Century Ago," and Sterndale's" Historical Account of the Calcutta Collectorate."

After the subjugation of Bengal by the English, the position of the Law Courts became more and more anomalous. The helm of administration was in the hands of the Mahommedan Subadar. Owing to grave political reasons, it was then deemed incumbent to keep the reins of Government in the hands of the Moslems. Thus the sovereignty and the right of administering Civil and Criminal justice were vested in them. The government of the provinces consisted of two parts; namely, the Dewani, *i.e.* the collection of revenue as well as the administration of the principal branches in the department of Civil justice, and the Nizamat, *i.e.* the Military Branch of Government with powers of superintendence in the criminal department of judicature. The Dewani was then subordinate to the Nizamat. It should be borne in mind that the East India Company was subject to the control of the King and the Parliament. This body was dependent on the constitution of England; and after the victory of the battle of Plassey the Company, although they became possessed of territories, found that they had a very difficult game to play. They became conscious of their anomalous position. Parliament intervened in their proceedings, and member after member discussed how far powers and responsibilities could legitimately be given to them. A Bill for the better government of India had been, from time to time, introduced defining the powers and control of the Sovereign over the Company. In India the effects of a double system of Government (namely one conducted according to English principles, and the other according to the existing Mahommedan form) soon began to manifest themselves.

The Company's primary object was anyhow to gain profit by their commercial ventures, and the grinding and fleecing of the Subadar often drove the people to maddening despair. I cannot do better than furnish here the statement of General Burgoyne, who was appointed Chairman of the Committee appointed to enquire into the state of affairs in the East Indies by the House of Commons in 1772. He said that such a scene of iniquity, rapine and injustice, such unheard-of cruelties, such open violation of every rule of morality, every tie of religion, and every principle of Government was never before discovered, * * * * that there were accounts of crimes shocking to human nature, and transactions that were carried into execution by perfidy and murder.

The year 1765 is associated with momentous changes. In that year, for the last time, Lord Clive came to Bengal with a commission to undertake duties as considerable and as arduous as those which devolved on William the Conqueror after the Battle of Hastings. It is not necessary here to enter into any details of the proceedings of the India Office at which the opponents of Clive made a show and afterwards retracted their statements upon which Lord Clive accepted the charge. Mr. Torrens, in his "Empire in Asia," has pithily described the situation. "Men's eyes turned once more on Clive. He was just beginning to enjoy the ease and luxury of the position he had won. His house in Berkeley Square, his equipage, and even his dress, betrayed his daily exaltation. He had a dozen votes in Parliament at his command, and rival statesmen, therefore, sought his society. He was the only living Commander who had actually won pitched battles, so he was made much of at the Horse Guards. He was the only Englishman who had added to His Majesty's dominion without adding to the national debt, so George III liked to talk to him at levee. Though quizzed by the fops of St. James's Street, and laughed at as ill-bred by women of fashion, he was regarded by the multitude as a hero, and by politicians as an administrator of signal power. If he could be only persuaded to return to Bengal, all would be sure to go well, so thought the proprietors of India stock. The Chairman, Mr. Sullivan, was, however, his personal adversary, and many of his colleagues shrank from submitting to one who they knew would prove to be their master. But bad times grew worse, and shortcomings grew shorter. How was a 10 per cent. dividend to be paid. After a stormy debate at the India House, in which Clive insisted on Sullivan being deposed, he was deputed to resume the reins of Government at Calcutta, and was named by the Crown, General-in-Chief of all the English forces in Asia." Clive, with an admirable resoluteness, first began to reform the officials which cost him great trouble afterwards, and then he placed the possession of the Company on a legal basis. From the Great Mogul at Delhi he obtained the grant of the Dewani which placed the Government of Bengal on a new footing, and established its relations to the natives on a footing of definite civil responsibility. Besides these arrangements for the internal administration of Bengal, Clive established relations with the other powers of India by several treaties. In these several administrative reforms and political undertakings Lord Clive was greatly helped by his Persian Secretary and Dewan, Maharaja Nubkissen Bahadur.* The text of the Firmaund of the Dewani is given below :—

" At this happy time our Royal Firmaund, indispensably requiring obedience, is issued; that, whereas, in consider-

* Memoirs of Maharaja Nubkissen Bahadur, by N. N. Ghose.

ation of the attachment and services of the high and mighty, the noblest of exalted nobles, the chief illustrious warriors, our faithful servants and sincere well-wishers, worthy of our royal favours, the English Company, we have granted them the Dewani of the Provinces of Bengal, Behar and Orissa from the beginning of the Fussel Rubby of the Bengali year 1172, as a free gift and ultumgan, without the association of any other person, and with an exemption from the payment of the customs of the Dewani, which used to be paid by the Court. It is requisite that the said Company engage to be security for the sum of 26 lakhs of rupees a year for our royal revenue, which sum has been appointed from the Nabob Nudjum-ul-Dowla Bahadur, and regularly remit the same to the royal Circar; and in this case, as the said Company are obliged to keep up a large Army for the protection of the Provinces of Bengal, &c., we have granted to them whatsoever may remain out of the revenues of the said Provinces, after remitting the sum of 26 lakhs of rupees to the royal Circar, and providing for the expenses of the Nizamut. It is requisite that our royal descendants, the Viziers, the bestowers of dignity, the Omrahs high in rank, the great officers, the Muttaseddees of the Dewani, the manager of the business of the Sultanut, the Jaghirdars and Croories, as well the future as the present, using their constant endeavours for the establishment of this our royal command, leave the said office in possession of the said Company, from generation to generation, for ever and ever. Looking upon them to be assured from dismission or removal, they must, on no account whatsoever, give them any interruption, and they must regard them as excused and exempted from the payment of all the customs of the

Dewani and royal demands. Knowing our orders on the subject to be most strict and positive, let them not deviate therefrom. Written the 24th of Sophar, of the sixth year of the Jaloos, the 12th August 1765."*

Though Clive obtained the Dewani, it was reserved for Hastings to make full use of this in the administration of the country. Clive left the administration of justice—civil, criminal and fiscal—in the hands of the Nabob, though he introduced a practical supervision over them which has been styled the "Double Government." The slight measure of improvement he thus introduced worked only for a time. Again misrule and oppression appeared on the surface. At last in 1771 the Directors declared their resolution "to stand forth as Dewan, and by the agency of the Company's servants to take upon themselves the entire care and management of the revenues." This involved the entire remodelling of rights of property in the soil, and the assumption of the administration of justice. It expressed the policy which has already been determined upon, *viz.* to abandon the government through the Nabob's hierarchy of officials subject to English supervision; and to transfer to the Company's servants the direct discharge of the duties of administration. The next event was that Warren Hastings was transferred from Madras to the Governorship of Bengal, where he landed early in 1772.† It was Warren Hastings who took the direct responsibility of the Government and gradually replaced Mahommedan Law and Offices by the regulations of the Company and its servants. Ultimately he transferred the seat of Government with the

* Cowell's Tagore Law Lectures, 1772.

† Life of Warren Hastings, by Colonel G. B. Malleson, C.S.I.

Chief Courts of Justice from Murshidabad to Calcutta. Rev. G. Gleig thus describes his work in these directions.

He found the Provinces, when he assumed the principal direction of their affairs, labouring under the accumulated vilse of an exhausted treasury and a Government destitute of influence. The revenues, collected nobody could tell how, proved year by year less productive. There were no tribunals to which men might appeal against the oppressions of the strong or the chicanery of the feeble. Bands of robbers wandered over the face of the country, setting the resistance of a wretched police at defiance, while poverty and sickness, the results of a terrible famine, appeared to paralyse the exertions of the scanty population that remained. With respect, again, to the commerce of the country, whether we look to its foreign or its domestic trade, that was totally destroyed, and partly through the misconduct of individuals, partly through the indifference of those at the head of departments; the native merchant was thrust absolutely aside, while the Company's investments fell to nothing, as much through the poverty of the weavers and contractors from whom they were obtained, as through the negligence of the Board whose business it was to look over them. Within the limited space of two years Mr. Hastings entirely reversed this picture. From the outrages of *dakoits* (robbers), and sannyasis, and other marauders, the Provinces were gradually delivered. He hunted them down wherever they showed themselves, and in the end they ceased to be troublesome. The revenue system, if not perfect, was the best which circumstances would allow him to form, for the five years' settlement could only be regarded as an experiment. The establishment of District Courts for the administration of justice likewise, and of district officers to maintain the public peace, were great steps taken towards better things. So also his division of the Supreme Council into committees, and his substitution of individual Superintendents for Boards which never acted, especially contributed to set the machine in motion and to render its movements certain and regular. And when we take into account that all this was done, often at the expense of private interests, oftener still in despite of old and deep-rooted prejudices, it seems impossible to deny to him who accomplished it the high praise of rare talent and industry such as no amount of labour could break down.*

While Hastings was developing his many schemes of reform with the help and co-operation of the India Office, the public in England became indignant with the servants of the Company, who, after a few years' residence in the country, returned home amassing immense fortunes and led there the life of Oriental potentates. The jealousies excited by this sudden change of fortune of the individuals were probably laid against them. The walls of Westminster Hall echoed with declamations against the Anglo-Indians, and Acts and Regulations were determined upon and passed to make the illicit gains impossible, and to administer the Indian Government on a sound basis.

In 1772, the Sadar Dewani Adalut, or a Court of last resort, was established in Calcutta by Warren Hastings. At first the President and three or more members of the Council

* Life of Warren Hastings, by Colonel G. B. Malleson, C. S. I.

formed the Court. It had jurisdiction over the Mofussil Courts where the amount in dispute exceeded more than Rs. 500.

By a Parliamentary Act, known as the Regulating Act of **1773**, the Supreme Court of Judicature came into existence. It was a signal triumph of the dominant party in England, who entertained a notion, almost bordering upon conviction, that Englishmen in India acquired their fortune through pillage and fraud. The ostensible object of the establishment of this Court was to separate the Judicial from the Executive branch of the administration. Their cherished notion seemed to be that gradually with aid from England the Supreme Court would be able to supervise and control the inferior Courts, and the whole administration of justice would be transferred from the control of the Executive. The Supreme Court consisted of a Chief Justice and three Puisne Judges who, besides being made independent of the Governor and Council, were armed with extensive Civil and Criminal jurisdiction. These judges arrived in Bengál with the prejudiced conviction that the natives were labouring under the accumulated injustice and grinding tyranny of the Agents of the Company. Their preconceived notions are illustrated in the following anecdote. "When the judges of the Supreme Court, who had come out with very strong notions of the oppression to which the people were subject, landed at the Chandpal Ghat and saw the natives with their legs bare, one of them said to the other: 'See, brother, the oppression to which the people have been subject. The Supreme Court was not established before it was needed. I hope our Court will not have been six months in existence before these poor wretches will be comfortably provided with shoes and stockings.'" Hence it is not surprising that these judges, on the very day of their arrival, commenced their crusade against the Executive. Thus the Supreme Council (which was created by the same Regulating Act of 1773 which brought into existence the Supreme Court of Judicature) and the Supreme Court jealously looked upon each other as rivals, and the consequences were that the judicial and political authorities were arrayed against each other as two contending factions. The Chief Justice and his associate Judges arrogated to themselves the supreme authority not only over Calcutta, but over the whole of the Company's territories. About this time stories and rumours began to circulate that as these judges derived their authority from the Crown and the Parliament, and were in no way subordinate to the Executive Head, they were quite empowered even to arrest the Governor-General and his Councillors. Although much coloured by high imagination and sentiment, Macaulay's glowing picture of the whole aspect of the situation will perhaps convey some idea. "No Mahratta invasion has ever spread through the Province such dismay as this inroad of English lawyers. All the injustice of the former oppressors, Asiatic and European, appeared as a blessing when compared with the justice of the Supreme Court."

The vagaries of the Supreme Court at last came to a crisis, when they began to question the legal status of the Provincial Courts. The Supreme Council and Supreme Court came to a direct collision in the well-known case of the Raja of Kossijorah, when the Governor-General and Council instructed the Raja not to obey the process of the Supreme Court. The Supreme Court also issued summons against the Governor-General and the Members of the Council individually. Ultimately the British Parliament was moved, and an amending Act was passed in 1781. It restricted the authority of the Supreme Court, made it subordinate to the Supreme Council, and recognized the Mafussil Courts established under the Dewani. Thus limited in its influence and power, the Supreme Court proved to be a blessing to the country and won the respect both of Europeans and Natives. The cool temper and sagacity displayed by Warren Hastings at this serious crisis averted a great catastrophe, and his judicious step in making Sir Elijah Impey the head of the Sadar Dewani Adalut put an end to the undesirable dissensions. This has called forth the criticism of Macaulay and his contempt upon the character of Impey. But "Bengal was saved; an appeal to force was averted." The Supreme Court has been compared to something like the English Court of Chancery and the Court of King's Bench combined in one. In or about the year 1801, a further change was introduced in its constitution, and two puisne judges from the Covenanted Civil Service were added; and afterwards the post of the Chief Justice was thrown open to the members of this service. Various other changes in the constitution took place until the year 1862, when the present Judicature of the High Court at Fort William was established. The two Courts known as the Sadar Dewani Adalut and the Supreme Court of Judicature were merged in the present High Court. The jurisdiction of the High Court embraces Bengal, Behar, Orissa and Assam. It has two departments—Original and Appellate. The Original side of the High Court represents to some extent the old Supreme Court of Judicature; the Appellate the Sadar Dewani Adalut. On its Original side it takes cognisance of the cases that come before it as a Court of first instance, and is only limited to the town of Calcutta. On its Appellate side it hears the appeals from decisions of the Original side and from the Mafussil Courts. It also acts as a Court of revision and reference, and for administrative purposes it acts by committees. It has also several jurisdictions—such as Insolvency jurisdiction, Ecclesiastic, &c. There are several offices attached to it—such as the offices of the Registrar and of the Accountant-General, and of Receiver, &c. Appeals from the Calcutta High Court in certain cases, not being of criminal jurisdiction, are allowed to lie to the Judicial Committee of the Privy Council. The value of the subject matters of appeal has been changed from time to time. The judicial functions of the Privy Council are exercised by a Judicial Committee established by 3 and 4 William IV, C. 41. The Committee is composed of the President of the Council, the Lord Chancellor and several of the judges of the highest rank in the kingdom, with power to the Sovereign to add any two Privy Councillors as members of the Committee, three members forming a quorum. The decision is with the majority. The Judicial Committee have power (i) to examine or direct the examination of witnesses at discretion, (ii) to remit the cause to the Court below for rehearing, either generally or with respect to certain points, and (iii) upon such rehearing to take further evidence, to admit evidence before rejected, to reject evidence before admitted, and to direct issues to be tried in any Court in His Majesty's Dominion abroad. The Privy Council stands as the last Court of appeal. It has had jurisdiction over India since 1726, when the Mayor's Court was established.

The Calcutta Small Cause Court was established in or about the year 1850, in the place of the Old Court of Requests.

During the administration of Lord William Bentinck, complaints of inefficiency and corruption of the Police became universal. The earliest attempts at reform were made in the Presidency towns by appointing Superintendents of Police separate from the Magistrate, and appointing non-official Justices of the Peace—Native and European. The result everywhere demonstrated the soundness of the principle of separation, while the Justices of the Peace discharged the duties entrusted to them in a very satisfactory manner. "In Calcutta, Act IV of 1866 of the Bengal Council has provided that the administration of Police in that town should be vested in an officer styled the Commissioner of Police and appointed by the Lieutenant-Governor, who can also appoint one or more Deputies to perform any of the Commissioner's duties under his orders. A special police force is provided for the Town of Calcutta, its strength being determined by the Lieutenant-Governor with the sanction of the Supreme Government. The Commissioner appoints them, and may fine, suspend or dismiss them. He may appoint special constables on emergency with the powers of ordinary officers of police."* At present there are two Courts established in Calcutta subordinate to the Calcutta High Court, where all Police, Municipal and Criminal cases are tried. For the convenience of the administration of justice, there are now three Criminal Magistrates presiding over three Courts, and a Municipal Magistrate presiding over the Court for the trial of Municipal cases. The powers of the Presidency Magistrates are those of Magistrates of the first class. Perhaps the Calcutta Police Court is the outgrowth of the old Zemindar's Court, as well the Court of the Justices of the

* Cowell's Tagore Law Lectures.

Peace which existed in the early part of the English Settlement at Calcutta. In early times there were also two jails situated in Calcutta—one in Lalbazar, which is described as "very clean and wholesome and only needs a separate apartment for the women"; and the other in Barabazar, said to be "a confined place and must occasion much sickness." It was also stated that Friday was fixed for the flogging of delinquents.*

In those days the authorities were frequently in collision with the lawyers. Asiaticus, in 1774, writes "the attorneys who have followed the Judges in search of prey as the carrion crows do an Indian Army on its march, are extremely successful in supporting the spirit of litigation among the natives, who, like children, delighted with a new plaything, are highly pleased with the opportunity of harassing one another by vexatious suits; and those pests of society called bailiffs—a set of miscreants hitherto little known in India—are now to be seen in every street, watching for the unhappy victims devoted to legal persecution. Even the menial servants are now tutored to breathe that insolent spirit of English licentiousness, which teaches the slave to insult his master, and then bring his action of damages at Westminster, if deservedly chastised for his impudence. Arbitrary fines are daily imposed on gentlemen who presume to correct their slaves; and the house of the Chief Justice of Bengal resembles the office of a trading Magistrate in Westminster, who decides the squabbles of oyster women, and

* The history of the Law Courts and Jails is chiefly based on The Tagore Law Lectures, 1872, Torrens' Empire in Asia, Rainey's Historical and Topographical Sketch of Calcutta, and Evidence of Our Transactions in the East Indies.

At present the Presidency Jail is situated at the extremity of the Maidan on the Northern side.

picks up a livelihood by the sale of shilling warrants." A Calcutta paper publishes the following epitaph:—

"God works wonders now and then—
Here lies a lawyer and an honest man."

Answered.

"This is a mere law quibble, not a wonder—
Here lies a lawyer and his client under."

Walter Hamilton in his *Gazetteer* states: "The law practitioners attached to the Supreme Court are 14 attorneys and 6 barristers. Enormous fortunes were made by lawyers in those times, and they fostered litigation among the natives" (*vide Calcutta Review*, Vol. XVIII, 1852). The Hartley House narrates: "No wonder lawyers return from this country rolling in wealth; their fees are enormous; if you ask a single question on any affair, you pay down your gold mohur, and if he writes a letter of only three lines, twenty-eight rupees! I tremble at the idea of coming into their hands; for what must be the recoveries to answer such immense charges! You must, however, be informed that the number of acting attorneys on the court roll is restricted to twelve, who serve an articled clerkship for three years only instead of five as in England. The fee for making a will is in proportion to its length—from five gold mohurs upwards; and as to marriage articles, I should imagine they would half ruin a man, and a process at law be the destruction of both parties." According to the late Babu Peary Chand Mitter, it was then considered a privilege to become an attorney's clerk; his attainments were "picked-up technical expressions, and when he made use of them he was dreaded."

Along with the institution of law courts* there has sprung up the body of practitioners called Vakils and Pleaders, and, unlike attorneys, they are empowered to conduct suits in these courts.† Day by day this class, along with the modern attorneys, is acquiring great influence, and is now an important and influential body in Calcutta Society. Its lucrative calling attracts young men to the field; and it is not too much to state that its ranks are filled up and adorned by all that is cultured and enlightened in the land. From very early days enormous fortunes have been earned by its votaries. The late Babus Romaprosad Roy, Krishna Kishore Ghosh, Prosonno Kumar Tagore, Mohinimohan Roy, and a host of others, left to their heirs properties that were of considerable value. Indeed, the large gains derived from this new opening are absolutely of British creation. Now-a-days, although the income arising from it is divided and distributed amongst the multiplying number of its professors, yet it is collectively on the increase. Litigation has been advancing with rapid strides, and the law's delay has become inevitable. Courts find it difficult to overtake the increasing work. There are, besides vakils, a large number of European and Indian barristers whose incomes are sometimes fabulous. The spirits of the writers who were aghast at the incomes of the old class of lawyers would be unquiet if they were to revisit their early scenes. Justice is not now to be easily got, nor can it be had cheap. It is looked upon as a game. In a vernacular satirical journal an amusing sketch is given, in which it is represented that two brothers are fighting for a milch-cow —one dragging the animal by the horns and the other pull-

* Sadar Dewani Adalut and the Supreme Court of Judicature.

† Attorneys can become Vakils after conforming to the prescribed rules.

ing it by the tail, and at the same time the lawyer quietly goes on milking the cow.

For want of space I have been obliged to leave out the history of many offices and departments established in Calcutta. It is quite undeniable that the modern machinery of Government has made a great innovation upon the habits, manners and sentiments of the people. Indeed, the western method of conducting government is altogether a new feature in this country. The heavy cost that falls upon the people is too severe to be lightly borne. The benefits and advantages of the modern system of government are dearly purchased. This exotic has its serious drawbacks. An excuse is to be found in the fact that our English rulers proceeded to reform the government of the country with high and enlightened ideas, and with honesty of purpose. But with all their good intentions, the benefit that has actually arisen is not an unmixed one. The histories of the several legislative measures affecting the intellectual, moral and material prosperity of the inhabitants of this great empire will confirm this view. The British legislature is indeed a progressive one. Since the direct assumption of government by the Crown, after the suppression of the Mutiny of 1857, the measures of Government have taken a definite turn. India is now a part and parcel of the dominion of His Majesty the King of England. Its interest is now also a matter of no mean consideration to the Imperial Government at home.

CHAPTER VIII.

THE PRESS.

IT can fittingly be ascribed that among the chief factors whose influence over the modern civilisation has greatly determined its present course, the Press has contributed vastly towards it. It is quite difficult to estimate its influence and to grasp at its proper situation. The Press has been described as the "Fourth State of the Realm." It is even greater. It arrogates to itself to represent *vox populi, vox dei.* As civilisation advances, its powers for good and evil increase and develop in rapid strides—by leaps and bounds. The great Chatham in one of his great speeches which have made him immortal, described it as "like the air a chartered libertine." Its arm-chair politician does not scruple to offer gratuitous advice to kings and commanders, statesmen and ecclesiasts and the people concerning their respective duties. Its domain and field of action are unlimited. It gives character to men who have no character. As Shakespeare has put it:—

> "And as Imagination bodies forth
> The forms of things unknown, the poet's pen
> Turns them to shapes and gives to airy nothing
> A local habitation and a name."

Such has been the character of the Press. Fortunate it is that Cicero and Demosthenes did not compose their orations when the powers of the Press have been felt. The modern orators labour under great difficulties in delivering speeches or reading discourses, for they are conscious that their speeches will be thoroughly exposed and criticised by the new power—which respects no person, no creed—ever self-conscious of its own importance. It has been observed that "Cæsar's wife must be above all reproach and suspicion." But before the majesty of the Press, she even will have to nod and bow down; otherwise the Press at some convenient opportunity will pounce upon her and not hesitate to expose her character. It, in fact, "teaches the teachers." It is interesting to find that within the course of four hundred years it has attained to such prominence and has come to wield such unspeakable power. It is recorded that the first newspaper was published in Germany in the year 1498.

Indeed, in the earliest ages, when science and arts of government were in a crude state, the advantage of publicity in bestowing praise or censure—the one to incite good and the other to restrain bad actions—was well understood. It is our nature to criticise and to approve of, or acquiesce in, the doings of our fellows. They say Truth and Justice are best promoted by the fullest publicity. The Press has also great educative force, and perhaps there is hardly any method yet invented or devised in disseminating knowledge so rapidly amongst a vast number of people in so short a space of time. It gives tone and character to the people, and its inestimable services to the growth of modern literature cannot be overrated. There is such a thing as intellectual honesty, which has derived great impetus by the creation of this new machinery of propagating knowledge. It, in fact, guides and shapes, reflects and controls, the opinion of a vast number of people. The so-called unrepresented "dumb millions" look upon this institution as the true champion, exponent and protector of their rights and liberties. Hence it is no wonder that it will acquire such power and consequence in the concerns of human affairs. The late Professor Henry Morley of the University College, speaking on the subject of "The Newspaper, Ancient and Modern," said that its first germ had been planted in the Middle Ages. The newspaper owed its rise to a custom which prevailed in Venice in the 16th century, of reading aloud in a public place a manuscript sheet of news of general interest prepared by the authorities; the sum paid by such as cared to hear the reading of this document being one "gazetta," a fractional coin then current, and from which subsequently the term "gazette" has come. In England, Mr. Morley traced that it owed its development with the merchants in the form of the news-letters which they carried on in different countries. During the 16th century news-sheets were issued on the occurrence of some event of extraordinary public interest. To Nathaniel Butler and Daniel Defoe belonged the credit of publishing the *Weekly News*, a periodical paper in England. During the Moslem period, and at the cost of the native princes, papers of news termed "Akbers" were produced, which were Court gazettes giving statement of occurrences, true or false, as matters of fact without comment or opinion. From the situation of writers under such government, it is clear that these Akbers bear no affinity to the English newspapers.

The Press in India has had a chequered history. It arose under almost overwhelming difficulties, and was beset with risk and danger. The situation was such that the authorities dreaded the appearance of a free Press in India. The French were still in the land causing anxiety. Add to that several Englishmen, missionaries in particular, were loud in their denunciation of native institutions, their manners and customs. It is no wonder that the English authorities should be jealous of the growth of the new powers under such circumstances. The English Government in this country were dependent on a corporate body at home, and it has oftentimes appeared that their English masters did not encourage them to bestow even the semblance of freedom on the Press. Perhaps the best defence that could be offered of such a system is to be found in the speech of Sir John Malcolm, published in the appendix to his History of India. The defence is a masterpiece of its kind. With reference to this question, Mr. William Digby has praised the Marquis of Hastings for the facilities given to the Anglo-Indian Press for the free expression of opinion.* But the chief credit and glory belonged to Sir Charles Metcalfe, afterwards Lord Metcalfe. Lord W. Bentinck hesitated to give liberty to the Indian Press. During his retirement Sir Charles Metcalfe temporarily succeeded him and took that opportunity to carry out the reform. He did so entirely of his own motion, and on his own responsibility. Macaulay helped Sir Charles Metcalfe to attain his object.

The freedom of the Indian Press dates from the 15th September 1835. Sir Charles Metcalfe has been rightly called the "Liberator of the Indian Press." I shall quote

* *Calcutta Review*, Vol. LXII.

from his own words, which bear testimony to the sentiments that impelled him. In reply to an address presented to him, he said: "If their argument be that the spread of knowledge may eventually be fatal to our rule in India, I close with them on that point, and maintain that whatever may be the consequence, it is our duty to communicate the benefits of knowledge. If India could only be preserved as a part of the British Empire by keeping its inhabitants in a state of ignorance, our domination would be a curse to the country and ought to cease............It cannot be that we are permitted, by divine authority, to be here merely to collect the revenues of the country, pay the establishments necessary to keep possession, and get into debt to supply the deficiency. We are, doubtless, here for higher purposes, one of which is to pour the enlightened knowledge and civilisation, the arts and sciences of Europe, over the land, and thereby improve the condition of the people. Nothing surely is more likely to conduce to these ends than the liberty of the Press."*

The inhabitants of Calcutta, in commemoration of this boon, erected a noble edifice on the banks of the river Hughli to "contain a public library, and to be applied to other enlightening purposes, and they called it the Metcalfe Hall. It was to bear an inscription declaring that the Press of India was liberated on the 15th of September 1835, by Sir Charles Metcalfe; and the bust of the liberator was to be enclosed in he building."

The Press was twice temporarily restricted, namely once in 1857 owing to that lamentable event—the breaking out of the Indian Mutiny; and a second time during the Vice-

* The Life and Correspondence of Lord Metcalfe, by J. W. Kaye.

royalty of Lord Lytton, in 1878, when the liberties of the Vernacular Press were curtailed. Lord Ripon repealed the obnoxious Act of 1878.

In 1768, Mr. Bolts put up a notice in the Council House and other public places to the effect that he had in his possession many articles of vital importance which most intimately concerned every individual, and he would be only too glad to allow anybody to read them, and was also ready to give the best encouragement to any person or persons who were versed in the business of printing to manage a Press, the type and appliances of which he would furnish. He complained of the great want of a Press in Calcutta. Mr. Busteed, in recording the above facts, says * :— "Yet for over eleven years more did the want, thus so publicly demonstrated by Bolts, remain unprovided for, and not till 1780 did the first city in Asia possess a medium which combined the object of conveying public intelligence in print, with that of promulgating the ordinary business or social wants of its European inhabitants." The *Bengal Gazette* was thus the first newspaper published on Saturday, January 29, 1780, and eight years previous to the appearance of *The Times* in England. It announced itself as "A weekly political and commercial paper open to all parties, but influenced by none." It consisted of two sheets about twelve inches by eight, three columns of printed matter on each side, much of which was devoted to advertisements : "The greater portion of the small budget was made up of correspondence from local and distant contributors, and occasional extracts from the news last received from Europe. The paper and printing were very poor." The proprietor

* *Vide* Busteed's Echoes of Calcutta.

was a Mr. James Augustus Hickey. From the accounts published by Mr. Busteed, it seems that Mr. Hickey's career, before he published his paper, had been full of adventures and troubles. He experienced many vicissitudes in life. Mr. Busteed goes on :—" In returning thanks for the first list of contributors, the proprietor states that, should he be so fortunate in his endeavours as to bring so useful an undertaking as a newspaper to perfection, he will think himself amply rewarded, as it may in a very little time prove an antibilious specific, from which he hopes his subscribers will receive more material benefit than from tincture of bark, castor oil, or columba root." During the first few months of its existence, the new undertaking seems to have led a tolerably prosperous and peaceful life. It is often dull and is invariably vulgar, but on the whole it is harmless. Its subscribers were recruited mostly from free merchants and traders and from the non-official European community. Its criticisms and personal attacks were directed against the English and the Indians alike; and the paper is famous for its attacks against Warren Hastings and Sir Elijah Impey. As for Francis, Mr. Busteed observes: " It cannot be said that his conduct was uniformly so immaculate as never to afford an opportunity for the moral platitudes so dear to Hickey; occasions which would fairly justify public comment, are either not availed of, or are employed in his favour. He almost alone amongst the official leaders of society is dealt gently with."

In another place, "many who are conspicuous in official or social life are assailed in terms indicative of malicious hostility, whilst the most prominent amongst them are given up to public odium and contempt, nay under the most obvious nicknames."

As to the style of his criticism, the following extracts will indicate its character: "A favourite method with the *Bengal Gazette* for pillorying those whom it desired to show up to public ridicule, was to announce a play or masquerade or concert (which were then fashionable amusement) and to assign certain suggestive parts or characters to members of society disguised under the thinnest veil."

Rev. Long states *:—"It grew so scurrilous that on November 14th, 1780, appeared an order of Government prohibiting its circulation through the channel of the General Post Office on account of its lately having been found to contain several improper paragraphs tending to vilify private characters, and to disturb the peace of the settlement. Hickey employed twenty *hurkarras* to distribute his papers, and stated he would persist in his opposition to Government, though he should have to compose ballads and sell them through the streets of Calcutta as Homer did. His career ended in a jail, after long battling it out." The author of the "Original Inquiry" describing a free Press in India puts altogether a different complexion on Hickey's *Bengal Gazette*. He observes: "Though a free Press never for a moment existed in India since the local governments were armed with the power of deportation, by the Act of 1793, yet at different times before the imposition, and since the discontinuance of a censorship at Calcutta, individual editors of newspapers have ventured, at their own peril, and to their own ruin, to try how far they might give publicity to facts and opinions respecting public affairs and public men. That any evil of a peculiar and local nature ever resulted from such attempts we have no evidence

* *Vide* "Peeps into Social Life of Calcutta a Century Ago," by Rev. Long.

whatever, nor the slightest grounds of presumption for believing. Of the great disorders produced by conflicting laws and jurisdictions, in 1780 for instance, we have incontestible proof; but of the serious evil which Sir John Malcolm supposes to have been occasioned by the circulation of Hickey's *Bengal Gazette*, he cannot produce one instance. On the other hand, it cannot be doubted that the files of that paper must throw singular light on the nature of the contentions which then agitated the public mind, and the character of the men who then held the highest stations; nor without access to such can a just view of that period ever be obtained."

Judging things from the present stand-point, the restrictions on the Indian Press of those periods would appear to be very strict. The rules prohibited the discussion of any topic involving the character or measures of the Government of India, whether at home or abroad, under pain of fine or imprisonment for a native of India, and deportation for a British-born subject. It is not easy to say if these restrictions were necessitated by the circumstances of the times, or if they proceeded from arbitrariness of the individuals who then wielded authority. But it is curious to observe that the "lashes of punishment" were levelled more against Englishmen than against the natives. It was Englishmen almost exclusively that managed the Press at that period. But after a few years, probably from 1816, the natives appeared in the field of journalism.

Much recrimination and quarrel ensued with Mr. John Adam in connection with the *Calcutta Journal*, the editor of which was the well-known Mr. James Silk Buckingham. The Hon'ble Mr. John Adam for some time became Governor. The latter gentleman was certainly to blame for his insolent, malicious and personal attacks on the Governor. At the same time it must be admitted that the punishment meted out to him, namely his banishment and the harassment he was constantly subjected to, was hardly to be justified.

During the administration of the Marquis of Hastings, the Press was managed by Englishmen alone, who received encouragement and kindness at his hands. In reply to an address, presented to the noble Marquis by the inhabitants of Madras, His Excellency said: "He has removed the restrictions from the Press and granted to Englishmen in India that freedom of publication which he regarded as the natural right of his fellow subjects." On another occasion, the noble Lord also said that, "while conscious of rectitude, authority can lose nothing of its strength by its exposure to general comments; on the contrary, it acquires incalculable addition of force."* It is gratifying to know that even in those early days the authorities felt the force and utility of public criticism. Of course, in those days it was too serious a task to publicly criticise the "person in power and authority;" and instances may be found here and there of the institution of Press prosecutions by the Government. But there can be no question as to the gradual development and the increase of power conferred upon and attained by the Press in India. That large-hearted Governor-General Lord Canning was conscious of the majesty of the Press, even in the bloody days of the Indian Mutiny.

* *Vide Oriental Herald*, Vol. I., 1824.

The noble Lord said: "The blessings of the liberty of the Press are so clear and so acknowledged as far to outweigh the mischiefs of its abuse—the evil is transitory, the good is immortal."

Various other newspapers appeared in the Town. There was the *Monitorial Gazette.* Rev. Long states that Mr. Kiernander had a Press so far back as 1780.* It may interest the general readers to know something of the early antecedents of the leading anglo-Indian journals of the present day:—

John Bull—which afterwards appeared as the *Englishman*—was first published in 1821, with a view to put down the *Calcutta Journal*, edited by Mr. James Silk Buckingham. Mr. Buckingham started his *Calcutta Journal* in 1818. The first outlay on this journal is stated to have been Rs. 30,000, but by repeated subsequent additions of capital, the concern rose to the value of four lakhs of rupees, and its net profit amounted to sixty to eighty thousand rupees per annum. During the first five years it rose to power and secured subscribers amongst all classes of people. But it soon fell into disfavour with the authorities, and suits for defamation were instituted against the editor. According to Mr. Buckingham, six other newspapers then existed in Calcutta. Of these the *Asiatic Mirror* was published under the editorship of Rev. James Bryce, D.D., Moderator of the Scotch Kirk, head of the Presbyterian religion in India. It is related that he had some violent

* According to H. E. Busteed, the earliest newspapers were published in the following chronological order:—*The Indian Gazette*, November 1780; the *Calcutta Gazette and Oriental Advertiser* (Mr. Francis Gladwin was the editor and it was exempted from postage), February 1784; the *Bengal Journal*, February 1785; the *Oriental Magazine* or *Calcutta Amusement*, April 6th, 1785; the *Calcutta Chronicle*, January, 1786.

altercations with the Hon'ble Mr. Adams, at which the European Society was thoroughly disgusted, and his paper began rapidly to decline. Now it was left to the *Calcutta Journal* alone to inveigh against the officials who happened to be not in its good graces. The paper *John Bull* appeared as a counterblast. The principal promoters and supporters of this paper were civil and military officers. It rapidly grew into consequence. A libel suit was instituted against the editor of the *John Bull* by the editor of the *Calcutta Journal.* Perhaps the nature and conditions of the English Press of that time can be best likened to the present day wrangling which goes on amongst so many vernacular newspapers. As to the origin of the *Englishman* the following account appears to me trustworthy :—

The *Englishman* originated in the opposite pole of political thought to that which inspired the *Indian Daily News.* In 1821, the year when the quarrel between George IV and his luckless queen attained its climax, "*John Bull* in the East" appeared as the "Supporter of Church and King, and the contemner of private scandals," which latter had hitherto been the mainstay of Calcutta journalism. Its title and platform were evidently borrowed from Theodore Hook's truculent organ. The venture obtained the support of many civilians of rank and became the channel of official utterances. But its stubborn hostility to reform soon told on the subscription list. The paper was moribund when it was purchased for a song, in 1833, by Mr. J. H. Stocqueller, who christened it the *Englishman* and gave it a new lease of life. Amongst his staff was Charles Thackeray, an uncle of the great novelist, who showed in his sober moments that his kinsman had no monopoly of the family's literary power

At the *Englishman* Press, Macaulay had rough proofs set up of his essays on Clive and Hastings. After the Mutiny, the *Englishman* was bought up by Mr. J. O'B. Saunders, father of the present chief proprietor.*

The *Statesman and Friend of India* first appeared under the name of *Friend of India* in the month of April 1818, as a monthly magazine. The late Dr. Marshman gave the title of the paper, and it was through the influence of the missionaries that it came into existence. Its principal object was to include original essays on questions connected with the progress of improvement in India, reports of the various societies which were coming into existence under the influence of Lord Hastings, and notices of the proceedings of Bible, Missionary, and Educational Societies in other parts of the world. In June 1820, Dr. Marshman began to publish its quarterly edition. It was found that the discussion of questions relating to the interests of the country increased its bulk and interfered greatly with its punctual appearance. He therefore established a quarterly periodical for "essays on subjects connected with India, and a review of such works, published either in Europe or in India, as might in any way affect the interests of the country." During its early career, it advocated the abolition of the Suttee rites, and its telling articles caused the late Hon'ble Mr. Adam to represent them to the Council as an infringement of the rule which prohibited "discussions having a tendency to create alarm or suspicion among the native population of any intended interference with their religious opinions or observances." Mr. Adam desired that editors be requested to

* From the *Life of Sir W. W. Hunter*, K.C.S.I., M.A., LL.D., by Francis Henry Skrine, F.S.S.

abstain from all such discussions in future. But the Marquis of Hastings saw nothing objectionable in the articles and refused to listen to Mr. Adam. At the same time, he assured Dr. Marshman that he was personally favourable to the entire abolition of the Suttee rites. The Press was in those days greatly fettered. The Marquis of Hastings, as already observed, was ever anxious to encourage the Press in India, but he was greatly hampered by the authorities at home and by his associates in the Council. He came to India with very enlightened views on the subject of the Press. To the students of Indian History, it is well known that in the year 1799, when the English were engaged in the struggle with Tippo Sultan, the rigid censorship of the Press was introduced by Lord Wellesley. "Every printer was required to affix his name to each number of his paper, and submit a copy of it, before its publication, to the inspection of the Government Secretary, under the penalty of a compulsory return to England." The censor drew his pen across any article which appeared to him likely to prove injurious to the interests of Government or of society, and it was not unusual for a journal to appear with one or more columns of asterisks.* On the 19th of August 1818, Lord Hastings abolished the censorship without recording any reasons, notwithstanding the remonstrances of his Council. He also made certain regulations for the editors. "They were forbidden to publish animadversions on the measures and proceedings of the India authorities in England, or disquisitions on political transactions of the local administration or offensive remarks levelled at the public conduct of the Members of Council, or the Judges of the Supreme Court, or the Lord Bishop. They were

* John Clark Marshman's Life and Times of Carey, Marshman and Ward, Vol. II.

likewise forbidden to admit discussions having a tendency to create alarms or suspicions among the native populations of any intended interference with their religious opinions or observances, or to republish from English or other newspapers passages coming under any of the above heads, as well as private scandal and personal remarks on individuals tending to excite dissension in society. Government was empowered to visit an infraction of these rules by a prosecution in the Supreme Court, or by cancelling the license of the offender and ordering him to return to Europe. These restrictions were so severe that, if literally enforced, they must have proved fatal to all freedom of discussion. But after they had been passed, the judges of the Supreme Court, who were known to be generally unwilling to interfere with the liberty of the Press, had on one occasion refused to grant a criminal information. Lord Hastings was, moreover, extremely averse to inflict on his administration the stigma of banishing one editor. The regulations, therefore, soon became a dead letter, and the Press became practically free.* In 1835, the weekly edition of the *Friend of India* was published. The editorial management was undertaken by Messrs. Marshman, Mack and Leechman. "It was resolved to give it rather a religious than a political character, and to make it the vehicle of discussion on all questions connected with the moral, social and material interests of India. It was established at a time when Lord William Bentinck had given the most liberal encouragement to the "ventilation" of such subjects. The earlier numbers were published before the close of his administration, and he was pleased to express his approbation of the spirit in which it

* Life and Times of Carey, Marshman and Ward, by J. C. Marshman, Vol. II.

was conducted. The missionaries of all denominations hailed, with pleasure the appearance of a journal not exclusively religious, but prepared to discuss public measures in an evangelical spirit, and it has always received their cordial support. But at the end of the first year the subscription list numbered only two hundred."*

In 1874,† Mr. Robert Knight purchased the good-will of the paper at Rs. 30,000 only. Its daily edition was issued under the name and style of *The Indian Statesman.* After a few months, the *Friend of India* was incorporated with it. Its present weekly edition appears as *Friend of India and Statesman.* The career of this distinguished journalist, Mr. Robert Knight,‡ who was regarded as exponent of the cause of the natives of this country, affords an interesting study. He served as an officer of the Bombay Government, and perhaps at a later stage as Assistant Secretary to the Government of India. But he is best remembered as a writer of conspicuous ability. Previous to his connection with the *Statesman*, he edited a journal of Calcutta, named the *Indian Economist.* There was a libel suit instituted by the Bengal Government against him, but it was settled in this way, *viz.*—Robert Knight was to get Rs. 20,000 as compensation for transferring the good-will of *Indian Economist* to the Government.

* Life and Times of Carey, Marshman and Ward, by J. C. Marshman.

† Some say 1875.

‡ The Bombay career of Mr. Robert Knight is condensed herein. He was an occasional contributor to the *Bombay Times.* He became its editor after the retirement of Dr. Buist. He remained editor for nearly seven years, from 1858 to 1864, and did much to render the paper popular. The Native proprietors and others who owned shares in the paper, parted with it in 1860, and sold it to their editor. During his management the *Bombay Times* took to itself the imperial name of the *Times of India.* The latter days of Mr. Robert Knight's editorship merged into the days of Bombay's wonderful prosperity owing to the cotton famine brought about by the American war. Crores upon crores of rupees flowed into the city. Mr. Knight retired at the height of this wave of prosperity, and his Indian friends gave him a purse of seventy-five thousand in recognition of the valuable services rendered by him.

There was hardly any Anglo-Indian writer among his contemporaries who excelled him in journalistic ability. He was an expert on economic questions ; and all his writings were distinguished by an independence, a breadth of sympathy, and a force and beauty of style which made his paper a power in the land and a special favourite of the educated native community. His attitude was really that of a friend of India, and the people of the country cannot forget their obligations to him. In regard to its financial condition the paper had some vicissitudes, but at his death he bequeathed it to his heirs, a most profitable concern, with full public credit and confidence. It is now one of the most largely circulated and successful papers in India.

The Indian Daily News attracted much notice and grew into consequence during the editorship of the late Mr. James Wilson. On 18th August 1864, the *Daily News* was incorporated with the old *Bengal Harkaru*. This paper was first started in 1795. The late Mr. James Wilson sometimes acted as sub-editor to the *Indian Daily News*, when its editor-in-chief was Captain Fenwick. One Mr. Parker also became one of the proprietors along with Wilson. But the latter gentleman afterwards became its sole proprietor. "The Bengal Printing Company" used to publish this paper when it had no press of its own. But as the venture proved a success, it ultimately secured a press of its own. When the late Mr. James Wilson retired from this country, he sold off this concern to a Limited Company. Its present editor is Mr. J. C. Wilson ; and a Limited Company manages its affairs.

A large and respectable section of the English Press has been built up by educated Indians. The best of them have proved themselves in no way inferior to their European compeers. Such men as Babus Srinath Ghosh, Girish Chandra Ghosh, Kshettra Chandra Ghosh of the Simla Ghosh family, Harish Chandra Mukherji, Ram Gopal Ghosh, Rev. K. M. Banerji, Keshub Chandra Sen, Sambhoo Chandra Mukherji, Kristo Dass Paul, Kasi Prosad Ghosh, Rev. Lall Behary Dey and others, wrote for newspapers, and some of them embraced the profession of journalism. Babu Kasee Prosad Ghosh was known as the editor of the *Hindu Intelligencer* (published about 1840), and it is said to have been the first native paper of note conducted in English. Babu Kasee Prosad was eminent alike as a writer of prose and verse. He was a well-known and favourite student of Captain D. L. Richardson. The *Hindu Pioneer* was edited by Ishan Chundra Dutt of the Rambagan Dutt family; but the *Hindu Patriot* has been the best known and the most successful of early native enterprises in journalism. As to the early history of this paper, we read in the Life of Babu Kristodas Paul by the late Babu Ram Gopal Sanyal that its first editors were Babus Sreenath Ghosh, Girish Chundra Ghosh and Kshettra Chandra Ghosh; and the idea was first conceived by one Madhu Sudan Roy of Barabazar, who had a Press at Kalakar Street and it was from his Press that the first number of the *Hindu Patriot* was issued in 1853. Mr. Skrine thus narrates its early history in the Life, &c., of the late Babu Sambhoo Chunder Mukherji, Editor of *Reis and Rayyet*. "The paper arose from the ashes of the *Bengal Recorder*, one of the ephemerides which heralded the awakening of a nation's literary spirit. The proprietor found it a losing speculation; and in 1854 offered the Press and good-will for a mere song. Harish Chandra, who had been one of the leading contributors, saw an opportunity of gratifying a darling ambition and became the purchaser. The transaction was veiled in secrecy, for his master, the Military Auditor-General, would hardly have approved of a proprietor-editor of a journal as one of his subordinates. The "man of straw" put forward was an elder brother Babu Haran Chandra Mukherji; but the entire labour of editing and management fell on Harish. The struggle was long and severe; and at one time the poor kerany's salary was taxed to the extent of Rs. 100 a month to meet the deficit in income. He bore the ordeal with heroic courage, which was at last rewarded by pecuniary success of his venture. His untimely death, however, robbed his family of the benefit they might have derived from a fine literary property. Babu Kaliprosonno Sinha, the Bengali translator of the Mahabharat, purchased the paper from the executor and satisfied the claim of the *benamdar* by a trifling solatium." Babu Ramgopal Sanyal says that the noble spirited Babu Kaliprosonno Sinha purchased the copyright of the paper at a cost of Rs. 5,000 and transferred it to the control of Pandit Iswar Chandra Vidyasagar. The venerable Pandit made over the management of the paper to Babus Kristo Das Paul, Kailash Chandra Bose and Nabinkrishna Bose, who undertook to edit the paper. Ultimately the paper came under the sole editorship of Babu Kristo Das Paul. In 1862, at the request of some prominent members of the Hindu Society, Babu Kaliprosonno Sinha transferred the management of the paper to a body of trustees composed of Maharaja Ramanath Tagore, Raja Dr. Rajendra Lala Mitra, Maharaja Bahadur Sir Jotindra Mohan Tagore, and Raja Protap Chandra Sinha. The trust-deed was drawn up in 1862. The income of the

Patriot was at this time very insignificant. Its subscribers then numbered 250 only. In 1863 its success became more assured. The *Patriot*, which used to appear every Thursday morning, began to be issued on Monday. During Kristo Das's period it was a weekly paper, but now it appears as a daily. Regarding the style and method of Kristo Das Paul's writing in *Hindoo Patriot*, Mr. N. N. Ghose observes that his writings "in the *Hindoo Patriot* were characterised by good sense, breadth of views and logical power, but seldom by superior artistic merits."* Add to that, Kristo Das was a social man, and he had the rare merit and tact of gaining confidence both among the ruling class and his countrymen. He was a representative of a large section of native Society. He infused into his paper his unfailing sweetness and sobriety. His turn of mind was essentially practical, and his writings bore the impress of his mind. He was independent in his criticisms, but his tone was dignified. He never betrayed a secret, never indulged in personal raillery. He had an admirable capacity of mastering facts and was above sentimental declamation.

The *Indian Mirror* owes its origin, in 1861, as a fortnightly paper to the public spirit of the late Mr. Monomohan Ghose, the eminent Calcutta Barrister, and the resources of the late Babu Debendra Nath Tagore. Babu Narendra Nath Sen used to write for the paper, and when Mr. Ghose went to England to prosecute his studies, the control of the concern devolved upon him. Under his able editorship, the paper became a weekly one, and to Babu Keshub Chandra Sen, the great Brahmo leader and orator, the idea of convert-

* *Vide* Kristo Das Paul, a study by Mr. N. N. Ghose.

ing it into a daily is attributable; Keshub Chandra Sen carried out the project in 1878 with another conspicuous Brahmo leader, Babu Protap Chundra Mazumdar, as its editor, and the late Babu Krishna Behary Sen, M.A., the cousin of the present editor, as its sub-editor. For many years it was the only anglo-native daily journal throughout all India. In or about the year 1879, the paper which was so long the joint property passed into the hands of Babu Norendra Nath Sen, who became its sole proprietor and editor. It had for some years a special Sunday edition, which treated of religious topics. The Sunday paper was edited by Babu Krishna Behary Sen.

The *Amrita Bazar Patrica* was originally a Bengali paper and was first published in Jessore, about 35 or 36 years ago, by Babu Sisir Kumar Ghosh and his brothers. It was named in honour of the sacred memory of their mother. In the introduction to the Indian Sketches by Babu Sisir Kumar Ghose, it is stated that "when Lord Lytton's Press Gagging Act was first broached, and it became evident that journals published in the vernacular would be more or less heavily shackled, the brothers Ghose, believing that the Press Act was specially aimed at their journal, determined that the *Amrita Bazar Patrica*, which at that time was printed both in vernacular and English, should in future be published in the English language alone." After some vicissitudes it has been able to establish itself as an influential and successful paper. In the early days of struggle, the proprietors derived much assistance and support from men like the late Hon'ble Raja Digambar Mitra Bahadur, C.S.I., Maharaja Kamal Krishna Bahadur, Babu Sambhoo Chandra Mukherji and Babu Bhudeb Chandra Mukherji, C.I.E.

In 1889 or 1890, the idea of converting the paper into a daily was conceived and carried into effect by the suggestion of the present writer, whose moral and material support at much sacrifice to himself proved very seasonable.

The *Bengalee* is now edited by the distinguished orator and educationist Babu Surendra Nath Banerji and appears as a daily. It is an influential and successful journal. It came into existence under the editorship of a well-known scholar and writer, the late Babu Girish Chandra Ghosh of the Ghosh family of Simla. In the year 1861, the first number of the *Bengalee* was struck out. It was then a weekly paper published every Saturday. Babu Girish Chandra Ghosh was then serving the Government as Registrar to the Military Pay-Examiner's Office. He remained in charge of the editorship till 1869, when he died. The late Babu Bacharam Chatterji, the associate of Babu Girish Chandra Ghosh, assumed the sole control of the paper, and several well-known scholars interested themselves in the undertaking, prominent amongst them being Babu Chandranath Bose, M.A., B.L., and the late Babu Rajkrishna Mukherji, M.A., B.L. In or about 1878, Babu Surendranath Banerji purchased the good-will and everything in connection with the *Bengalee*. There arose some dispute in connection with the above transaction, but at the happy intervention of the late Maharajkumar Neelkrishna Bahadur, the elder brother of the writer, the matter came to a happy settlement. About the year 1900, the *Bengalee* came out as a daily at the earnest suggestion and co-operation of the present writer and Kabiraj Upendra Nath Sen.

The *Indian Nation*.—Of the weekly anglo-native papers, there are so many that it would be quite wearisome to give here even a brief description of each one of them. I shall therefore allude to the *Indian Nation* only. It came into existence in 1882, during the Viceroyalty of Lord Ripon, in the stormy days of the Ilbert Bill controversy. Its editor is our thoughtful and remarkable writer of vast erudition, Mr. N. N. Ghose, F.R.S.L., Barrister-at-law and the Principal of the Metropolitan Institution.

I pass on to a notice of the Vernacular Press. In entering upon this task, I would only echo the sentiments which have been so happily expressed by Mr. N. N. Ghose in the remark that "the connection of England with India is a divine dispensation."* The services of Englishmen, both official and missionaries, towards the development of the vernaculars have been very great. The labours of the missionaries were first directed towards acquainting themselves with the language of the people. They then bestirred in improving the vernaculars. The phrase "national education" means "instruction imparted to the masses through the medium of their mother tongue." Such men as Drs. Carey, Marshman and Ward, David Hare, Dr. Duff and high officials like Lords Hastings, Wellesley, Hardinge, Sir Charles Trevelyan, Halliday and others animated with high motives, have rendered conspicuous services to the growth and advancement of the vernaculars of the country. That the outlook of the Bengali language is full of hope, there can be no doubt. About 50 years ago, a writer in a magazine† thus spoke of the Bengali language :—"The Bengali language, fifty years ago, was as crude as Italian before Dante's time. Dante rose, and single man

* *Vide* Last Chapter of the Memoirs of Maharaja Nubkissen, by Mr. N. N. Ghose.
† The *Calcutta Review*, Vol. XXII.

by single work, the 'Divine Comedie,' showed that his country's language was capable of expressing the most lofty and abstract ideas. What may we not expect in Bengal?" Looking at the rapid and unprecedented growth of Bengali, the writer's prognostication has been remarkably verified.

The Brahmo Somaj movement in Calcutta, which owes its origin to Raja Ram Mohan Roy, gave a great impetus not only to the growth and development of Bengali journalism, but all along the line to Bengali language and literature. Amongst the prominent Brahmo workers may be mentioned Keshub Chandra Sen, Akshoy Kumar Dutt, Pandit Sib Nath Sastri, Chiranjib Sarma, Gour Govinda Roy, Babus Rabindra Nath Tagore, Dwijendra Nath Tagore and others. The writings of the early Brahmos were directed against the ancient religion of the land, which they deemed to be full of superstition and based upon no immutable truth. Under the guise of restoring to pristine condition the Vedantic principles, a new creed was organised—many of its ideas were derived not only from European theology, but also from several European political institutions. The doctrines of individual conscience as the guide to action, of liberty, equality and fraternity and a crusade against real and fancied oppression that afflicts the land, destruction of the priestly class, the abolition of the entire caste system, the uplifting of Hindu women from their so-called humiliating and degenerated condition to a state equal to that enjoyed by men with full powers and privileges, have been openly preached. The iconoclastic zeal of these gentlemen has been most striking. They have seceded from society, ancestral religion, kith and kin, and sacrificed their prospects of life to crusade against what they regarded as serious and growing evils that menaced society and hindered progress. Never in the annals of the Bengalee race have the destructive systems of English and French thinkers been so warmly appreciated and boldly accepted as a panacea for the ills of the land. The eloquent writings of a certain school of European philosophers have so far overpowered them, and have carried them to such an excess, that they treat the whole social question and its constitution like problems of geometry with an almost complete disregard for the traditions and special features and characteristics of the Hindu race. And like Father Malebranche they inveighed against imagination by employing imagination. Thus by the aid of bigotry, the ancient rules of society and its organism have been violently disturbed. To Raja Rammohan Roy belonged the credit of having been the practical founder of modern Bengali prose. His prose writings were simple, and for the first time the abstruse branches of the Hindu philosophy were taken in hand with a masterly grasp. The Raja started, in1821, a Bengali periodical named the "Brahmonical Magazine." The paper was said to be fiery and meteoric. Its attacks were mainly directed against the missionaries. The paper had only a short existence. The *Sangbad Kaumudi* newspaper was started to counteract the influence of *Samachar Chandrika.* Raja Rammohan Roy and Pandit Gourisanker Tarkabagis were its editors. There was another paper named *Banga Doot,* in which the Raja was associated with Mr. R. Martin, Dwaroknath Tagore and Prosanua Kumar Tagore.* The Raja had successfully cultivated the Sanskrit, Persian and Arabic languages, and while he was an officer under the Collector of

* *Vide Calcutta Review,* Vol. XIII.

Rungpur, cultivated the English language with such assiduity that in a few years he was able to comprehend the most profound treatises on metaphysics and divinity. He travelled in several parts of India, visited France, England and other countries, conferred with great men and the Western *savants*. He possessed a great influence. His activities and his noble efforts to make his race rise in the scale of civilisation and progress, bear the stamp of a reformer, statesman, and pioneer of English education. He was born at Radhanagore, in the district of Hooghly, in 1780, and died in the year 1833, at Bristol, in England.

Babu Akshai Kumar Dutt was a friend, associate and co-worker of the late Babu Debendra Nath Tagore.

The *Tattabodhini Patrika*, at first a fortnightly, then a monthly magazine, was started with Babu Akshai Kumar Dutt as its editor. During his editorship, its writing evoked so much interest that people all over Bengal awaited its issue with eagerness. Mr. Romesh Dutt says :— "Discoveries of European science, moral instructions, accounts of different nations and tribes, of the animate and inanimate creation, all that could enlighten the expanding intellect of Bengal and dispel darkness and prejudices, found a convenient vehicle in the *Tattabodhini Patrika*."* The *Tattabodhini Patrika* still exists, and its present editor is Babu Dwijendranath Tagore, the eldest son of Babu Debendranath Tagore. Babu Akshai Kumar Dutt had the rare power of introducing into the Bengali language many scientific technical words and phrases. He was of an extremely good disposition, kind and affable to a fault, studious, quiet and a silent worker in the

* R. C. Dutt's Literature of Bengal.

cause of progress. He was born in 1820 and died in 1886. His treatises on scientific and other subjects have been deservedly prized as the best text-books for juvenile pupils not only in Calcutta, but in all parts of Bengal. Babu Keshub Chandra Sen's labours in the field of journalism, both English and Vernacular, have been of an abiding nature. I have already observed how he identified himself with the *Indian Mirror*. The Sunday *Mirror* owed its origin to him, and that paper at first treated of pure theology and ethics. That one-pice paper, the *Sulava Samachar*, he published in vernacular, and he may be fitly called the originator of cheap vernacular journalism conducted on this side of India. From the *Nava Bidhana* or the New Dispensation Church it took up amongst others the subject of Bengali literature. Its services towards the growth and development of Bengali literature deserve recognition. Those acquainted with and taking an interest in what is passing, cannot but fail to observe the services of the unostentatious Brahmos who did yeoman's service to Bengali literature. Perhaps field-preaching in Bengali first took its cue from Babu Keshub Chandra. He was to be seen among a motley group in Beadon Square preaching his Theism against the preachers of Gospel. Undoubtedly, oratory in the Bengali language derived a great stimulus from him. Female education received great encouragement and a practical turn from his unceasing toil. The Albert Hall—the only public hall in the native portion of the town—owes its existence mainly to his efforts, where the people are allowed to convene meetings, to discuss political, social, religious and all other topics freely. The native stage, games and athletic sports, found in him a practical supporter and reformer. The India Club was started by him, its patron being his distinguished son-in-law,

His Highness the Maharaja of Cooch Behar. It was established in the year 1882, and its chief object was to promote social feeling between the English and the Indians. His activity was many-sided. He was the second son of the late Babu Peari Charan Sen of the Colootolla Sen family, and was born on the 19th November 1838. In his early days, he was very fond of theatrical representations, and it is said that he spent no less than Rs. 10,000 on this hobby. He was educated in the Hindu Metropolitan College, and it is stated that before he became a Brahmo and abjured his ancestral faith, he earnestly read for a series of years the Bible and standard Theological and Philosophical works in order to befit himself for the great mission for which he was destined. For a time he joined the Adi Brahmo Somaj of which the late Babu Debendranath Tagore was the founder and the head. But such a stubborn soul and mighty spirit it was too difficult for a Debendranath to control. Keshub seceded from Debendranath, set up a church, and soon acquired the natural position worthy of his great character and talents. I will not enter into the details of his career. His biography has been ably written by his admirer and associate, the worthy Babu Protap Chandra Majumdar, from which much can be learnt about him. He was the first Indian whom our Gracious Sovereign, then Empress Victoria, delighted to make acquaintance with, and he and his family were in correspondence with the Royal family in England. If Raja Rammohan Roy is the founder of the new creed, Keshub Chandra may be styled as its best exponent, and through his efforts and toil the Brahmo Somaj has become so much respected. He died in 1883.

I have already alluded to the good work done by the missionaries. It was the Serampur missionaries who heralded the growth and development of the Vernacular Press. Not only was the first newspaper, *Samachar Darpan,* started by them in 1818, but Bengali printing types and press were first successfully introduced. The late Rev. Lall Behary Dey* writes:—"The printing press brought from England by Mr. Ward was set up. A fount of Bengali type was cast through the assistance of a Bengalee blacksmith named Panchanon, who had learnt to cut punches from Dr. Wilkins. On the 18th of March 1800, an ever-memorable day, Carey took an impression of the first page of the Gospel of St. Matthew. The last page was printed on the 10th Feb., 1801. There was the New Testament printed. Christian tracts followed in rapid succession. For the support of the mission, a boarding school under Mr. and Mrs. Marshman was opened." As the English Government did not allow the missionaries to settle at Calcutta, Revs. Marshman, Ward, Grant and Brausdon were obliged to settle at Serampur. Although Rev. Carey spared no pains to obtain settlements for them at Calcutta, his efforts met with no success. The Danish Government treated them with kindness. A suitable house was bought and the missionaries were installed at Serampur, and Carey joined them at their new settlement. The late Dr. Carey was the first European who learnt the Bengali language and delivered a speech, for which he was much complimented by the then Governor-General.† Previous to the publication of the *Samachar Darpan*, a monthly magazine called *Digdarshan* was issued a few months before by Rev. Marshman and his friends; and a weekly newspaper named *Sangbad Timir-Nashak* (Destroyer of Darkness) was edited by Krishnamohan Das, which was published a few days after the appearance of

* The Bengal Magazine, February 1875.
† Do. Do.

the *Darpan.* This weekly paper was intended to support the doctrines and to protect the interests of Hinduism; and it is significant that among its subscribers was Babu Dwarkanath Tagore.*

Through the good offices of the Marquis of Hastings Dr. Marshman was able to circulate the *Darpan*, by post, at one-fourth the usual charge. It appears that a Brahmin named Gangakishore Bhattacharjea, as editor, published the first paper in Bengali named *Bengal Gazette* in 1816. According to Rainey† the Bengali typography was introduced in 1778, and the first book, a grammar in Bengali characters, was printed at Hooghly; it was written by Mr. N. B. Halhead, an eminent Orientalist, whose patron was Warren Hastings. The Bengali types were first prepared by Charles Wilkins, then a Lieutenant of the Bengal Army, from whom Panchanan learnt this art. This native blacksmith charged Re. 1-4 per letter. Among the native converts, the late Rev. Dr. K. M. Banerji, D.L., has rendered valuable services to his mother-tongue. He edited and conducted many newspapers in English and vernacular. When he was almost a student, he conducted a paper called the *Enquirer*, and he wrote articles in the columns of *Parthenon*, which was issued under the direction of Derozio, but the paper was stopped by the order of Dr. Wilson. He also edited another paper called the *Evangelist*. Among his works, both Bengali and Sanskrit, may be mentioned "Sarvadarsan-Sangraha" (published in 1861-62), editions of Raghubansam, Kumar Sambhab, Vatty Kabya and Rig Veda with notes of his own. In 1846, under the patronage of the Government of

* Life and Times of Carey, Marshman and Ward, Vol. II.
† Rainey's Topographical Sketch, &c.

Bengal, he published his Vidyakalpadruma, or Encyclopædia Bengalensis, and dedicated it by permission to the Governor-General of India. He was known as a great scholar in English, Sanskrit, Latin, Greek, French and Bengali, and was deservedly respected for his unassuming manners, good disposition, humility of spirit and true piety. In 1876, the Calcutta University conferred upon him the degree of D.L. for his high literary attainments and culture. He was a public-spirited citizen and was connected with many public movements. Rev. Dr. Banerji was born at Calcutta in 1813. His father was Jeebon Krishna Banerji.

Whatever may have been the motives that induced the early missionaries to ransack and learn the languages and literature of the Hindus and Mussalmans, it is unquestionable that their services in the cause of the republic of letters were of an abiding nature. Governors like Warren Hastings rendered signal services in this connection. It was through his active sympathy that Dr. Wilkins first published an English translation of the Bhagbat Gita ; and such eminent scholars and linguists as Sir William Jones, Colebrooke, Gladwin and others interested themselves in publishing Oriental works for the inquisitive Europeans. The efforts of the European traders and merchants in the field of the Oriental languages and literature have solved many knotty problems for the antiquarians and philologists. It has opened "many wonders of the primitive world." As to the literary importance a writer has observed, "an event inferior only to the revival of the Greek learning, and in a religious and philosophic point of view, pregnant, perhaps, with greater results; ...." The same writer goes on: It has "carried the torch into the dark caverns of the earth, traced by its light the physical revolutions of our globe, and discovered the remains of an extinct world of nature;..........." It has also "explored the inmost recesses of language," and "brought to light the fossil remains of early history, discovered the migrations of nations and the changes of empire and regained the lost traces of portions of our species."*

The Hindus are ever noted for their zeal in learning. Perhaps no other race on earth appreciates and values knowledge so much as do the Hindus. To what extent their noble passion for learning carried them, is best illustrated in the anecdotes given below :—

When Maharaja Nubkissen Deb Bahadur made a large offer to Pandit Jagannath Tarakapanchanan of presenting a zemindary yielding a lakh of rupees (£10,000) a year, he refused it on the ground that riches were demoralising, and his descendants, if they were wealthy, would not care for learning and give themselves up to luxury.† Another illustration is given below. When Raja Iswarchandra of Nuddea in Bengal paid a visit to Pandit Ramnath Tarkasiddhanta, the latter spoke to that nobleman in response to a kind enquiry about the Pandit's earthly wants and requirements, with the lofty dignity and stubborn pride of Diogenes answering Alexander the Great.

On this subject Rev. Mr. Ward says: "No reasonable person will deny to the Hindus of former time the pride of very extensive learning. The variety of subjects upon which they wrote prove that almost every science was cultivated among them; the manner also in which they treated these

* *Vide* Von Schlegeb's Philosophy of History, translated by J. B. Robertson.

† *Vide* Memoirs of Maharaja Nubkissen Bahadur.

subjects proves that the Hindu learned men yielded the place of learning to scarcely any other of the ancients. The more their philosophical works and law books are studied, the more will the enquirer be convinced of the depth of wisdom possessed by the authors."* In Calcutta, Maharaja Nubkissen Deb Bahadur was celebrated for his open-handed generosity to the Pandit class, and helped them to found their *tols* or *chatuspaties*. He invited them to come and settle in Calcutta, presented rent-free lands and money to them, and otherwise encouraged them. It was at his instance that Hatibagan† became famous as one of the centres of learning in Bengal. It was he who brought to the notice of the authorities the claims of the Pandits, and secured for them titles, pensions and other kinds of recognition. His solicitude to promote the interests of the Pandits has called forth the following eulogy from Babu Sambhoochandra Mukherji:

"A warm patron of letters, his palace was the centre of association of all the learned of the surrounding districts, and the resort of those of distant parts of India who chanced to come to Calcutta. In accordance with a hoary-headed but most unexceptionable custom of this country, great men are attended by a number of Pandits, who give them the benefit of their opinion on all occasions and often discuss logical and metaphysical topics before them. Naba Krishno's council of the learned was splendid, as the names of two of its distinguished ornaments—Jagannath Tarkapanchanan and Vaneswar Vidyalankar—will indicate, and discussions in it were always encouraged by large presents to the wranglers.

* Rev. Ward's View of the History, Literature, Mythology, &c., of the Hindus. Vol. IV.

† Hatibagan is a local place situated on the North-East side of Calcutta. It was the place of abode of the learned Pandits.

His wealth and influence procured him many rare Persian and Sanskrit manuscripts."*

The *Samachar Chandrika*, edited by Babu Bhabani Charan Banerji, was noted for its advocacy of Hinduism. It was started in 1821, and was the organ of the Dharma Sava. The editor, Bhabani Charan, was also its Secretary, and the late Raja Gopeemohan Deb Bahadur was its founder and President. In truth, it was the earliest Hindu organisation set on foot with a view to safeguard its interest. J. C. Marshman† writes of Bhabani Charan: "A brahmin of great intelligence and considerable learning, though no pandit, but remarkable for his tact and energy, which gave him great ascendancy among his fellow countrymen......... ....During the life of its able and astute editor it was considered the great bulwark of the current superstition. Its success was owing not only to the popularity of the opinions which he advocated, but also to the charm of its pure and simple style." The *Chandrika* ceased to exist only in recent years. The *Sangbad Provakar*, another influential Hindu paper, was started in 1830 A.D. under the editorship of the poet, Iswar Chandra Gupta. From a tri-weekly, ultimately it became daily in 1837. Such talented writers as the late Rai Bahadurs Bankim Chandra Chatterji, C.I.E., Dinabandhu Mitra and Babu Monomohan Bose served as apprentices to Iswar Chandra. His influence upon society was then unbounded. In the latter stage of life he met with reverses, but he lived peaceably under the fostering care of the late Maharaja Kamalkrishna Bahadur in his suburban garden house at Khardah

* *Vide* Memoirs of Maharaja Nubkissen.

† Life and Times of Carey, Marshman and Ward, Vol. II.

near Barrackpur, where a bower, named Iswar Chandra's kunja, still exists. About his literary merits, Mr. Romesh Dutt* thus writes: "His fame rests on his smaller poems alone, which sparkle with true wit and are very popular. His subjects are the every-day occurrences of life, and specially of Hindu life in all its phases. The turmoil and joys and sorrows of the Hindu household during the Puja season, or during the *Amoni* festival in winter, the amiability as well as the faults of Hindus, their hopes and fond wishes and ardent love, their jealousies and disputes, the vices of young Bengal and their pride and pretensions, all these and much more have been described with a faithful minuteness really striking. It is only necessary to read the poems to see the scenes which the author paints, to live and move among the imaginary actors and speakers. Satire is the *forte* of Iswar Chandra, and the richest wit sparkles in every line of his easy and flowing poetry. In all the great qualities of a poet, however, pathos and true sublimity for instance, Iswar Chandra is sadly wanting." Another vernacular journal which made some stir at the time was *Sangbad Bhaskar*. Its editor was the well-known Pandit Gourisankar Bhattacharjia, nicknamed Gur-gurè Bhattacharjea. He also published another journal named *Rasoraj*. It is interesting to record how native society was regaled by the wit-combats of Iswar Chandra and Gourisankar. It has been remarked that much indecency, personality and vulgar taste were freely indulged in by them; but compared to the present day wranglings by certain sections of the Vernacular Press, they are moderation itself. During the days of the mutiny, the late Maharaja Kamal

---

* *Vide* The Literature of Bengal.

Krishna Bahadur used to contribute regularly articles to the *Sangbad Bhashkar*. I give at the end of this chapter a list of the newspapers and magazines. The compilation is by no means an exhaustive one. Amongst the vernacular journals, Pandit Dwarkanath Vidyabhusan's *Shome Prokash* deserves more than a passing notice. He was a vigorous Bengali writer, and his penmanship has been greatly admired by such good judges as the late Pandit Iswar Chandra Vidyasagore. He was, so to speak, the landmark between the older and the latter-day journalism. His paper became the most influential of his time. He was a great Sanskrit scholar, and was noted for his independence of character. He was born at Chingripota in 24-Pergunnas. With the passing of the Vernacular Press Act, the paper ceased to exist. It re-appeared with its former editor, but with its lustre gone. The late Babu Bhudeb Mukherji, C.I.E., conducted with great ability and wisdom the *Education Gazette*, a weekly vernacular paper, to which the Government has accorded its patronage. This paper is still in existence. Amongst the monthly periodicals, the *Bibidharta Sangraha*, published in 1851 and edited by the late Raja Dr. Rajendra Lala Mittra, C.I.E., occupies a prominent place. It was an illustrated monthly vernacular magazine chiefly devoted to science, arts and literature. It came latterly under the control of the late Babu Kali Prasonno Singha, who changed its name to *Rahasya Sangraha*. The late Rai Bahadur Bankim Chandra Chatterji, C.I.E., published his *Bangadarsana*, which also attained much celebrity. Many Bengali writers, since distinguished, were among its early contributors. Bankim's constructive power and capacity of writing were extraordinary. He has, so to speak, given a new turn to modern Bengali literature. His incisiveness, his wisdom and power of observation, his witticism and the power he displayed in character painting, were really extraordinary.

To the founders of the *Bangabasi* belong the credit of successfully introducing cheap vernacular journalism in this country. That journal was started during the Viceroyalty of Lord Ripon by a number of public-spirited persons, notably Babu Upendra Krishna Singha Roy and Babu Jogendra Chandra Bose, its present editor and proprietor. From its early days its articles caught the attention of the readers, and the paper rapidly rose to importance and influence. Its success became unprecedented, and for the first time a Bengali journal could boast of subscribers ranging from 15 to 20 thousand. This extraordinary success is attributable mainly to the ability of Babu Jogendra Chandra Bose. During his management, not only has the paper attained an unrivalled position and prosperity, but such eminent writers as Babu Akshai Chandra Sarcar, Chandra Nath Bose, M.A., B.L., and Indranath Banerji, identified themselves with its ideas and sentiments. Its advocacy of Hinduism also drew a large circle of educated men under its banner. About this time, and under its auspices, Pandit Sasadhar Tarkachuramani began to preach and interpret Hinduism in a manner which his admirers regarded as scientific. Sree Krishna Prasanno Sen, otherwise called Krishnananda Swami, ranged himself for a time under its banner. For the first time the remote villagers, rude shopkeepers and even the itinerant sellers in the interior villages came under newspaper influence. The modern phase of Hinduism has been much invigorated by the new method of preaching. About this time the *Bangabasi* commenced a regular crusade against the Indian National Congress by exposing some of its methods and ideas and its great extravagance. In some quarters the necessity was felt of a journal that should represent the opposite political creed. A joint-stock company was formed to launch the *Hitabadi* newspaper with Pandit Krishnakamal Bhattacharjea, an eminent Sanskrit scholar, as its editor. Babu Rabindra Nath Tagore and other distinguished writers were among its early contributors and supporters. As the concern did not prove paying, it was ultimately sold off to Pandit Kali Prasanna Kavyabisarad, its present editor. Under his management the *Hitabadi* has secured thirty to forty thousand subscribers. Pandit Kaliprasanna is a versatile gentleman, who is not only a master of Bengali prose, but is a skilled hand in verse, and is not only a Sanskrit scholar, but well-read in English. His ability and independence have made the journal deservedly a success and a power in the country.

The *Sanjibani* newspaper is a weekly vernacular, started at the instance of the advanced section of the Brahmo community of Calcutta, known as the Sadharan Brahmo Somaj. Its present editor is Babu Krishna Kumar Mittra, the Superintendent of the City College. Although it represents Brahmo interests, it deals with several interesting and learned subjects for the welfare of all classes and sections in a fair and reasonable way. It is conducted on catholic principles and with much good sense.

There are several other periodicals, magazines and journals which have not been noticed in this chapter. The limited space at my disposal has unfortunately precluded me from making even a bare allusion to such high-class literary magazines as the *Bharati* or *Nabyabharata*. These and such other journals are conducted with singular ability and thoroughness.

It would be a prodigious task to sketch out in a chapter the mental activities of the Hindu race that have found expression in the entire field of human knowledge embracing Religion, Arts, Science and Literature. It was in 1822 that the late Raja Sir Radhakanta Deb Bahadur, K.C.I.E., published the first volume of his *Magnum opus*, the *Sabdokalpa-druma*, an encyclopædic lexicon in sanskrit in 8 thick quarto volumes. It was the first publication of the kind, and required unbounded erudition, herculean labour, an extensive research, an immense outlay, to achieve it, when printing itself had been but very recently introduced in India. The late Babu Ramkamal Sen published his Dictionary from English to Bengali at Serampur, in 1830, with the help of the late Dr. Carey. The idea was taken from Todd's edition of Johnson's Dictionary; and its second volume appeared in 1834. It was dedicated to His Excellency the Right Hon'ble Lord William Cavendish Bentinck. Before its publication, many other dictionaries * were published in India with the encouragement and assistance of the Government.

I shall now allude to the services rendered by the late Babu Ram Gopal Ghose to the cause of journalism.

* The names are:—

(1) Gilchrist's Hindi English dictionary, and *vice versâ* 2 Vols. (2) Forster's Bengali and English Dictionary, 2 Vols. (3) Hunter's Hindi and English Dictionary. (4) Gladwin's Hindi, Persian and English Dictionary. (5) Wilson's Sanskrit and English Dictionary. (6) Carey's Bengali and English Dictionary. (7) Hough's Burman and English Dictionary. (8) Molesworth's Maharatta and English Dictionary.

In *Jnananeshwana*, under the signature of "Civis," he wrote on the Indian transit duties. Babu Ram Gopal Ghose started a paper called the *Spectator* and was one of those who founded the British Indian Society, afterwards the British Indian Association, along with Mr. George Thompson. Its first name was the *Landholders' Association*. He was coadjutor with Mr. David Hare, D. Bethune, and Dr. Mowat in several schemes of improvement for the natives of Bengal, and was one of those who encouraged Babu Dwarkanath Tagore in sending four students to England for acquiring the necessary training for different professions. Above all, he was the first Bengali Orator, and is best remembered by his countrymen for his celebrated defence, at a meeting of the Justices of the Peace, of the practice of cremating the dead bodies of the Hindus on the banks of the Ganges. "As a speaker and writer," says his biographer, "he had a singular command of pure idiomatic English, and he so thoroughly identified himself with the subject he discussed or advocated that it was difficult to believe that English thoughts and expressions were foreign to him, and that he had not been brought up in the English household. Mr. Cochrane, the well-known barrister of Calcutta, on one occasion remarked that he seldom listened to any one who was more eloquent, never to one who was more zealous than Babu Ramgopal was in advocating all measures which had any tendency to benefit his countrymen."* Babu Ramgopal Ghose was, by caste, a Kayastha, son of Babu Gobind Chunder Ghosh. He was born at Calcutta in October 1815 and died on the 25th February, 1868. He was also among the first to inaugurate the Joint-Stock Company, and was one of the early natives appointed, in 1850, a member of the Bengal

* *Vide* Ghose's Modern History of the Indian Chiefs, &c.

Chamber of Commerce. Babu Ramgopal Ghose's habits and manners were open to objection from the orthodox Hindu point of view; and during the *sradh* ceremony of his venerable mother, he was placed in great difficulty. However, it was removed by the good offices of the late Maharaja Kamal Krishna Deb Bahadur, whose admiration for Babu Ramgopal was very great. Ramgopal Ghosh bequeathed Rs. 40,000 to the Calcutta University, 20,000 to the District Charitable Society, and Rs. 40,000 he paid to his friends who were indebted to him.

The late Babu Peary Charan Sircar, Professor of the Presidency College, was well-known as a veteran educationist and philanthropic gentleman. He was styled "the Prince of Indian teachers" and "the Arnold of the East."† He started a Bengali paper, *Hitasadhak*, and afterwards an English magazine, the *Well-wisher*, in 1865 or 1866. He was associated with the Temperance Movement in Bengal. A Temperance Society was formed with Raja Kali-Krishna Deb Bahadur, and afterwards with Maharaja Kamal Krishna Deb Bahadur as its President, when Babu Keshub Chandra Sen identified himself with the question. Babu Peary Charan Sarkar took charge, for a short time, of the *Education Gazette.* He was known as a great patron of the students, particularly of the poorer sections. His English primers—First Book of Reading, Second Book of Reading, &c.—are still held in high repute and used as standard text-books; the books are now published by Sir Roper Lethbridge, who has purchased the copyright. He was born in Calcutta on the 23rd January 1823, and died on the 23rd September 1875. The late Babu Prasana Coomar

† *Vide* the *Hindu Patriot* of the 5th October 1875.

Sarbadhicary was some-time the Principal of the Calcutta Sanskrit College. Perhaps he was the first native who composed, in Bengali, books on Arithmetic and Algebra. It was not an easy thing to do in those days, for one had to coin several technical terms. He was well-known as a veteran educationist, and he helped to spread English education in the country by establishing schools and supplying many students with funds and other requirements. He died in November 1886. Babu Kissory Chand Mitter in his day was known as one of the brilliant English writers in newspapers, magazines &c. He was a great friend and was the biographer of the late Babu Dwarkanath Tagore. Babu Peary Chand Mittra was born at Calcutta in 1814. His services in the field of Bengali journalism, and generally in that of Bengali literature, are not of an evanescent nature. Rev. J. Long styled him the Dickens of Bengal. His acquirement in English and Bengali was vast; and Lord Albemarle brought to the notice of the House of Lords his article on zemindar and rayat which appeared in the *Calcutta Review*, Vol. VI.* He wrote several articles on social, moral and religious subjects. Perhaps he was the first in composing satirical pieces—Alaler Gharer Dulal, &c.—in Bengali. His biographer states: None of his books are large, but all of them are written in clear and simple language; in a language in which every one of us speaks, and all of them are entitled to this praise—the praise of originality. In his satirical writings there is none of the concentrated venom, the fierce indignation, the sustained spirit of malignity which characterise inferior works. He started a monthly Bengali magazine named *Masik Patrika*. He

* See London *Times* of the 8th July, 1853.

conducted the Bengali *Spectator* with Babu Tarachand Chakrovertee. When the British Indian Society was established, with Mr. George Thompson as its president, he acted as its secretary. It is impossible to withhold high praise for the efforts of the late Babu Kaliprasanna Singha of Jorasanko in the field of Bengali language and literature. It was at his instance and under his immediate supervision, the grand epic, the Mahabharat, was translated into Bengali. Perhaps hardly any Bengali translation has yet appeared which can be compared to Kaliprasanna Singha's edition in point of faithfulness and purity and dignity of style. Such men as the late Pandit Iswarchandra Vidyasagar and several other eminent Pandits and scholars looked after its proper translation and accuracy. It is difficult to estimate the never-to-be-forgotten services which this noble spirited gentleman rendered to the Bengali language. Unfortunately the Bengali language is yet a sealed book to Western *savants*, otherwise it is certain that his labours would have met with due recognition. To serve the Bengali language in those days required an amount of patriotism and disinterested self-sacrifice which few are capable of. He is therefore entitled to the deep gratitude of his countrymen. He was a patron and friend of several meritorious persons who have since become famous in different spheres of life. He assisted much in developing the Bengali stage. His comical and satirical social sketch, the *Hutumpencha*, graphically delineates in a humorous vein several points, good and bad, of the state of society which prevailed at the time. It is a masterpiece of its kind and has never been eclipsed by the latter-day productions in the line. Time may come when one may not read *Hutumpencha*, but the time will never come when it will fail to give pleasure and profit to its readers. He was the descendant of Dewan Santiram Singha and grandson of the late Babu Joykrishna Singha, who was early associated with the development of the Hindu College. Kaliprasanna Singha was by profession a zemindar. He was a Kayastha by caste and his descendants are still living.

The services of the late Madhusudan Dutt, especially in the domain of Bengali poetry, are of a really transcendental character. Mr. Romesh Dutt says*—"Nothing in the entire range of Bengali literature can approach the sublimity of Meghnadbadha Kavya, which is a masterpiece of epic poetry. The reader who can feel and appreciate the sublime will rise from the study of his great work with mixed sensations of veneration and awe, with which few poets can aspire him, and will candidly pronounce the bold author to be indeed a genius of a very high order, second only to the highest and greatest that have ever lived, like Vyasa, Balmiki, or Kalidasa, Homer, Danté or Shakespeare." He was born in 1828 at Jessore. He embraced Christianity at the age of sixteen, and after completing his studies, he was for a time at Madras. In 1836 he returned to Bengal and composed three dramas, two farces, three works in Bengali blank verse, the first of its kind ever produced, and one in rhyme. He then went to England with the assistance of Pandit Iswar Chandra Vidyasagar and was called to the bar. He died in 1875. Indeed, it is hard to believe on perusing his works that they came from the pen of a Christian.

* The Literature of Bengal.

According to Romesh Dutt* second only to Madhusudan, was the renowned poet Hem Chandra Banerji. His poetry had a fine sensibility, a quick, sportive imagination, and an exquisite sense of the beautiful as well as chasteness of thought and grandeur of conception. His smaller poems breathe a lofty spirit and intense feeling. Babu Hem Chandra has left several poetical works. He was Senior Government Pleader of the Calcutta High Court, was born in 1838 and died in the year 1902. Babu Nabin Chandra Sen's poetry has much pathos, sensibility, and a richness of imagination. It has a sparkling beauty and freshness. There are other poets: the late Madan Mohun Tarkalankar, Babu Monomohon Bose, Robindra Nath Tagore, the late Rangolal Banerji, and poetesses Girindramohini Dasi, Kamini Sen, Mankumari, and several others.

Rai Bahadur Dinabandhu Mitter, Monomohan Bose, Girish Chandra Ghose, Amrita Lall Bose, Beharilal Chatterji and Rajkrishna Roy, have been also eminent and distinguished writers in the field of Bengali literature, and especially on its dramatic side. Dinabandhu's works aimed at the correction of society, painting men in their true colours, and it is impossible not to praise him for his representing the characters in their true light, even in their vulgarity and wickedness. So also do the writings of Babu Amritalal, whose satirical and telling social sketches have won for him a permanent name.

The Rambagan Dutt family has for generations been noted for its literary works. Among its members, who have made the name of the Bengalees respected, Nilmani Dutt,

* *Vide* Dutt's Literature of Bengal.

Russomoi Dutt, Rai Bahadur Sashi Chandra Dutt, Gobin Ghandra Dutt, Ishan Chandra Dutt, Jogesh Chandra Dutt, a lady writer Miss Toru Dutt, O. C. Dutt, and last, but not the least, Romesh Chandra Dutt, C.I.E., may be mentioned. This galaxy of writers in a single family is really very striking. The late Babu Nilmoni Dutt, almost the founder of the family, was among the first Bengalees who knew the English language, and was a friend and associate of the late Maharaja Nubkissen Bahadur.† Russomoi Dutt was the first native judge of the Calcutta Small Causes Court. Rai Bahadur S. C. Dutt's English works on various subjects show the versatility of his talents; and the important services of Romesh Chandra Dutt, C.I.E., have won for him the gratitude of his countrymen. His admirable works of fiction are greatly admired by his countrymen. His annotated edition of the Rigveda has been highly spoken of by the learned societies of Europe. His historical works bear the impress of a great writer. He is at once an historian, a novelist, a poet, a scholar, and a voluminous general writer.

Sir Raja Radhakanta Deb was one of the founders of the Hindu College, and was a member of the Committee of Management of that institution for 34 years. In those days English education was viewed with jealousy and even alarm by the Hindu community, but the Raja used his influence in its favour and made the College a success. He was a constant visitor and for some time Honorary Secretary of the Government Sanskrit College, of which he often conducted the annual examinations. He was advanced

† *Vide* Deposition of Nilmani Dutt in the case of Raja Rajkrishna *versus* Gopimohan Deb and *vice versâ*.

enough to appreciate female education. In the language of the Hon'ble Mr. Bethune, "to him belongs the credit of being the first native of India who, in modern times, has pointed out the folly and wickedness of allowing women to grow up in utter ignorance." In his house the pupils of the girls' schools assembled to receive prizes; and what he preached in pamphlets he practised in his own home by educating the female members of his family. He was an active member of the Calcutta School Book Society, then much dreaded for the supposed tendency of its publications to undermine the Hindu faith and he wrote and published several vernacular school books on his own account.

Great and varied was the activity of the Raja. He was the first president for life of the British Indian Association, and gave to its Councils a guidance that was at once wise and loyal. He was Vice-President for a time of the Agricultural and Horticultural Society. He contributed to many papers on the agriculture of Bengal, and prepared an English translation of a Persian work on Horticulture, which was published under the auspices of the Royal Asiatic Society of Great Britain and Ireland. The greatest work of his life was the Encyclopœdic Sanskrit Dictionary called *Shabdakalpadruma*, a work which involved stupendous labour, occupied him for over forty years, and absorbed a fortune. For its publication the Raja established a press at his house and had type specially prepared; the work brought him world-wide fame. The Royal Asiatic Society of Great Britain and Ireland, the Asiatic Society of Paris, the Royal Society of Northern Antiquities at Copenhagen, the German Oriental Society, the American Oriental Society, the Imperial Academy of Sciences at St. Petersburgh, the Royal Academy of Sciences at Berlin, sent him diplomas of honorary or corresponding membership. The Czar of Russia and King Frederick VII of Denmark sent him medals, and Her Gracious Majesty Queen Victoria not only admitted him to the Most Exalted Order of the Star of India, but sent him a splendid gold medal as a personal present, "appreciating the spirit of loyalty" in which the work had been transmitted to her. The title of Raja Bahadur had already been conferred on him, and he discharged for many years the duties of Justice of the Peace and Presidency Magistrate.

Learned in Eastern and Western languages, devoutly religious, rigidly pure, liberal in sentiments, progressive in life, actively helping education, literature and the expansion of society, the Raja has greatly influenced life and thought in the country by his work and his example. His broad sympathies and refined manners gave him universal popularity; and Sir Lawrence Peel, after a long and intimate acquaintance with him, was pleased to say that "he was a pattern of gentlemanliness which we would do well to imitate."

I have not mentioned in this chapter, while dilating on the progress and development of the Bengali language and literature, the very important part played by the *yatras*, theatres and other kindred amusements. They have in no inconsiderable degree developed the tastes, manners and refinement of the Indian population. The essence of the Vaisnava religion, the ethics inculcated in our grand religious works—the Mahabharata and the Ramayana—nay the principles of Hindu philosophy, have been instilled, in an impressive way, into the minds of the people. Even the females and tender-aged boys and girls have not escaped the blessed influence. In recent times, the efforts of the Brahmo sects and the theatre-people towards the growth of modern Bengali songs and their tunes and intonations have been conspicuous. Fashion now eschews out the *yatra* songs and no longer they are relished, and in their stead the songs composed by the cultured Brahmos and the theatre songs, set to light tunes, are much in vogue. And it is unquestionable that to the Brahmo sects and to the popularity of the theatre we owe the modern Bengali songs.

Hindustani and Mahommedan songs at one time held their sway. It was the songs that were encouraged by the polite and the fashionable. They were very often set to high tunes and were generally known as *Kalwati* songs. The Bengali songs, except the religious songs, were then at a discount. Such sweet and melodious varieties of songs as *Tappa* and *Gazels* were much appreciated and popularised by Maharaja Raj Krishna Bahadur.* The late Dr. Sambhu Chandra Mukherjea, Editor, *Reis and Rayyet*, thus writes about the late Maharaja:

"Rajkrishna's passion for music was unbounded. He was himself a remarkably good songster and player on instruments............Those who pretended to proficiency in the art travelled from the North-Western Provinces and from the Deccan to receive Rajkrishna's approbation and reward. His ear was exceedingly good, and he was one of the best judges of the art. Fakirs and ascetics who excelled in it, to whom worldly goods offered no temptation, went to receive from Rajkrishna the compensation from the world's dulness."†

* Histoir de-Literature, Hindui et Hindostani par, &c., Gracin de Tassy, Vol. I.

† *Mukherjea's Magazine*, Vol. I, No. 4, 1861.

Kabi, Panchali, Kathakata, Akhrais, &c., also formed a part of the national amusement, and it is difficult to lightly pass over the important services done by Maharaja Nubkissen Bahadur in these directions. Mr. N. N. Ghose in his Memoirs says:—

"His appreciation of the fine arts, of music in particular, was in every way worthy of himself. Haru Thakur and Nitai Das, well known as composers of songs, were his *protegés*, and he introduced into Calcutta Society and popularised the *nautch* which Englishmen believe to be the chief of our public amusements. It is *Bai-nautch*. The songs of Kabis were a favourite entertainment of Hindu Society. They were a curious illustration of the blended powers of metrical composition and of controversy, songs composed by one person or party and sung before an assembly were then and there answered by another. The answer brought a reply, and so the song duel went on till one side was fairly exhausted. The full name of Haru Thakur was Harry Kristo Dirghangi. He was called a Thakur because he was a Brahmin among Kabies. It was in Nubkissen's house that this species of entertainment had its origin, its first exhibition. Haru Thakur was so attached to Nubkissen, that after the Maharaja's death he gave up his profession. Of another kind of musical entertainment known as *Akhrai*, the Maharaja was a distinguished, probably the first patron. Kului Chandra Sen, who was not only competent in *Akhrai*, but probably its founder, received great encouragement. A cousin of Kului—Ram Nidhi Gupta—popularly known as Nidhoo Babu, made great improvement in the art. Distinguished musicians, singers and players on instruments, came to him, attracted by his fame as a votary of Muses, and none went disappointed."*

* Memoirs of Maharaja Nubkissen, by N. N. Ghose, Esq.

I cannot dismiss this topic without giving prominence to the services of the talented Raja Sir Sourindra Mohan Tagore, Kt., D.L., C.I.E., who has spared no expense and devoted his whole life for the restoration and development of Indian music. No Indian in modern times can be compared with the noble Raja in this respect. He has, so to speak, raised and elevated the noble muses from the hands of the vulgar in which they had recently fallen, to their proper place in genteel society. He devoted himself to the study of higher music and published many books and pamphlets on the subject.

On pages 246—249 will be found a comprehensive list of Bengali Newspapers and Periodicals ranging over the period 1818—1855.

A Catalogue of Bengali Newspapers and Periodicals which issued from the Press from 1818 to 1855.

Names of Newspapers and Periodicals.	When first published.	How long continued.	Names of Editors.	Monthly Price. Rs.	A.	P.
Bengal Gazette	1816	1 year.	Gangadhar Bhattacharjea ...	1	0	0
Samachar Darpan	1818	21 ,,	J. Marshman, Serampore ...	1	0	0
Sangbad Kaumudi	1819	33 ,,	Baboo Tarachand Dutt and Bhobani Charan Bandopadhia ...			
Samachar Chandrika	1822	...	Bhabani Charan Banerjee ...	1	0	0
Sangbad Timirnasak	...	10 years.	Kristomohan Dás			
Banga Duta	...	16 ,,	Nilratna Halder			
Sangbad Provakar	1830	25 ,,	Iswar Chandra Gupta	1	0	0
,, Sudhakar	...	3 ,,	Premchand Roy			
Anubadika	...	2 ,,				
Jnaneshwan	1831	13 ,,	Dakhinaranjan Mukherji and Rasik Mallik			
Sukhakar	...	1 ,,	P. Ray			
Sangbad Ratnakar	...	1 ,,	Brojomohan Singha			
Samachar Suvarajendra ...	...	...	Dulub Chandra Chattopadhea ...			
Sashtra Prokash	...	1 year.	Lakshminarain Nayalankar ...			
Vigan Sebadhis	...	...	Ganga Charan Sen			
Gyanan Sindu Taranga ...	...	...	Rasik Kristo Mallik			
Ganadoy	...	...	Ram Chunder Mitter			
Pashably	...	...	Ram Chunder Mitter			
Sangbad Ratnabali	1832	...	Mohesh Chunder Pál			

Sangbad Sarsangraha ...	...	...	Benimadhab Dey			
„ Purnachandrodoy ...	1835	2 years.	Huro Chundro Banerji	1	0	0
„ Sudha Sindhu ...	1837	1 „	Kalisankar Dutt	0	8	0
„ Dibakar	1837	6 months	Ganganarain Bose	0	8	0
„ Gunakar	1837	6 „	Grish Chunder Bose	0	8	0
„ Sadamani	...	2 years.	Kalachand Dutt			
„ Mrinujai	...	...	Parbati Charan Dass			
„ Bhaskar	...	...	Srinath Roy	1	0	0
Rasoraj	1838	17 years.	Gourisankar Bhattacherjee ...	0	8	0
Sangbad Arunoday	...	...	Jugonnarain Mukherji			
Sujan Ranjan	...	...	Heramba Charan Mukhopadhai ...			
Bengal Govt. Gazette ...	1839	17 years.	J. Marshman			
Moorshidabad Patrika ...	1840	1 year.	Gurudoyal Chowdhuri			
Gayandipika	...	1 „	Bhabani Chattopadhea			
Bharat Bandhu	...	...	Samacharan Bandopadhea ...			
Banga Duta	...	1 year.	Nilcomul Dás			
Baden Darshan	...	...	Ukhoy Kumar Dutt and Prosonno Chunder Ghose			
Bengal Spectator	...	2 years.	Ramgopal Ghose and others ...			
Aynbad Darshan	1843	1 „	Srinarayan Roy. Barrakpur ...	1	0	0
Tatuabodhini Patrika	1843	12 „	Akhoy Kumar Dutt	0	8	0
Sangbad Rajrani	1844	6 months	Ganganarain Bose			
Subborosoranjini	...	...	......			
Jagatbandhu Patrika	1846	2 years.	Sitanath Ghose and others ...			
Satyarnab	1850	5 „	Rev. W. Smith	0	1	6
Pashand Piran	...	1 „	Iswar Chandra Gupta			
Samachar Gyan Darpana ...	...	3 „	Umakant Chatterji			
Jagut Dipak Bhaskar	.	...	Maulavi Bazurally	0	4	0
Nitya Dharma Ranjika ...	...	...	Nund Kumar Kaviratna ...	0	8	0
Bhairab Dando	...	...	......			
Durjan Daman Mahanoboni ...	...	...	Mathuranath Guha			

A Catalogue of Bengali Newspapers, &c.—(*contd.*)

Names of Newspapers and Periodicals.	When first published.	How long continued.	Names of Editors.	Monthly Price. Rs. A. P.
Kabyaratnakar	1847	1 year.	Umakant Bhattacherjea ...	
Gyananjan	...	1 ,,	Chaitanya Charan Adhikari ...	
Hindu Dharma Chandrodoy ...	...	1 ,,	Horinarayan Gaswami ...	
Rungpur Bartabaha	...	...	Guru Charan Roy	0 4 0
Gyan Sancharini	...	2 years.	Ganganarayan Bose	
Sadhuranjan	...	...	Iswar Chunder Gupta	0 4 0
Dikbijaya	...	...	Dwarkanath Mukhopadhea ...	
Sujan Bandhu	...	...	Nobin Chunder Dey	
Bandhu Hindu	...	...	Umacharan Bhaddro	
Aukkel Gurum	1847	4 months	Brojonath Bose	
Manoranjan	1847	...	Gopal Chunder Day	
Kanotubh	1848	1 year.	Mahes Chunder Ghose	
Gyanchandrodoy	1848	2 months	Radhanath Bosé	
Gyan Ratnakar	1848	1 year.	Tarini Churan Roy	
Bhringo Dut	1848	1 ,,	Anonda Chunder Barma ...	
Sangbad Arunadoy	1848	1 ,,	Panchanan Banerji	
Sangbad Dinaminy	1848	6 months	Gopal Chunder Dey	
,, Ratnabarsan ...	1848	...	Madhab Chundra Ghosh ...	
,, Rosaundjar ...	...	...	Khetter Mohan Banerji ...	0 8 0
Baranasi Chandradoy ...	...	2 years.	Woomakant Bhattacharjea ...	
Muktabali	...	...	Collykant Bhattacharjea ...	
Rasamudgar	1849	...	Gobind Chunder Banerji ...	
Rasasagar	1849	5 years.	Rangalál Banerji	
Rasoratnakar	...	...	Jadunath Pál	

Sujanranjan ...	...	...	...	Gobind Chandra Gupta ...	
Mahajan Darpan ...	...	...	...	Joykali Bose ...	
Kaustab Kiran ...	...	...	...	Rajnarayan Mittra ...	
Gyan Pradayini ...	...	...	...	Biseswar Banerji ...	1 0 0
Satya Dharma Prokashika	...	...	...	Gobind Chund Dey ...	
Sarva Subhakori ...	...	...	...	Motilal Chattopadhea ...	
Satya Pradip ...	...	...	1 year	M. Townsend ...	0 8 0
Sangbad Burdwan ...	...	...	...	Kalidas Bandopadhea ...	0 8 0
Burdwan Chandradoy	...	...	...	Ramtaran Chattacharjea ...	
Sangbad Sudhangsu ...	...	1852	1 year.	Rev. K. M. Banerji ...	0 4 0
Upadeshak ...	...	...	9 ,,	Rev. J. Wenger ...	0 2 0
Satya Sancharini ...	...	...	2 ,,	Samacharan Bose ...	
Sangbad Nisakar ...	...	...	...	Nilcomul Dás ...	
Dharmamarma Prokashika	...	...	...		
Bhakti Suchak ...	...	...	...	Ramnidhi Dás ...	
Durbikhanika ...	...	...	...		
Gyanodoy ...	...	...	...	Chundraikhar Mukherji ...	0 4 0
Gyna Durshan ...	...	...	...	Sreepoti Mukherji ...	
Kasiborta Prokashika...	...	...	...	Kasidass Mittra ...	0 8 0
Midnapur and Hijli Guardian	...	1852	2 years.	H. V. Bayley, C.S. ...	
Bibidharta Sangraha ...	...	1852	4 ,,	Rajendra Lala Mittra ...	0 3 0
Gyanarunadoy ...	...	...	...	Keshub Chandra Karmokar ...	0 4 0
Sulab Patrika ...	...	1853	...	Taranath Dutt ...	0 2 0
Sudha Bardhan ...	...	1854	...		1 0 0
Banga Bartabaha ...	...	1854	...		0 4 0
Sarbha Subhakori ...	...	1854	...		0 4 0

This Catalogue was submitted to Government by the Rev. J. Long in 1855.*

* *Vide* Selections from the Records of the Bengal Government, No. XXII, page 145.

CHAPTER IX.

EUROPEAN SOCIETY.

IT is a bold task to attempt to speak of the manners and customs of a foreign people. It is not easy to enter into their feelings and to sympathise with their tastes and idiosyncracies. One has to change an instinct before one is expected to have an appreciation of foreign manners. A close contact and free association are indispensable to make a true estimate of social life. Eminent European writers, whose honesty of purpose and goodness of heart cannot be doubted, have committed sad blunders in describing the social life and ideas of the Hindus. No wonder the Hindus, as judges of foreign life and character, are no exception to the rule, and they have sometimes made egregious mistakes in attempting to judge of European institutions. The following from the *Calcutta Review** will illustrate how far the judgment is coloured by prejudice.

"Ladies' dancing makes a curious impression on the natives. One of them, many years ago, gave a description of the English dinner party;" he ends with "after dinner they dance in their licentious way, pulling about each other's wives."

* Vol. XXXV. *See* foot-note page 205.

I shall therefore, instead of speaking authoritatively upon such a delicate subject, try to place before the readers the early state of European society in this country as depicted by Europeans themselves.

A writer has remarked that "no people has been so much subject to tyranny of fashion or custom as Englishmen appear to be." Fashion is said to be the chief of their idols; and they hold no sacrifice too great to propitiate that deity. The following serves to illustrate the obstinacy of national habits and prejudices: "Much of the disease in Calcutta and in other parts of India has been owing to the English not conforming their mode of living, dress, &c., to the climate. The Anglo-Saxon in every part of the world has wished to carry his home system on with him, he is the *topi-wala* in Calcutta as in London; he is like the Dutch at Batavia, who in the swamps made canals and fetid ditches run through their capital because Amsterdam had them—the results were pestilential fever, hence the canals have slain more Dutch in Java than the swords of the natives. We find Calcutta people warned in 1780 from the many sudden deaths which have happened lately; gentlemen should be cautious not to eat too freely during the continuance of the heat (June); the surgeon of an Indiaman expired in the street after eating a hearty dinner of beef; the thermometer was at 98."*

Apropos of the early state of European society in this country, several European writers observe that little morality was then to be found. In 1780 there was published the following satirical catechism in Hickey's Gazette.†

* *Calcutta Review*, Vol. XXXV.

† *Vide* Long's Peeps into Social Life.

Q.—What is commerce?

A.—Gambling.

Q.—What is the most cardinal virtue?

A.—Riches.

Q.—What is the amor patriae?

A.—Amor sui.

Q.—What is fraud?

A.—Detection.

Q.—What is beauty?

A.—Paint.

Q.—What is punctuality?

A.—An observation of the appointments of duelling and intriguing.

Q.—What is gentility?

A.—Extravagance.

Q.—What are public taxes?

A.—Pack saddles.

A.—Who are the people?

Q.—Nobody.

The following is from an old Calcutta newspaper of 1781.*

WANTED.

A resolution not to bribe, or a determination not to be bribed.

LOST—the dignity of high life in inattention to trifles.

STOLEN—into the country, the inhabitants of the Esplanade.

* *Vide Calcutta Review*. Vol. XXXV.

On Sale—For ready money whatever ought to be purchased by merit only.

In regard to European marriages in India, a writer in the *Calcutta Review* writes:—"The marriage question is one that occupied an important place in old Calcutta, in the days when Edinburgh was called the flesh market for the Indian marriage mart." London, too, sent out supplies. Grand Pre writes: "From a knowledge of this general predilection in favour of matrimony in India, the English, who are inclined to every sort of speculation, send thither annually whole cargoes of females who are tolerably handsome and are seldom six months in the country without getting husbands.* These cargoes were impatiently expected by such as not liking the orphans, are tired of celibacy and are on the look-out for the arrival of the ships. They were eager, as in other places, for a freight of merchandise to make purchases of goods. What is more extraordinary, these marriages in general are happy."†

The same writer makes a further statement altogether different from the one quoted above. The consequences of hasty marriage were often deplorable, Calcutta having been noted for its *affairs de cœur* almost as much as the Court of Verasilles, and a husband was often regarded by the lady as an Italian lady generally views hers. On the slightest attack of illness the wife found a pretext for leaving (for Europe) a husband to whom she had no attachment nor had

* A satirical poem, in 1813, called the "Anglo-Indian" thus described some of the ladies imported:

Pale faded stuffs, by time grown faint
Will brighten up through art;
A Britain gives their faces paint,
For sale at India's mart.

† *Calcutta Rivie*w, Vol. XXXV.

he for her; in various cases the ship had scarcely reached Kedgiri, before the husband had supplied himself with a seraglio of black dames. Cases have been even known when the doctor was bribed by the husband to give an order for a change of climate. Men old enough to make a girl guilty of a breach of the canonical articles which positively forbid you marrying your grand-father, were wedded to girls in their teens with little or no attraction. No wonder it was remarked of those marriages, "Hymen in Calcutta is seldom attended at the nuptial ceremony by Cupid." Marriages were celebrated in the evening; we find it so in 1778—how much earlier the practice may have arisen we do not know. "Weddings here are very joyous things to all parties; especially, I should suppose, to the padre or clergyman, who frequently receives twenty gold mohurs for his trouble of performing the ceremony. The bride and bridegroom's friends assemble, all elegantly dressed, at one or other of the young couple's nearest relatives and are most sumptuously entertained; and the congratulatory visits on the occasion put the whole town in motion."*

In those days, it appears, even the authorities preferred married men for their service. An extra sum of Rs. 200 a month was allowed to married civilians, a premium held out to bachelors to enter into matrimony.†

Stavorinus, the well-known Dutch Admiral, describing the European ladies in 1770 observes. "Domestic peace and tranquility must be purchased by a shower of jewels, a wardrobe of richest clothes, and a kingly parade of plate upon the sideboard; the husband must give all these, or

* *Vide Calcutta Review*, Vol. XXXV.
† Rainey's Historical and Topographical Sketch.

according to a vulgar phrase "the house would be too hot to hold him," while the wife never pays the least attention to her domestic concerns, but suffers the whole to depend upon her servants or slaves. The women generally rise between eight and nine o'clock. Dinner is ready at half-past one; they go to sleep till half-past four or five; they then dress in form and the evening and the part of the night is spent in company or at dancing parties which are frequent during the colder season. They are fond of parties of pleasure which are frequently made both upon the delightful banks and upon the pleasant waves of the Ganges."* Mackintosh's description of European life is given below: "About the hour of seven in the morning, his durwan (porter or door-keeper) opens the gate and the verandah (gallery) is free to his sircars, peons (footmen), harcarrahs (messengers or spies), chobdars (a kind of constable), huccabardars and cunsummas (or stewards and butlers), writers and solicitors. The head-bearer and jemadar enter the hall and his bed-room at eight o'clock. A lady quits his side and is conducted by a private staircase either to her own apartment or out of the yard. The moment the master throws his legs out of bed, the whole posse in waiting rush into his room, each making three salams, by bending the body and head very low and touching the forehead with the inside of the fingers and the floor with the back part. He condescends, perhaps, to nod or cast an eye towards the solicitors of his favours and protection. In about half an hour after undoing and taking off his long drawers, a clean shirt, breeches, stockings and slippers are put upon his body, thighs, legs and feet without any greater exertion on his own part than if he was a statue.

* *Calcutta Review*, Vol. XXXV.

The barber enters, shaves him, cuts his nails, and cleans his ears. The chillumjee and ewer are brought by a servant, whose duty it is, to pour water upon his head, to wash his hands and face, and present a towel. The Superior then walks in state to his breakfasting parlour in his waist coat; is seated; the consummah makes and pours out his tea and presents him with a plate of bread or toast. The hair-dresser comes behind and begins his operation, while the huccabardar softly slips the upper end of the snake or lute of the hucca into his hand. While the hair-dresser is doing his duty, the gentleman is eating, sipping and smoking by turns. By and by his banian presents himself with humble salams and advances somewhat more forward than the other attendants. If any of the solicitors are of eminence, they are honoured with chairs. These ceremonies are continued perhaps till ten o'clock when attended by his cavalcade, he is conducted in his palanquin, and preceded by eight to twelve chobdars, harcarrahs and peons with the insignia of their profession and their livery distinguished by the colour of their turbans and cumarbands (a long muslin belt wrapped round the waist) they move off at a quick amble; the set of bearers, consisting of eight generally, relieve each other with alertness and without incommoding the master. If he has visits to make, his peons lead and direct the bearers; and if business renders his *presence only* necessary, he shows himself and pursues his other engagements until two o'clock, when he and his company sit down, perfectly at ease in point of dress and address, to a good dinner, each attended by his own servant. And the moment the glasses are introduced, regardless of the company of ladies, the huccabardars enter, each with a hucca, and presents the tube to his master, watching behind and blowing the fire the whole time. As it is expected that they shall return to supper, at four o'clock they begin to withdraw without ceremony and step into their palanquins; so that in a few minutes the master is left to go into his bed-room, when he is instantly undressed to his shirt and his long drawers put on, and he lies down on his bed, when he sleeps till about seven or eight o'clock. Then the former ceremony is repeated and clean linen of every kind as in the morning is administered; his huccabardar presents, the tube into his hand, he is placed at the tea-table and his hair-dresser performs his duty as before. After tea, he puts on a handsome coat and pays visits of ceremony to the ladies: returns a little before 10 o'clock, supper being served at ten. The company keep together till between twelve and one in the morning, preserving great sobriety and decency, and when they depart, our hero is conducted to his bed-room, where he finds a female companion to amuse him until the hour of seven or eight next morning. With no greater exertions than these, do the Company's servants amass the most splendid fortunes.* The hucca was then in extensive use everywhere and among all classes, from a petty clerk to the Governor-General. The following copy of an invitation from the Governor-General and his lady will explain:

"Mr. and Mrs. Hastings present their compliments to..........and request the favour of his company to a concert and supper on Thursday next at Mrs. Hastings' house in town. 1st October 1779.

The concert to begin at eight o'clock. Mr............is requested to bring no servants except his huccabardar."†

* Mackintosh's "Travels..............." Letter L. V. dated Dec. 23, 1779, page. 219
† Rainey's "Historical and Topographical Sketches.".

Walter Hamilton says that it was usual with the Europeans in Calcutta to rise early to enjoy the cool air of the morning, which is particularly pleasant before sunrise; such places as the present Circular Road and Perrin's Garden* were once the resort of the fashionable. Other favourite places of recreation were mentioned lying between the Chandpal ghat and the fish-pond now known as Lal Dighi. The practice of walking was also then in vogue, and it is stated that Sir William Jones made a regular habit of walking from his house at Garden Reach at Kidderpore to the Supreme Court near the Old Court House Street.† Then the Governor and the members of the Government walked in solemn procession to the church every Sunday. But the great place for exercise, *i.e.* lolling in a carriage, was a very good race ground at a short distance from Calcutta, a place of Vanity Fair for morning and evening airings, where people "swallowed ten mouthfuls of dust for one mouthful of air;" the course was not watered in those days."‡

Calcutta Society was then full of gaiety, and there was no dearth of amusements. Billiards were then as, now, a favourite game. "The sums won and lost must keep the blood in a perpetual fever. In private families, the billiard is a kind of state-room. At the coffee-houses you are accommodated with tables and attendants for eight annas or half a rupee, by candle-light, a certain number of hours—every

* Perrin's Garden was situated somewhere near the present Bagbazar at the Perrin's point. It was sold in 1752 by Mr. Holwell.

† The Respondentia Walk appears to have been a favourite place for the European inhabitants to resort to of a morning or evening, as it was reserved for them exclusively between 5 and 8 P.M., and natives were prohibited from entering it at any such time; sentries were placed near the sluice bridge, to enforce the order. The walk was situated between Chandpal Ghat and the Fort. (Rainey's Historical and Topographical Sketch of Calcutta.)

‡ *Calcutta Review*, Vol. XXXV.

coffee-house having at least two tables: so that men of spirit have as many fashionable opportunities of themselves here, as you Europeans can boast. Selby's Club was a famous gambling one, but Lord Cornwallis put down public gambling with a high hand." Mrs. Fray writes of *card playing*. "After tea, either cards or music fill up the space till ten, when supper is generally announced. Five card loo is the usual game, and they play a rupee a fish limited to ten. This will strike you as being enormously high, but it is thought nothing of here. Tré, dille and whist are much in fashion, but ladies seldom join in the latter, for though the stakes are moderate, bets frequently run high among the gentlemen, which renders those anxious who sit down for amusement, lest others lose by their blunders."

Boating, in long handsome boats called snake-boats, was much practised, in the evening particularly, with bands of music. Gentlemen kept their pleasure yachts and went occasionally in them with their friends to Chandernagore or Shuksagaur on pleasure trips. English as well as Dutch, fond of parties of pleasure, frequently made both upon "the delightful boats and upon the pleasant waves of the Ganges." Europeans do not call the treacherous Ganges "pleasant waves." Stavorinus states in 1770: "Another boat of this country, which is very curiously constructed, is called a Mour-pankhy; these are very long and narrow and sometimes extending to upward of an hundred feet in length and not more than eight feet in breadth; they are always paddled, sometimes by forty men, and are steered by a large paddle from the stern, which is either in the shape of a peacock, a snake, or sometimes other animals; the paddles are directed by a man who stands up and sometimes makes use of a branch of a plant to regulate their motion, using much gesticulation and telling stories to excite either laughter or exertion. In one part of the stern is a canopy supported by pillars on which are seated the owner and his friends, who partake of the refreshing breeze of the evening. These boats are very expensive, owing to the beautiful decorations of painted and gilt ornaments, which are highly varnished and exhibit a considerable degree of taste." It is mentioned of Warren Hastings' friends, when he was leaving Calcutta, "their budgerows were well stored with provisions, and every requisite, &c., so with pendants flying, and bands of music, to the last man and instrument to be found in Calcutta, they attended him to Sagaur, the extremity of the river." Lord Valentia in 1803 says: "He came up the river in Lord Wellesley's State barge, richly ornamented with green and gold, its head a spread eagle gilt, its stern a tiger's head and body; the centre would convey twenty people with ease." The fact is the only drive was the dusty course; there was no Strand Road and no country drives; they had then to betake themselves to the river. Racing was always popular in old Calcutta.* An old race course was at the foot of Garden Reach on what is now the Akra farm; there was another, however, on the maidan. In 1780 a subscription plate of 2,000 rupees was advertised, and it was stated that at the close of the race the stewards will give a ball to the ladies and gentlemen of the settlement. Allied to racing is sporting, which, besides the exercise it gave to inactive Ditchers, was of great use to the natives, numbers of whom used to fall a prey to wild animals, at the time when leopards

* Lord Wellesley for some time stopped racing in Calcutta, and according to Rainey, "despite the frowns of the Governor General, some sportsmen managed to get up * * * *; (Rainey's Historical and Topographical Sketch.)

infested the suburbs of Calcutta. Hog-hunting was the favourite sport, and Buckra, 15 miles south of Calcutta, was last century the chosen spot."*

Lotteries were then the order of the day. Shopping was also greatly indulged in by fashionable Society. Asiaticus writes: "Europe shops, which are literally magazines of European articles, either of luxury or convenience, early in the morning are the public rendezvous of the idle and the gay, who here propagate the scandal of the day, and purchase at an immoderate price the toys of Mr. Pinchenbeck, and the frippery of Tavistock Street." Tailors formerly made a rich harvest by their trade, and it is related of one Martin that after ten years' business he returned to Europ with two lakhs. The milliners also settled early in Calcutta. The ladies of Calcutta dressed like the ladies of London, except that their fashions were some twelve months old.†

The business of undertakers was very profitable, and a good-will of a rainy season was worth half a lakh of rupees. In 1780, it is stated that the rent of an upper house consisting of two small rooms and a hall was 150 rupees in Calcutta. In a fashionable part it was 300 to 400 rupees. The rent of the bungalows was equally high. Captain Williamson gives an interesting account of several kinds of edible articles which, for want of space, will not be mentioned here in detail. It is stated that in Stavorinus's time, *i.e.* about 1768, "peas, beans, cabbages were to be had in Calcutta only during the cold season; in the hot season nothing was to be had but some spinage and cucumbers, but about 1780

* *Calcutta Review*, Vol XXXV.
† *Calcutta Review*, Vol XXXV, page 192.

potatoes, peas, and French beans were in high repute. The Dutch are said to have been the first to introduce the culture of the potato, which was received from their settlement at the Cape of Good Hope." From them the British received annually the seeds of every kind of vegetable useful at the table as well as several plants of which there appeared much need, especially various kinds of pot-herbs. They likewise supplied us with vines from which innumerable cuttings have been dispensed to every part of Bengal and its upper dependencies. The Dutch seemed to have communicated the taste for gardens to the English; they had one themselves at Chinsura, made on three stone terraces, raised one above the other, with groves of trees behind. The French also at Gyrette had a magnificent garden. In 1780 appear notices and advertisements in Hickey's *Gazette* of garden houses in Baitakhana, Ballygunge, Tannah near Holwell place opposite Murkar Thannah; Commodore Richardson's, delightfully situated at Ducansore, Russapagla; John Bell's, eastward of the Sepoy Barracks at Chowringhee, a piece 400 yards from the main road leading to the Salt-water Lakes; one with a hall, three rooms, and two verandahs on the Culpi Road near Alipore, for many years Mr Croft entertains the Governor-General (W. Hastings) and his lady with several other persons of rank and quality at his plantation at Sook Sagaur, now in the river bed.*

Distinctions of rank among Europeans were rigorously insisted on, but Lord William Bentinck was said to be the first man in high position who abolished this state of things. He opened his levees at the Government House to society

* *Calcutta Review*. Vol XXXV.

in general, much to the displeasure of the civilians and others of an aristocratic disposition. Mrs. Kindersly in her travels (1760-1768) observes: "There is no part of the world where people part with their money to assist each other so freely as the English in India." It is indeed remarkably true even now. Anglo-Indian fellow feeling filled with wonder and admiration the mind of so great a scholar as the Right Hon'ble the late Professor Max Muller.*

The hospitality of the old Anglo-Indians has been spoken of with admiring gratitude by many travellers, and it is said that a guest finds in his host's house, servants and money at his disposal. The following description will, I have no doubt, be very interesting: Breakfast is described as the only *degagé* meal, every one ordering what is most agreeable to their choice and in elegant undress chatting *á lá voloute*; whilst on the contrary, dinner, tea and supper are kinds of State levees. At twelve a repast is introduced, consisting of cold ham, chicken and cold shrub. Supper was light at 10 o'clock, a glass or two of a light wine with crust, cheese, then the hookah and bed by 11. Lord Cornwallis on the New Year's Day 1789 invited a party to dinner at 3½ at the Old Court House. Turtle and turkey courted the acceptance of the guest, a ball opened at 9½ in the evening, supper at 12, they broke up at 4 in the morning.

Hartley House says as to drinks:—Wine is the heaviest family article; for whether it is taken fashionably or medi. cinally, everybody, even to your humble servant, drinks at least a bottle per diem, and gentlemen four times that

* Read "India, what can it teach us."

quantity.* Beer and porter were little used, being considered bilious; the favourite drinks were madeira and claret, cider and perry also formed part of the beverages; ladies drank their bottle of claret daily, while gentlemen indulged in their three or four, and that at five rupees a bottle. This was far inferior to the beer drinking propensities of various men twenty years ago, when a dozen a day was thought little of in mofussil districts. A drink was in use called country beer. "A tempting beverage suited to the very hot weather and called 'country-beer' is in rather general use, though water artificially cooled is commonly drank during the repasts; in truth nothing can be more gratifying at such a time, but especially after eating curry. Country beer is made of about one-fifth part porter, or beer with a wine glassful of toddy or palm wine which is the general substitute for yeast, a small quantity of brown sugar and a little grated ginger or the dried peel of Seville oranges or of limes which are a very small kind of lemon abounding in citric acid and to be had very cheap."†

Mrs. Kindersly speaking of the furniture states: "Furniture is so exorbitantly dear, and so very difficult to procure, that one seldom sees a room where all the claims are of one sort; people of first consequence are forced to pick them up as they can either from the captains of European ships or from China, or having sets made by blundering carpenters of the country, or send for them to Bombay, which are generally received about three years after they are bespoke; so that those people who have great good luck generally get their houses tolerably well equipped by the time they are quitting

* *Calcutta Review*, Vol. XXXV.
† *Calcutta Review*, Vol. XXXV.

them to return to England." Glass windows were very dear. Warren Hastings was one of the few that had them.

Mrs. Fay writes of the Christmas festival: "Keeping Christmas, as it is called, prevails here with all its ancient festivity. The external appearance of the English gentleman's house on Christmas day is really pleasing from its novelty. Large plantain trees are placed on each side of the principal entrances, and the gates and pillars being ornamented with wreathes of flowers fancifully disposed, enliven the scene. All the servants bring presents of fish and fruits, from the Banian to the lowest menial; for these, it is true, we are obliged in many instances to make a return, perhaps beyond the real value; but still it is considered as a compliment paid to our *burrah-din* (great day). A public dinner is given at the Government House to the gentlemen of the Presidency, and the evening concludes with an elegant ball and supper for the ladies. These are repeated on New year's Day and again on the King's birthday. No doubt the influence of the Portuguese servants, who like pomp and show connected with religious festivals, contributed to this feeling. On Christmas 1780, the morning ushered in with firing of guns; the Governor-General gave a breakfast at the Court House, and a most sumptuous dinner at noon, several royal salutes were fired from the grand battery at the Lall Diggy, every one of which was washed down with *Lumba pealas of lall sharab.* The evening concluded with a ball."

Previous to the battle of Plassey, only the Governor and the senior member of Council used carriages.* Hardly

* According to Rev. Long: "The kiraunchi also now so despised * * * * was a fashionable vehicle for native gentlemen; it was an imitation of the old English family coach." There were also other kinds of carriages then in vogue.

any metalled road then existed as now, where the carriage drives could be performed with ease and comfort. The streets swarmed with Brahmini bulls, camels and elephants, and up to 1805, mention is made that elephants were allowed to pass through the streets of Calcutta.* The palanquin was greatly in vogue as a convenient conveyance; and Sterndale mentions that the palanquin bearers charged double fare for going to Chowringhee, which was then considered out of town.

As for hotels, it is stated that, "the Wilson's of 1800 was at Fulta, where a large establishment was maintained for families and single ladies who had to embark and disembark there on account of the tide. On the increase of strangers and temporary residents in Calcutta, the cost and inconvenience of furnishing a whole house led to the setting up of boarding houses. The increase of rent of late in Chowringhee is leading many now to adopt the Parsi fashion of having a suite of rooms in a house. In 1780, however, we find an advertisement of an hotel in Calcutta to be kept by Sir E. Impey's late steward and Sir J. Rumbold's late cook——Turtles dressed, gentlemen boarded and families supplied with pastry."

Mr. Sterndale writes: † "In one respect Calcutta of a century ago was better off than it is at the present day." He mentions the existence of eight hotels in Calcutta They were the "London," the "Harmonic"—which occupied

* The *Bengal Harkaru* dated the 16th April 1805, writes:--"A few evenings ago Mr. and Mrs. Hutteman. with three of their children, were returning home in a carriage. They met an elephant on Esplanade Row, opposite the tank, upon which the horses got wild and ran the carriage on to the chain close to Mr. Brady's house aup upset it."

† *Vide* Colonel R. C. Sterndale's Historical Account of the Calcutta Collectorate.

the present Police Court building—the "Union," "Wright's New Tavern near St. John's Church," the "Calcutta Exchange," the "Crown and Anchor"—the present Exchange buildings—Beard's Hotel and Moor's Tavern in Dacre's Lane, then a fashionable quarter. Monsieur de le Gallais' Tavern was famous for public breakfast and masonic banquets. Besides these, there were in 1800, eleven punch-houses and several European foreigners and others opened eating and lodging-houses in different parts of the town for the reception of the sailors and others. Billiard tables were kept in those houses, and liquor of various kinds were sold in them under the denomination of beer, lemonade, &c.

It is stated that a theatre existed before the sack of Calcutta by Siraj-ud-doulah; the ex-subadar and his army converted it into a battery to attack the Old Fort. But it was rebuilt in 1775-76 by public subscription. Among the subscribers were Warren Hastings, General Monson, Richard Barwell., Sir E. Impey, and several others. The theatre was generally performed by amateur performers. A ball room was also attached to it. Asiaticus gives the following lively description:—

"For my own part, I already begin to think the dazzling brightness of a copper-coloured face infinitely preferable to the pallid and sickly hue, which banishes the rose from the cheeks of the European fair and reminds me of the death-struck countenance of Lazarus risen from the grave. The English ladies are immoderately fond of dancing, an exercise ill-calculated for the burning climate of Bengal; and in my opinion, however admissible in cooler latitudes, not a little indelicate in a country, where the inhabitants are covered with no more clothes than what decency absolutely requires. Imagine to yourself the lovely object of your affections ready to expire with heat, every limb trembling, and every feature distorted with fatigue and her partner with a muslin handkerchief in each hand employed in the delightful office of wiping down her face, while the big drops stand impearled upon her forehead."

Lord Valentia in 1803 writes: "Consumption is very frequent in Calcutta, which I attribute in a great measure to their incessant dancing, even during the hottest weather; after such violent exercise they go into the verandah, and expose themselves to the cool breeze and damp atmosphere."

CHAPTER X.

HINDU SOCIETY.

NO subject at the present moment excites so much interest, or demands such serious treatment, as the one which forms the subject of this chapter. It is painful to observe that the importance of the question is generally not recognised. A dispassionate study of social problems, or rather of the principles on which they are to be solved, has become an imperative necessity. Our social polity has reached such a stage that the sooner we grapple with the problems and face the present situation, the better for all of us. Coming events cast their shadows before; and to judge from them, the symptoms that have already developed are, in all conscience, alarming. They do not indicate progress. "All that glitters is not gold." The easy-going present may be, in every way, pleasant and comforting; but the after-effects are likely to be damaging to a degree. Let one and all be conscious of the serious aspect of the present condition of society. The glare and pomp of the so-called superior civilisation of the West has blinded our vision, and we are so much enamoured of the captivating present that, lightly and in a most listless manner, we dispose of all the important questions of our social life. There is no mistake that Hindu Society is being broken up. Every day its organisation is receiving rude shocks; and it is doubtful whether ultimately it will be able to withstand the catastrophe that threatens it. A silent revolution has been working behind us and all that has been built up in antiquity, and cemented through ages, is about to be swept away by its mighty and resistless tide. Let us seriously examine the character of this revolution and of the philosophy that underlies it. In one word, it may be termed Anarchy; and its inevitable result is destruction. We are not satisfied with the ideal which the Hindu Society has set before us. All sorts of schemes and plans, are eagerly discussed and methods pursued in order to realize some foreign ideal for the moment may seize our fancy. There is a vagueness in our ideas. The bonds of society are being loosened; but the mischief wrought has to be boldly faced. It is an evil day for human happiness, when social ties disappear and men no longer feel a strong attachment and an abiding inclination to work in the interests of society. The spirit of defiance is abroad. The harmony of society is disturbed. It is not my purpose to decry the spirit of independence. On occasions it leads to noble deeds. At the same time, one must feel an attachment for his country and an affection for its social institutions. No man can ever really be a citizen of the world. There are characteristics and peculiarities of each race which mark it out from others; and while ultimately all the races work out the destiny of mankind, each does so in its own peculiar way according to its own environments and to the light vouchsafed to it. Individuality, a great virtue in the West, has here often degenerated into rank selfishness; and the high living, which in the West has proved to be such a stimulus to many ennobling virtues, has an opposite effect upon us. History shows how the peculiarities of races are developed. They are worked out silently through ages. They are attributed to the religion, the manners, the habits and occupations of a people. The climate, too, is no mean factor in determining the result as Buckle * has shown.

Every nation has a religion of its own, peculiarly suited to it, in which it thrives and prospers. Even the spread of Christianity among the aborigines has produced no enlightening effect. It has not been able to raise the moral or the intellectual status of some of the savage tribes. Although these savages imitate European manners, no compensating advantage has been gained by them. It is said that nations are born, or are rather sent forth into the world and appointed by the Lord to work out in practical life His behest—some grand comprehensive idea—"Logos" as it is termed, which runs through all their thoughts and actions and manifests itself in the national life on important occasions. To the Hindus, such a "Logos," to some extent, seems to have been Dharma—a term which, in its true sense, I am afraid, cannot be rendered intelligible in English. But it comprises the idea of religion pervading the soul and manifesting itself in man's thoughts, words and actions, and forming the active principle of his nature, life after life, till emancipation of the soul is attained. The idea is so wide and comprehensive that the whole universe, in its general and particular aspects, comes within its range. Be it said to the credit of the Hindu people that they have performed their task with the strength vouchsafed by the Lord for the salvation of mankind. They have illustrated in their

* History of Civilisation, Vol. I.

own lives that man can raise himself to the realisation of God, and they have opened the path which leads him on to God. In the course of working out their destiny, the Hindus have evolved a philosophy and religion which is unique in the world. They were not satisfied with making observations by the ordinary senses, but they developed their faculties to an unlimited extent, and they had a clearer insight and perception through processes known by the general term of *yoga*. This enabled them to annihilate distances of time and place, and the past, the present and the future were to them as clear as the mid-day sun. Developing such powers with the higher moral sense, the *rishis* or sages of ancient India renounced *Swarga* (heaven), the place of unmixed happiness and thus became the *guru* or spiritual preceptors of mankind. It is they who shaped the outward form of the society and religion of India suitable to the growth of spiritual life. The Hindus believe in the essential unity of the manifested universe; they find no difference, in essence, between a man and a mineral, all being manifestations of the same Supreme Being. As an illustration of the practical result of this doctrine may be cited the universal fellow-feeling of the Hindus extending to the worms or even to the trees. Thus, while aiming at the highest, the Hindus have recognised the necessity of the meanest, and have evolved a religion styled "*Sanatan Dharma*," or religion for all times, which can satisfy the cravings of man in all stages of development. The Hindus also believe that the present life is only a link in an infinite chain of lives through which one must pass before he can realise the "Self" in him, and thus pass the bounds of all nations which tie him down to the manifested universe, and reach the Absolute and thus become really free. They therefore set very little value on mere earthly affairs, and strive to keep on developing their spiritual nature with equanimity of temperament—neither elated by prosperity nor depressed by misfortune. The Hindus hold a distinctive idea about good and evil. To them no action is meritorious or sinful except in relation to the *dharma* of a person. The dharma of each person indicates the stage of his evolution. It is a well-known fact that nations as well as individuals vary in the stages of their development; and an action which is useful to one is regarded as harmful to another. Conscious of this elementary principle of evolution, the ancient Hindu rishis (saints or seers) divided the entire Hindu nation into four divisions or castes—Brahmin, Kshatriya, Vaisya and Sudra. Birth fixes the caste of a person; and the Hindu firmly believes it is determined by Higher Powers in consequence of one's *karma* or actions in his past existence. To the Hindus, the doctrine of "As you sow, so you reap," is true not only of the physical world, but also of the spiritual. Thus the doctrine of *karma* is the key to the Hindu religion; and it has profoundly influenced the ideas of the Hindu race. The doctrine asserts that no action (which includes thought and desire also) goes without producing its necessary consequences; that the consequence attaches itself to the person who performs the action through the interest of the person in the action and he must taste the fruits either in this life or in future lives. The good he enjoys or the evil he suffers in the present life, without any sufficient apparent cause, is the result of his actions in his past existence. So long as the consequences of actions attach themselves to a person, he must be born again and again to taste the fruits of his *karma*. The connection between the action and the person is cut off, if it is performed without any desire or affection, that is, without any interest in the action and any regard for consequences; and this can only be done by the person's annihilating his sense of separate existence and realising "The Self" in him. In this way the consequences of his actions fall on the universe and not on himself, and thus become much more potent. This is the salvation which the Hindus aim at; and their *shastras* throw light on the path leading to it. The special duty of the Brahmins is to keep the torch burning, as they are the fittest persons for the task by the life they are enjoined to live. The practical result of belief in the doctrine of *karma* is general contentment, each person believing that his lot has been of his own making. I have touched only some of the main features of the Hindu faith.

"Hinduism," says Mr. N. N. Ghose, in his *Memoirs of Maharaja Nubkissen Bahadur*, "is not only a code of morals, but an interpretation of the unseen. It has something very distinctive to tell us about man's origin and destiny. It points out to us the means of getting at spiritual realities and of placing ourselves in contact with the world beyond this." Emancipation and not happiness is the aim of the Hindu, and to him the present life is valuable only so far as it enables him to prepare himself for his great journey, life after life, till salvation is attained. The functions and rules of conduct for the four castes are to be found embodied principally in the *Sanhitas*, named after the rishis who promulgated them; and they are collectively called *Smritis*. Their texts are regarded as authoritative.

It is a lost legend when or how the divisions of castes came into operation.* Indeed, the practical Hindu religion has been styled the *Varnasrama Dharma* or the rules of conduct for the four great castes or *Varnas*. "The original division that into four castes, rests more clearly upon a distinction of moral temperament than upon distinction of pursuits. Classification by calling is recognised, is in fact apparent on the face of division, but arises out of, and is dependent on, the former principle, *viz.* that of classification by temperament and character. The castes constitute a hierarchy, and their dividing line is rigidly fixed. The caste of an individual is the caste of his father. Whatever might have happened in ancient times, when the Hindu Kings reigned and rishes made and applied the law, it is certain that today no one can be transferred, or can transfer himself from one caste to another. He can neither be promoted to a higher caste for his virtuous acts or qualities, nor degraded for his sins. The caste of a man is supposed to be a necessary consequence of his acts in his previous existence; and the life that he now lives will, it is believed, determine his caste in his next birth."† The caste system is the basis of the social polity of the Hindus. The peculiarity of the system lies not in its division into different sections but upon the principle underlying the whole system and the method followed for reducing the principle into practice.

Broadly speaking, there never was any state where the people attained some degree of refinement and culture, which ultimately was not obliged to recognise the utility of classi-

* In Rig Veda, mention of caste system is found. The Western *savants* fix the date of the composition of Rig Veda 3000 B.C. The Hindus aver that it existed "from before all time."

† Memoris of Maharaja Nubkissen Bahadur, by Mr N. N. Ghose.

fication or division within itself. Religion is not one of the factors that ordinarily determine it. But the ultimate result *viz.* the division, has always been there, whatever might have been the principle of division. The inclinations of the people, or their occupations in life, were the chief factors that determine the classification; and the Sovereign also is no insignificant a factor in this division, who enjoys the rare power of altering the social status of his subjects. The scope of the present article would be greatly enlarged, were I to make an attempt to describe and trace the history of European societies as affected by the prerogatives of Sovereigns. The Hindus as well as other civilised races set a high value upon noble deeds, but they widely differ in their estimate of rewards. The noble and meritorious acts of an individual, according to the Hindu ideal, will entitle him, not in the present, but in the future lives to higher and holier stations. And thus it is not surprising to discover, even to this day, that a Sudra enjoying high posts and emoluments is not in social estimation, placed higher than the Brahmin.

It is interesting to note that there have been no revolutionary disturbances in our society like the great socialistic movements in Europe, such as the rise of the Nihilists in Russia, or the social convulsion and anarchy that paralysed France at the end of the 18th century. It has been said that "the test of the pudding is in the eating;" and the virtue of the Western social polity has already begun to manifest itself on the many and varied complications of social life in Europe.

To secure all the happiness and luxury which arts and science can provide, and wealth can command, has been the

Western ideal. What a contrast to the old Hindu ideal! To material happiness and misery the Hindu is absolutely indifferent. How to know himself, to attain perfection, to be always in communion with his Maker—that is his ideal. Mons. Royer Collard says: "Human societies are born, live and die on the earth. It is there their destinies are accomplished * * * * after (he) man has engaged himself to society, there remains to him the noblest part of himself, those high faculties by which he elevates himself to God, to a future life, to an unknown felicity in an invisible world." It is sad to contemplate the falling off from the old standard. It is distressing to observe that symptoms have already come to the surface, which indicate a loosening of the foundations of society. From the Family the Individual has become the unit of society. Burke has very truly said—"Nothing is more to be dreaded than a shock in which old and traditional manners should perish. When ancient opinions and rules of life are taken away, the loss cannot possibly be estimated. From that moment we have no compass to govern us."

What an ideal, what heroic sacrifices, noble and divine characters are depicted in the lives of the true and noble Hindu? In the burning words of Babu Surendra Banerji—"Where shall we find a nobler character than that of a Rama or Yudhisthira? Where shall we find sublimer precepts of morality than those taught in the Ramayana and the Mahabharata? The solemnity of pledges, the great duty of filial obedience, the absolute necessity of self-sacrifice in the discharge of solemn obligations, the supreme virtue of chastity, the sacredness of truth, heinousness of perjury, are all enforced with a degree of eloquence, of pathos, of sincerity of depth, of conviction, as cannot fail to leave an impression on the mind of even the most casual reader of the Ramayana. The Purans say: "The world cannot bear a liar." The Ramayana quotes the remark with approbation. When Rama visits Agastya Muni in his hermitage, the great sage tells him that the perjurer feeds on his own flesh in the next world."*

A story is related that when the Lord Buddha was confronted, in his meditation in hermitage, by a widow who seriously demanded life to be restored to the body of her only son, the saint is stated to have promised to restore life, if the widow could get him some quantity of *Til* seed from a household where death had never paid his visit. The widow exultingly went round in search of such a household; but alas nowhere could such a house be found. She returned discomfited and reported to the great sage that there was not a single household which did not complain of the loss of any of its dear inmates. As there is no household without its death, so there is no society without its evils. If we carefully examine the constitution of any society, we shall not fail to discover many evils. But appreciation is more useful than fault-finding.

A society cannot be rotten which has witnessed many vicissitudes, has withstood the shocks of time, and has been able to produce men remarkable in every sphere of life. It is easy to declaim against prejudices and superstitions, but in spite of its so-called prejudices, our society has had wonderful vitality and retained its character, intellect and spirituality. Prejudices, however, are not always an evil. As Burke says: "It is not invariably a sound policy to wage war against prejudices; for, it is never wise to put men to live and trade, each on his own private stock of reason; and

* Speeches by Babu Surendranath Banerji, Vol. I.

this stock in each man is so small, that individuals would do well to avail themselves of the general bank and capital of nations and of ages." Superstition has been called the religion of feeble minds, and they must be tolerated in an intermixture of it in some trifling or some enthusiastic shape or other; else, to quote Burke once more, "you will deprive weak minds of a resource, found necessary even in the strongest."

Hindu society has passed many an ordeal. Here the natural development of Society was arrested by frequent foreign invasions and conquests. It has been able to survive the onslaughts. It owes its existence to the peculiarities of its religion, which has worked itself into the basis of social organisation and made the Hindu quite unique even among the Eastern races. In grappling with the social problem, therefore, we cannot avoid facing the question of religion. It is a remarkable fact in the history of the country that the conflict between Buddhism and Hinduism came to a close before the Mahommedans knocked at the gate of Hindustan, since Hinduism has coiled and sheathed itself within its own case. Fortunate it was for the Hindus that at this momentous and critical period of the world's history, namely, that of the rise and progress of the Mahommedan power which was coeval with the commencement of that epoch of darkness which divides the ancient from the modern world, they were blessed with guides who had their lights direct from heaven to shape their conduct and mould their institutions. The Mahommedans, as Prescott has observed, "came like a torrent, sweeping down and obliterating even the landmarks of former civilisation." Half the ancient world was converted to Islamism; but India alone stood firm and preserved its distinctive features

The caste system and the village community proved veritable little republics in a social polity. The force of Islamism was quite inadequate to break through the strong and compact organisation. The patient fortitude developed by this system, while heroically resisting fire and sword, has built itself into the Hindu character. "Mild," as applied to the Hindu, is not an epithet of reproach. He is not aggresive, but he is firm in his religion and patient in his suffering.

Experience has proved that imitation and adaptation are not necessarily conducive to the progress and happiness of society. They are not always to our best advantage. Lecky has well said, "The seeds will germinate which suit the soil, and men will often adopt sweeping principles and conclusions, and completely neglect all the qualifications, safeguards, and counterpoises by which they had been elaborately fenced round." Hence innovations are to be introduced not recklessly, but due regard and attention should be paid to the peculiarities of the society concerned. Max Muller's pronouncement, touching this question, appears to me very pertinent. He observed, "A people that can feel no pride in the past, in its history and literature, loses the mainstay of its national character."

Our society like every other is not only capable of, but even demands, reform in several respects. It is only to be hoped, however, that in conceiving and carrying out reforms, the principles here briefly dwelt upon may not be ignored; that there may be no haste or rashness; and that nothing may be destroyed on mere abstract principles without regard to circumstances.

THE END.

APPENDIX.

LIST OF THE 38 VILLAGES THE ENGLISH COMPANY WERE PERMITTED BY THE EMPEROR TO BUY FROM THE ZAMINDARS IN 1717.

(1) *On the Howrah side of the river—*

1. Salica (Salkeah).
2. Harirah (Howrah).
3. Cassundeah (Kasundiah).
4. Ramkissnopoor (Ramkristopur).
5. Batter (Betor, modern Bantra)

(2) *On the Calcutta side of the river—*

6. Dackney Packparra (Dakshin Paikpara).
7. Belgashia (Belgachhia).
8. Dackney dand (Dakshindaree).
9. Hogulchundey (Hogulkuria).
10. Ultadang (Ultadinghi).
11. Similiah (Simla).
12. Macond (Makonda).
13. Comorparrah (Kamarpara).
14. Cancergasoiah (Kankurgachhi).
15. Bagmarrey (Bagmari).
16. Arcooly (Arkuli).
17. Mirsapoor (Mirzapur).
18. Sealda (Sealdah).
19. Cooliah (Kuliah).
20. Tangarah (Tengra).
21. Sundah (Surah).
22. Bad Sundah (Bahir Surah).
23. Shekparra (Sheikhpara).
24. Doland (Dalanda).
25. Bergey (Birji).
26. Tiltola (Tiljula).
27. Topsiah (Topsia).
28. Sapgassey (Sâpgachhi).
29. Chobogah (Chowbagah).
30. Cherangy (Chowringhee).
31. Colimba (Colinga).
32. Goborah (Gobra).
33. Badokney dand (Bahir Dakshindaree).
34. Sicampur (Serampore).
35. Jola Colimba (Jala Colinga).
36. Gendalparah (Gondolpara).
37. Hintaley (Entally).
38. Chittpoor (Chitpur).